How Can We Forgive Murderers?

And Other Answers to Questions about
A Course in Miracles®

Greg Mackie

Book #26 in a Series of Commentaries on
A Course in Miracles®

THE CIRCLE OF ATONEMENT

This is the 26th book in a series, each of which deals with a particular theme from the modern spiritual teaching, *A Course in Miracles*®. The books assume a familiarity with the Course, although they might be of benefit even if you have no acquaintance with the Course. If you would like a complete listing of these books and our other publications, a sample copy of our newsletter, or information about the Circle of Atonement, please contact us at the address below.

The Circle of Atonement
Teaching and Healing Center
P.O. Box 4238, West Sedona, AZ 86340
(928) 282-0790 Fax: (928) 282-0523
E-mail: info@circleofa.com
Website: www.circleofa.com

ISBN 1-886602-21-2

Published by The Circle of Atonement: Teaching and Healing Center
Printed in the United States of America
Cover design by Kathy Simes
Design and layout by Phillips Associates

Library of Congress Cataloging-in-Publication Data

Mackie, Greg, 1963-
  How can we forgive murderers? : and other answers to questions about a course in miracles / Greg Mackie.
      p. cm. -- (A series of commentaries on a course in miracles ; bk. #26)
  Includes bibliographical references and index.
   ISBN 1-886602-21-2
   1. Spiritual life--Christianity. I. Title. II. Series.
   BV4501.3.M235 2003
   299'.93--dc21
                                   2003000510

Acknowledgments

Many people contributed to the creation of this book. In particular, I want to thank Robert Perry and Allen Watson for their contributions to this work. Both of them consistently offered insightful feedback on these pieces before they were posted, thus greatly improving the final versions. Allen also contributed a Q & A of his own to this volume, an excellent piece on how to distinguish between the voice of the ego and the Voice of the Holy Spirit.

I also want to thank the many people who asked such thoughtful questions. The questions I've received have led me to research and reflect on important Course issues and ideas in a way that I may never have done had I not been asked for help. These questions have enabled me to deepen my own understanding, and I am very grateful for that. They have also blessed others: Based on the feedback I've received, I can think of countless examples where an answer of mine was helpful not only to the original questioner, but also to many other people who were wrestling with the same issue.

Without all of you, this book would not exist. Thank you for inspiring me to write it, one question and answer at a time.

All references are given for the Second Edition of the Course, and are listed according to the numbering in the Course, rather than according to page numbers. Each reference begins with a letter, which denotes the particular volume or section of the Course and its extensions (T=Text, W=Workbook for Students, M=Manual for Teachers, C=Clarification of Terms, P=*Psychotherapy*, and S=*Song of Prayer*). After this letter comes a series of numbers, which differs from volume to volume:

> T, P, or S-chapter.section.paragraph:sentence; e.g., T-24.VI.2:3-4
> W-part (I or II).lesson.paragraph:sentence; e.g., W-pI.182.4:1-2
> M or C-section.paragraph:sentence; e.g., C-2.5:2

Contents

Course Theory and Terminology

Living the Course

Forgiveness and Relationships

Topical Issues

Jesus and Religion

Introduction

Welcome! This book is a collection of some of the "Course Q & A's" that I have been writing and posting on the Circle of Atonement's website since November of 1999. (Web address: www.circleofa.com.) I am very pleased to make this collection available, both to those who do not have Internet access and to those who prefer to have this material in book form.

By way of introduction, I'd like to present a brief account of how these Q & A's came to be. As I answered people's questions about the Course in my role as one of the Circle of Atonement's teachers, I noticed that certain questions were asked very frequently. So I thought: Wouldn't it be great if there were a place where people could find answers to common Course questions twenty-four hours a day?

Thus the "Course Q & A" feature on the Circle's website was born. The purpose of the feature, as described on the website, has been to serve as a place where people could submit questions they have about Course theory, interpretation, practice, and application. I would answer those questions, and post my answers on the website. I'm pleased to report that people have responded very well to this feature. Many people—both the original questioners, and others who have read the Q & A's—have let me know that my answers were helpful to them.

Having discussed the origins of this material, I'd like to provide other information that will be helpful to readers. First, this book assumes some familiarity with *A Course in Miracles*, since the people who originally submitted the questions were generally experienced Course students. Therefore, you won't find answers here to the most basic questions beginners ask, such as questions about what the Course is and how it was written. However, I think beginners will still find this book useful, as it does address many topics beginners ask about, such as why and how the separation occurred, how to distinguish between the ego and the Holy Spirit, and why the Course uses masculine pronouns.

For basic information about the Course, I recommend that beginners consult the introductory material on the Circle's website, and Robert Perry's booklet *An Introduction to 'A Course in Miracles,'* which is available from the Circle and from Miracle Distribution Center. I also recommend Robert Perry's *A Course Glossary*, which is an excellent introduction to the Course's unique terminology, useful for both beginners and experienced Course students. It is available both online on the Circle's website, and in book form from the Circle.

Each Q & A in this book originally appeared as a separate, self-contained essay on the Circle's website; therefore, there is no need to read the book sequentially. The questions are not arranged in any particular order, although I did group them into broad categories. There is plenty of overlap between the categories, of course; many of the questions fit more than one. That being said, I do hope these general categories will aid you in finding questions of a particular type or on a particular topic.

You will notice that each Q & A (with the exception of Allen Watson's) follows the same basic structure. Underneath the heading for each question is a "short answer," which is my brief summary answer to the question, usually no longer than a paragraph. This is followed by a longer answer, in which I discuss the main points of the short answer in more detail. Sometimes the longer answer will also contain a Course-based practice for applying the ideas discussed, which I encourage you to do.

Those who have read these Q & A's on the Internet will notice some differences between the online versions and book versions. In compiling them for this book, I took the opportunity to do some revisions. Many are not revised at all, or have been revised very little; others have been revised significantly. My basic answers to these questions have not changed—in no case have I felt the need to drastically reverse my stance on something—but I have revised some answers for greater clarity, to conform them to the short answer/long answer format, and to reflect new insights based on my continuing study of the Course.

Many people have found these Q & A's helpful to them, and it has been a real joy for me to write them. I hope this book will be helpful to you on your continuing journey with the Course.

Course Theory and Terminology

1

Why and how did the separation occur?

Short Answer

Why did the separation occur? The Course's answer is basically as follows:

1. The Sonship consists of parts even in the Oneness of Heaven.

2. Some of these parts wanted special love from God, but God could not grant this request because He loves everyone equally.

3. So these parts of the Sonship chose to rebel against God, usurping His role as Creator by remaking themselves, giving themselves the specialness that He didn't give them.

How did the separation occur? The Course's answer is basically as follows:

1. The separation did *not* occur in reality.

2. We who made the separation and the ego originally are remaking it every moment of the day through our ongoing denial of God. Recognizing this process at work in the present is the key to understanding and undoing it.

3. There is no intellectual answer to the question of how the separation occurred; the only real answer is the experience of Heaven, which *ends* the separation once and for all.

☾ ☾ ☾

The question of why and how the separation occurred is probably the single most-frequently-asked question among Course students. I know it was one of the first ones I asked. The Course has a few things to say about this question, which I'd like to summarize here.

I'll say right off the bat that the Course does not offer any airtight, intellectually satisfying answers to this question. Since the state of Heaven cannot really be described in words, the words we use to describe it (and how we could have left it) confront us with all sorts of paradoxes, which I believe are intellectually irresolvable. I think we just have to accept the fact that there are certain things words simply can't describe. With that little disclaimer in mind, let's look at the questions of "Why?" and "How?" one at a time.

Why did the separation occur?

Why would part of the Sonship want to separate from God? Given how glorious and joyous Heaven is according to the Course, it is certainly hard to imagine why we would ever want to leave it. That being said, the Course's own take on why we decided to leave can be boiled down to the following three points:

1. The Sonship consists of parts even in the Oneness of Heaven.

To understand the Course's answer to the question of why we separated, it is important to recognize that even in the Oneness of Heaven, the Sonship consists of "parts." The Course says or implies this in a number of places, such as this line from the Workbook: "Creation is the sum of all God's Thoughts, in number infinite, and everywhere without all limit" (W-pII.11.1:1). Note the references here to "sum," "Thoughts," and "number," all words which suggest multiple parts. The Course even has at least one clear reference to individuals in Heaven (see T-4.VII.5:1). In a nutshell, the Sonship contains parts (the Sons of God) which in some inscrutable way are distinct from each other, yet at the same time are absolutely one: "The Sonship in its Oneness transcends the sum of its parts" (T-2.VII.6:3). This, as you have probably guessed, is one of those irresolvable paradoxes.

2. Some of these parts wanted special love from God, but God could not grant this request because He loves everyone equally.

As paradoxical as the idea of a kind of "partness" in Heaven's

　　　　　　　　　　　　　　　　　　　　　　Greg Mackie

Oneness is, the idea is crucial to understanding how part of the Sonship would want to separate. Why is it crucial? Because the Course tells us that the main reason we separated was because parts of the Sonship wanted special love from God: "You were at peace until you asked for special favor" (T-13.III.10:2). The root desire that started the separation was none other than "the tiny, mad desire to be separate, different, and special" (T-25.I.5:5). In other words, parts of the Sonship wanted more of God's Love than the others. They wanted to be His favorites. They wanted Daddy to single them out and shower them with more affection than He gave to any of His other children.

Of course, God could not give any part more love than any other. The very request was meaningless "for the request was alien to Him, and you could not ask this of a Father Who truly loved His Son" (T-13.III.10:3). Giving more love to some—and thus less to others—is a violation of the very nature of love. Being a violation of the nature of love, the request for special love was really a request for pain, and God could not and would not give pain to His Son. And so, God turned down the request for special love. True love, by definition, is limitless, and our loving Father can only give true love.

3. So these parts of the Sonship chose to rebel against God, usurping His role as Creator by remaking themselves, giving themselves the specialness that He didn't give them.

Unfortunately, we—parts of the Sonship who craved special love— wouldn't give up that easily. And so we decided that if God would not make us special, we would cut off all ties with this deadbeat Dad and strike out on our own. We would usurp His creative power and re-create ourselves, making for ourselves the specialness that God wouldn't give us. And this is exactly what the Course says we did. We declared our independence, and thus the whole process of separation began. And the rest, as they say, is history.

Before moving on to the question of how this separation occurred, one more important thing must be said about this third point: This rebellion happened only in the *minds* of the Sonship. It isn't real. We are not really capable of re-creating ourselves and overturning the Laws of Heaven. The entire drama occurred only in the Son of God's imagination.

How did the separation occur?

How could part of the Sonship actually accomplish the feat of separating from God? This is basically the same thing as asking, "How did the ego originate?" There are three main places in the Course that discuss the general issue of the origins of the separation and the ego, and each gives us a slightly different (but related) answer:

1. The separation did not occur in reality.

One place that discusses the issue of how the ego originated is Section 2 of the Clarification of Terms, a section written for the very purpose of defining the term "ego" (along with the term "miracle"). It has something very thought provoking to say about our venture of trying to pin down the ego:

> Who asks you to define the ego and explain how it arose can be but he that thinks it real, and seeks by definition to ensure that its illusive nature is concealed behind the words that seem to make it so.   (C-2.2:5)

In reality, the separation (and the separate self, the ego) did not occur at all. As I said above, it only *seemed* to occur—it is purely a figment of our imagination. By asking how the separation occurred, we are just affirming our belief that it did in fact occur. By trying to resolve the conundrum of the ego, we are just making it more real in our minds. And that is the whole point behind our questioning: to affirm the reality of the separation. Thus the question "How did the separation occur?" is essentially an ego ploy designed to reinforce our belief in the ego's reality.

2. We who made the separation and the ego originally are remaking it every moment of the day through our ongoing denial of God. Recognizing this process at work in the present is the key to understanding and undoing it.

Another place where this issue is discussed is in Chapter 4 of the Text, which gives us another interesting and unexpected spin on this line of questioning:

> Your own state of mind is a good example of how the ego was made. When you threw knowledge away, it is as

if you never had it. This is so apparent that one need only recognize it to see that it does happen. If this occurs in the present, why is it surprising that it occurred in the past?

(T-4.II.3:1-4)

Here, Jesus is appealing to a phenomenon that all of us are familiar with: the phenomenon of denial. Denial is a psychological defense mechanism in which a person suppresses thoughts, feelings, or memories from her conscious awareness and thus forgets all about them, even though they are still buried deep in her mind. It is obvious that we do this all the time with all sorts of things; indeed, denial is such a part of everyday life that we frequently speak of people being "in denial." So, the Course suggests, the theory of separation that it presents should not be too difficult for us to grasp. Since we deny so many things so frequently in the present, the Course's theory of how the separation and the ego originated—that we denied our knowledge of God and our true Self in the past—should at least be plausible to us.

But the key point is that this denial was not just an event of the ancient past (see especially T-4.II.1:1-3). On the contrary, we are still actively burying our knowledge of God and our true Self *now*, every second of our lives, thus keeping the separation and the ego going. And so, our focus should not be on trying to answer the question of how the separation occurred in the past. Rather, our focus should be on noticing how the separation is occurring right now in the ongoing decision-making process of our minds.

If we keep this present focus, the question of how the separation occurred can be transformed from an ego ploy to reinforce our belief in the separation into "the best question [we] could ask" (T-4.II.1:2). This present focus allows us to recognize the ongoing process of separation at work in our minds, and this recognition is what allows us to undo it. By becoming aware of our denial, we free ourselves to choose again and reclaim the knowledge that we have denied.

3. There is no intellectual answer to the question of how the separation occurred; the only real answer is the experience of Heaven, which ends the separation once and for all.

Our final reference is from the Introduction to the Clarification of Terms. Like the other two references, it casts doubt on the whole enterprise of asking about the origins of the separation and the ego:

The ego will demand many answers that this course does not give....The ego may ask, "How did the impossible occur?", "To what did the impossible happen?", and may ask this in many forms. Yet there is no answer; only an experience. Seek only this, and do not let theology delay you.   (C-In.4:1,3-5)

I love the way the Course phrases the question in the second sentence quoted above. This is its form of the question of how the separation, the ego, the world, etc. originated. It is, of course, a nonsensical, absurd question: "How could that which could not possibly happen actually happen?"

How could anyone possibly come up with an answer to such an absurd question? "There is no answer; only an experience." I think that the "experience" referred to here is the experience that the Course is leading us toward: the experience of reality, the experience of Heaven. So, what Jesus is saying here is that there is no intellectual (or theological) answer to the question of how the separation occurred; rather, the only real answer is the experience of Heaven, which brings an end to the separation—and this is what we should be shooting for. Rather than answering the *question* of the ego by explaining it, this experience answers the *problem* of the ego by dispelling it. And with the problem of the ego resolved once and for all, who has need to ask the question?

Conclusion

As I said, these questions confront us with all sorts of paradoxes that I think will forever escape the power of words to resolve. Some people have seen this as a weakness in the Course, but I do not—or perhaps I should say that if it is indeed a weakness, then it is a weakness shared by every religious, metaphysical, or scientific system that attempts to explain the nature of ultimate reality and how things came to be. All of them, at least the ones I'm aware of, end up in irresolvable paradoxes.

The question of why and how the separation occurred is a form of the famous "problem of evil" question: "How could a loving, all-powerful God allow evil?" I've never seen a fully intellectually satisfying answer to that question from any religious or metaphysical system. I think it finally comes down to which of the various explanations speaks to you on the deepest level. For me, that is the explanation given by the Course.

2

Are all the events and circumstances in our lives predetermined, or do we have free choice?

Short Answer

All events and circumstances are predetermined in the sense that they are part of the Holy Spirit's script of our journey through time and space, a journey that has already been completed. We have free choice in the sense that we can freely give and receive miracles, which both shifts our perception of events in the script and "fast forwards" us through parts of the script. In short, while the script is already written (determinism), our experience of the script and the speed of our journey through it is up to us (free choice). Thus there are many ways that the Holy Spirit's script can actually play out in the world.

☾ ☾ ☾

The Course's stance on the age-old question of determinism versus free will is rooted in its ideas about the nature of time. The Course's ideas about time are mind-boggling to say the least, and I know I still don't fully understand them; nevertheless, we can certainly grow in our understanding of them if we read the Course carefully. Here, then, is my current understanding of the Course's position on the determinism versus free will issue. (Henceforth I will use the term "free choice" instead of "free will" since, strictly speaking, "free will" in the Course refers not to choice but to the undivided will we share with God.) I am indebted to Robert Perry for his research on the Course's view of time, which I have drawn on in this answer.

All events and circumstances are predetermined in the sense that they are all part of the Holy Spirit's script of our journey through time and space, a journey which has already been completed.

The Course is emphatic that our journey in this world is not a haphazard affair subject to the vagaries of random chance, but in fact follows a preordained script:

> Yet there is a plan behind appearances that does not change. The script is written. (W-pI.158.4:2-3)

Who wrote this script? Well, certainly our own choices contributed to it, and this is one sense in which we have free choice—in fact, the Course says that we ourselves have chosen *all* of the particular events and circumstances of our individual lives (see, for instance, T-21.II.2-3). But the Holy Spirit is actually the author of the script; the Course alludes to this when it refers to "Him Who wrote salvation's script in His Creator's Name" (W-pI.169.9:3). He took all of the "story material" that we gave Him and incorporated it into His all-encompassing script, a script of our entire journey through time and space, a journey from separation to salvation. (The fact that our own ego material is incorporated into the script leads some Course interpreters, including Ken Wapnick, to conclude that there are two scripts: the ego's and the Holy Spirit's. However, I don't find support for this in the Course.)

This idea that the Holy Spirit incorporated our choices into His script for salvation helps to reconcile two seemingly contradictory aspects of the Course's thought system: the idea that all events are the result of our choices (as in T-21.II.2-3), and the idea that all events are lovingly planned by the Holy Spirit (as in W-pI.135.18:1-4). It also helps answer the nagging question, "If the Holy Spirit wrote the entire script, why are there so many painful events in it?" Faced with this question, we might hastily pin responsibility for our pain onto the Holy Spirit, but the Course assures us that "He would never offer pain to [us]" (W-pI.135.18:2). Who, then, is responsible for our pain?

The answer to this question is that painful events are the result of our own ego choices, which the Holy Spirit *had* to incorporate into His script because He couldn't violate our free choice—love never imposes itself by force. And so, He took our choices—both painful and pleasant—and placed them into His script. But because His goal for us is salvation, He did more than that: He also *reinterpreted* our choices in the light of His salvific purpose. He took even our darkest dreams and wove them into a tapestry of light. The bottom line for us is that because the Holy Spirit wrote the script and everything in it serves His purpose of salvation, we can trust that no matter how things may appear to us, all is well:

> What could you not accept, if you but knew that everything that happens, all events, past, present and to come, are gently planned by One Whose only purpose is your good? (W-pI.135.18:1)

Our lives, then, follow the Holy Spirit's loving script. Yet the Course also tells us that in truth, the error of separation and the Holy Spirit's correction happened instantly—the entire separation lasted only a "tiny tick of time" (T-26.V.3:5) that came and went quicker than a flash of lightning. Time, and our entire journey through it, is in fact an illusion that is already over and done with. Why, then, do we experience it as this long timeline? Because even though the separation is over, a part of our minds still wants to hold onto it. And since it is over, the only way we can hold onto it is to hold onto our memories of it. That, says the Course, is exactly what we are doing: "You keep an ancient memory before your eyes" (T-26.V.5:6). As we go through the Holy Spirit's script, we are actually "reviewing mentally what has gone by" (W-pI.158.4:5). As Robert Perry puts it: Like a senile person, we are living in our memories.

Our experience of our journey through time and space can be likened to watching a movie on a VCR (only in this case, we are part of the movie). The script is written and all we are doing is watching a movie that has already been shot. Because the movie has already been shot, we cannot really do anything to change the movie itself. In this sense, all events and circumstances in our lives are in fact predetermined (including, fortunately, the happy ending of our movie, which is salvation). However, there is one significant thing that we can do to change our *experience* of the movie: We can give and receive miracles.

We have free choice in the sense that we can freely give and receive miracles, which both shifts our perception of events in the script and "fast forwards" us through parts of the script.

There are two main ways in which miracles change our experience of our journey through time and space. First, and most important, they change our *perception* of the events and circumstances scripted into our lives. Miracles awaken us to Christ's vision, and with this vision, physical events are seen in an entirely different light. Miracles allow us to see "the love beyond the hate, the constancy in change, the pure in sin, and only Heaven's blessing on the world" (W-pI.151.11:3). They reveal to us the Holy Spirit's salvific purpose behind the events of His script. We will go through the same script regardless of how we perceive it; however, our experience of the script will be profoundly different if we choose to view it through the holy perception that the miracle brings to us.

Second, miracles actually alter our journey *through* the script by allowing us to skip over parts of it and thus go through it faster. We are told that "the miracle is the only device at your immediate disposal for controlling time" (T-1.I.48:1). The miracle thus comes from outside of time, outside the script; "it establishes an out-of-pattern time interval not under the usual laws of time" (T-1.I.47:2). In other words, our choice to give and receive miracles is not predetermined by the script; it is a truly free choice. According to the Course, this is the only free choice we have.

What about the other things the Course says we can freely choose? It tells us in some places that our only free choice is whether to listen to the ego or the Holy Spirit (C-1.7:1), and in other places that we can't choose the curriculum, but can choose when we want to learn it (T-In.1:3-5 and M-2.3:6-7). In my opinion, these are just different ways of saying the same thing: We can choose the miracle (which is the choice for the Holy Spirit, and the choice to learn His curriculum), or we can refuse the miracle (which is the choice for the ego, and the choice to delay learning the Holy Spirit's curriculum).

So, miracles control the script of time. How do miracles control time? The following passage gives us the answer:

The miracle minimizes the need for time. In the longitudinal or horizontal plane [the time line] the recognition of the equality of the members of the Sonship [the end of the journey] appears to involve almost endless time. However, the miracle entails a sudden shift from horizontal to vertical perception [a shift into timelessness]. This introduces an interval from which the giver and receiver both emerge farther along in time than they would otherwise have been. The miracle thus has the unique property of abolishing time to the extent that it renders the interval of time it spans unnecessary. There is no relationship between the time a miracle takes and the time it covers. The miracle substitutes for learning that might have taken thousands of years....The miracle shortens time by collapsing it, thus eliminating certain intervals within it. It does this, however, within the larger temporal sequence. (T-1.II.6:1-7,9-10)

This is an amazing passage. It tells us that by working miracles (or receiving them), we can skip over huge chunks of time. This doesn't mean that we skip over chronological time; it's not as if I experience a miracle in the year 2000, save a thousand years, and then find myself in the year 3000. Rather, it bumps both giver and receiver ahead on the timeline of their *spiritual development*. It thus "renders the interval of time it spans unnecessary," meaning that it literally skips over the part of the Holy Spirit's script that we otherwise would have needed to plod through in order to reach that level of spiritual development. Miracles thus allow us to hit the "fast forward" button on our VCR and skip entire scenes of the movie. The entire aim of *A Course in Miracles* is to save time (see T-18.VII.4:5); miracles are its means for accomplishing that aim.

In short, while the script is already written (determinism), our experience of the script and the speed of our journey through it is up to us (free choice). Thus there are many ways that the Holy Spirit's script can actually play out in the world.

Applying the time-saving aspect of miracles to our question about determinism versus free choice, what this tells me is that even though there is a single, unchangeable script, there many possibilities for how that script actually plays out in the world. Everything that happens is indeed part of the script (except for the choice to give and receive miracles), so in that sense there is determinism. But since different people are progressing through their "sub-scripts" at different rates— some working more miracles than others, some receiving more miracles than others, each saving a hundred years here, a thousand years there—the number of possibilities for how things actually unfold in space and time must be truly staggering.

To me, this means that all bets are off when it comes to predicting specific events with certainty. Jesus himself was apparently unable to do this concerning Helen and Bill's lives; commenting on a particular situation Helen and Bill were facing one day, he said, "I do not yet know what decisions those who are involved in [what is] happening later today will make" (*Absence from Felicity*, by Ken Wapnick, p. 290). Thus it seems clear that no particular event in our lives is actually predestined in the sense that there's absolutely nothing we can do to keep it from happening. Yes, it is in the script, but it doesn't have to happen as an event in time because we can use miracles to skip over parts of the script.

To illustrate this with an example, let's assume for the sake of argument that the Holy Spirit's script says I'm going to get cancer (remembering that the Holy Spirit wrote my cancer into the script only because I insisted upon it—it was my choice). This cancer is part of the script, so it's predestined in that sense. But I still have a choice: I can work a miracle or receive a miracle from someone else, and if I do, I may skip over that part of the script completely and not get cancer at all. Since our choices jump us to different parts of the script, our choices make a huge difference in determining what actually happens in our lives. Thus I don't think there is predestination in the absolute "it's going to happen and you're powerless to do anything about it" sense.

This idea that there is one predetermined script but many ways we can choose to go through it raises all sorts of questions about how it all fits together. I think it's just far too vast and complicated for our limited minds to ever figure out. That being said, one analogy I have found helpful is to liken the Holy Spirit's script to the "Choose Your Own Adventure" books for children. These are interactive storybooks in which the reader is essentially the "hero" of the story, who must make choices that determine how the story will play out. At the bottom of each page, the reader is given a choice about what will happen next in the story, and is then told something like: "If you choose Option A, go to page 23; if you choose Option B, go to page 26." Each choice will lead to a different outcome, which presents the reader with a new set of choices, and so on. Thus the same, predetermined book (the book is, of course, already written) can nonetheless be gone through in a variety of ways, depending on the reader's free choices.

Perhaps the Holy Spirit's script is something like this. Events unfold in our lives, all of which are part of the Holy Spirit's predetermined script, a script which leads to the inevitable happy ending of salvation. Yet as the events of the script unfold, we are constantly presented with choices which will determine how we experience the script, how fast we go through it, and what parts of it will actually happen in our lives. As we go through the "book" of our lives, every instant we are presented with our options: "If you choose a miracle, then experience joy, skip a thousand pages, and go to page 10,214. If you choose the ego, then experience pain and go to the next page." I'm not entirely sure this analogy is accurate, and it still leaves all sorts of unanswered questions about how our individual "books" all work together. But it is at least one possible explanation of how we can have a predetermined script and real free choice at the same time.

Fortunately, I don't think that we need to know exactly how it all works. All I think we need to remember is this:

1. Because the script has already been written, and at the end of that script is our salvation, our return to God is inevitable. If indeed we have already journeyed through the script and all we are seeing now is only a dim memory of an ancient instant, we have already returned to God. In fact, since the whole journey is an illusion, we never really left God.

2. Yet we have meaningful choices to make in this world. We can choose miracles, which will both shift our perception of the events and circumstances of our lives to a more joyful perception, and help us and our brothers move faster toward our happy reunion with the God we never really left.

Let us, then, choose miracles. Let us save time. And let us remember as we do so that "every collapse of time brings everyone closer to the ultimate release from time, in which the Son and the Father are One" (T-1.V.2:4).

3

What does the Course mean when it says its goal is to save time?

Short Answer

It means that through walking the path of the Course, we can awaken from the dream of separation much sooner than we otherwise would. In truth, the dream of separation is already over, and all we need to do is *accept* that fact to fully awaken. We will inevitably accept that fact, but *when* we do so is up to us. We can come to this acceptance sooner, and thus save time, by turning away from delaying tactics of the ego and following a path of awakening—any path that teaches forgiveness. The Course saves time because it makes forgiveness its central message, because it teaches us how to enter the holy instant, and because it teaches us how to give and receive miracles, "the only device at your immediate disposal for controlling time" (T-1.I.48:1).

ꙫ ꙫ ꙫ

In truth, the dream of separation is already over, and all we need to do is *accept* that fact to fully awaken.

As real and inescapable as our present experience in the world seems to be, the Course tells us in no uncertain terms that "this world was over long ago" (T-28.I.1:6). The entire dream of separation, which from our perspective has lasted billions of years and will likely last billions more, took place in the blink of an eye, a "tiny tick of time" (T-26.V.3:5). The only reason the separation seems to still be going on is that we are reliving it in our minds, as if we were watching a videotape of an old movie. And the only reason we are reliving it is that part of our minds has refused to accept that it is over and done with. Like a person who loses herself in memories of a loved one in order to push away the realization that he has passed away, we lose ourselves in memories of the separation in order to push away the realization that the separation is over.

This refusal to accept that the separation is already over produces the illusion of time. One could say that the illusion of time is our resistance to awakening, our desperate attempt to delay our inevitable homecoming. We have already come home, and in fact we never left to begin with. But our resistance to that fact produces the illusion that we are trudging through time, traveling a long, arduous journey to an awakening far in the future, if at all. From our normal perspective, this seems to be our only choice, but since our only problem is our resistance to awakening, this long journey through time isn't really necessary. All we really need to awaken is willingness to give up our resistance and accept the fact that the dream is gone, and we never left our Heavenly home: "You can accept what has already happened at any time you choose, and only then will you realize that it was always there" (M-2.3:5).

We will inevitably accept that fact, but *when* we do so is up to us.

"The acceptance of the Atonement by everyone is only a matter of time" (T-2.III.3:1). Our resistance to awakening may be strong, but we can only stave off the inevitable for so long. However long it takes us to become willing to awaken, willingness will come, and when our willingness is complete, the truth we had been resisting for so long will dawn upon our open minds. This is why the Course tells us that our only real choice is not *whether* we will awaken, but *when*:

> As the course emphasizes, you are not free to choose the curriculum [the lessons which lead to awakening], or even the form in which you will learn it. You are free, however, to decide when you want to learn it. And as you accept it, it is already learned. (M-2.3:6-8)

One might get the impression from all this that the choice to accept our awakening is a single, all-or-nothing choice. Indeed, ultimately it is. However, since we believe we are in time, our path to this single choice is a gradual one. Our curriculum is not a single pass/fail test, but a "slowly evolving training program" (M-9.1:7). Over time, in the context of the countless choices we make in our daily lives, we gradually learn that choosing to remain in separation brings us pain, while choosing to let go of separation brings us joy. As we come to realize this, we become more and more willing to let go of the separation, until finally our willingness is total, and the single, final choice to accept our awakening is made without reservation.

Our journey through time, then, could be characterized as *the gradual making of a single choice*. Making that single choice will take time; how much time it takes, however, is up to us. And this leads to the whole idea of saving time.

We can come to this acceptance sooner, and thus save time, by turning away from delaying tactics of the ego and following a path of awakening—any path that teaches forgiveness.

As we have seen, the good news is that in the end, all of us will choose to accept our awakening. Unfortunately, the bad news is that "the end can be a long, long way off" (M-1.2:9). This bad news is not something the Course takes lightly; as much as it emphasizes the fact that the final outcome is certain, it also makes it clear that the journey to that outcome can be an arduous one, at least as long as our resistance is strong:

> It is time alone that winds on wearily, and the world is very tired now. It is old and worn and without hope. There was never a question of outcome, for what can change the Will of God? But time, with its illusions of change and death, wears out the world and all things in it.   (M-1.4:4-7)

I think most of us can probably relate to this passage. Who among us does not feel weighted down by the onslaught of time, especially as we grow older and our bodies begin to slow down and wear out? It is precisely because time is so wearying that the Course considers saving time to be so important. Yes, a happy ending is assured no matter what we do with our time, but why suffer unnecessarily? The Course wants above all to spare us pain, and so it encourages us to save as much time as possible.

How do we save time? Speaking in very general terms, we save time by turning away from the ego, and listening to the Holy Spirit. The ego always delays us, because it does not want us to experience the joy of awakening; the Holy Spirit always speeds us up, because He does not want us to suffer the pain of delaying our awakening. As I said above, the journey is a gradual one of becoming more and more willing to let go of the pain of separation (the ego) and to accept the joy of release from separation (the Holy Spirit). The more willing we become to listen to the Holy Spirit, the faster we speed toward the endpoint of the journey. To get a sense of how this works, let's trace the journey through time that the Course envisions for us, a journey which starts slowly but gathers speed as we go along, until we ultimately make that final choice to accept our awakening.

At first, we listen almost exclusively to the ego, and it counsels us to seek happiness through following the paths of the world. And so we go off on our merry way, searching for money, sex, companionship, career, or any of a thousand other things that we think will make us happy. But none of these paths really deliver happiness, and that is precisely the ego's purpose for them. It wants us to waste our time looking for happiness where it can't be found, and in so doing delay making the choice that alone will truly bring us happiness: the choice for God.

We may persist in following the ego's paths for a long time. But over time, it slowly dawns on us that the paths of the world are all dead-ends; no matter how promising they may seem at first, in the end they all "lead to disappointment, nothingness and death" (T-31.IV.2:3). This recognition can be a devastating experience; the Course tells us that "men have died on seeing this" (T-31.IV.3:4), either through literal suicide or simply losing hope and giving up. It seems that there is no way out, no alternative but the inexorable march to the grave. At this point in the journey, progress through time is slow, because we are mired in the ego's delaying tactics.

Yet, this moment of despair can also become a turning point. "The learning that the world can offer but one choice [death], no matter what its form may be, is the beginning of acceptance that there is a real alternative instead" (T-31.IV.6:1). The real alternative is the way of God, the path on which the Holy Spirit would lead us. Once we see the real alternative, however dimly, we begin to turn away from the paths of the world, and embark on a path of awakening, some form of the "universal curriculum" (M-2.1:2) chosen for us by the Holy Spirit (remember M-2.3:6 above, which said that we ourselves don't choose "the form in which [we] will learn" the curriculum). It is at this point that we really begin to save time. Saving time is the very function of the universal curriculum, and of the teachers of God who teach it (see M-1.2-4). Once we begin the transition from the paths of the ego to a path of awakening, progress through time begins to accelerate.

Now, the question may arise: What forms can a path of awakening take? Certainly the world's spiritual paths come to mind, but actually, the options are broader than this. The *Psychotherapy* supplement tells us that psychotherapy under the Holy Spirit's guidance saves time (see P-1.5:4-6), which certainly makes it a path of awakening. Given this, I think that any kind of recovery program that aims to heal the mind would qualify. The *Psychotherapy* supplement goes so far as to say that "to be a teacher of God, it is not necessary to be religious or even to believe in God to any recognizable extent" (P-2.II.1:1). Since a teacher of God, by definition, teaches a path of awakening, it can safely be said that even overt belief in God is not required to be on such a path.

What, then, *is* required? The sentence which immediately follows the one just quoted above gives the answer: "It is necessary, however, to teach forgiveness rather than condemnation" (P-2.II.1:2). Therefore, a path of awakening is *any path that teaches forgiveness*. Indeed, the Course sums up the core teaching of the universal curriculum as follows: "God's Son is guiltless, and in his innocence is his salvation" (M-1.3:5). This statement, of course, is a statement of the recognition that forgiveness brings.

The implications of this are truly staggering. The Course is saying that the active ingredient in every single path of awakening is forgiveness, whether that active ingredient is consciously acknowledged or not. Whatever outward doctrines or practices a path may have, forgiveness is the fuel that really propels followers of that path to God. Even if a person is not on any kind of outwardly acknowledged "healing" path at all, as long as he is teaching and learning forgiveness, he is on a path of awakening. Forgiveness is the path that brings the moment of acceptance of our awakening nearer; it is through teaching and learning forgiveness that we save time.

The Course saves time because it makes forgiveness its central message.

While all paths of awakening save time, the Course will save even more time for those who are called to follow *its* path. How? First, it saves time simply because it expresses the teaching of forgiveness much more clearly and directly than other paths do. True, many paths value forgiveness, and the Course tells us that forgiveness is the central teaching of all of them, regardless of their external form. Yet the Course makes forgiveness front and center. With many other paths, one may need to sift through a lot of superfluous material or at least do some reinterpretation to find the message of forgiveness, but the Course makes the message of forgiveness almost impossible to miss. This can only make its path faster, because it focuses like a laser on the vehicle that drives all paths of awakening to God.

The Course saves time because it teaches us how to enter the holy instant.

Teaching us how to enter the holy instant is a major thrust of the Course; Chapter 15 of the Text, in particular, is devoted to this subject. But perhaps the best discussion of the holy instant as a way of saving time is in the Text section "I Need Do Nothing" (T-18.VII). In this section, the Course contrasts its means of salvation—the holy instant—with two other means: "fighting against sin" (T-18.VII.4:7) and "long periods of meditation aimed at detachment from the body" (T-18.VII.4:9). These two means express, in a nutshell, the main spiritual emphases of the West (fighting sin) and the East (meditation); therefore, the two means discussed here end up capturing the essence of most of the world's spiritual practices.

The Course does not condemn these means; it tells us that they do work eventually, and thus they are worthy means for those who are called to those paths. (It also must be said that undoubtedly other paths have their own ways of achieving what the Course calls the holy instant.) However, it also tells us that both of these means "are tedious and very time consuming" (T-18.VII.4:11), because both assume that we must travel a long, hard road to a goal that lies far in the future. In other words, both assume that the illusion of time, and our long journey through that illusion to our eventual awakening, is real.

In contrast, the Course offers its means: the holy instant, which we invite into our minds through remembering that "I need do nothing" (T-18.VII.5:7). The holy instant saves time in at least three ways. First, the holy instant is the birthplace and home of the holy relationship, the Course's main means of extending forgiveness. Second, it is the instant in which the miracle, the Course's main time-saving device (see below), is given and received. Third, it is an instant in which we shift from time into timelessness, a foretaste of the end of our journey through time, a temporary experience of our present, awakened state. The whole reason we need do nothing is that the journey through time is already over, and so there is really nothing to be done. Thus, unlike the other means, the holy instant doesn't assume that the illusion of time is real; on the contrary, it demonstrates that time is actually unreal. In so doing, it brings the end of time nearer—it saves time.

The Course saves time because it teaches us how to give and receive miracles.

The miracle, we are told, is "the only device at your immediate disposal for controlling time" (T-1.I.48:1). Since miracles are the means by which forgiveness is received by us and given to others, they are the Course's primary means of saving time. (It *is* a course in miracles, after all.) Of course, people on other paths of awakening can and do give and receive miracles as well. But as with forgiveness, the Course makes the miracle front and center, thus speeding us ever faster toward God.

How does the miracle save time? The Course tells us that by giving and receiving miracles, we can skip over huge expanses of time—not chronological time, but rather our *developmental* time, the time it will take us to learn the curriculum and finally accept our awakening. (See T-1.II.6 for the Course's best description of how the miracle saves time.) How much time can we save? Apparently, quite a lot: "The miracle substitutes for learning that might have taken thousands of years" (T-1.II.6:7). Drawing on an image I used earlier, if the dream of separation is a videotape of an old movie, then the miracle is the fast forward button on our mental VCR. By giving and receiving miracles, we can zip through large portions of this tedious and depressing movie, and thus reach the inevitable happy ending that much sooner.

How can we give and receive miracles? We can do so in a variety of ways. As alluded to above, we experience the miracle whenever we enter a holy instant. We experience the miracle whenever we enter into a holy relationship, which the Course at one point calls "a miracle of joining" (T-20.V.1:6). We experience the miracle any time we do a Workbook-style practice period; doing Course practices, we are told, can save us countless years of effort (see, for instance, W-pI.27.4:6; W-pI.97.3; W-pI.123.7:3; W-pI.127.7:1; and W-pI.127.10:1).

And finally, we experience the miracle every time we actively *extend* a miracle to another person. The extension of miracles to others is precisely what this course in miracles aims to teach us how to do, and it wants to teach us this because extending miracles saves time for both giver and receiver. Whatever form the miracle takes, "It establishes an out-of-pattern time interval not under the usual laws of time" (T-1.I.47:2). In doing so, it brings the moment of acceptance of our awakening that much closer. If this is so, then what better use for our time is there than to give and receive miracles? It is because miracles are such a potent means of saving time that the Course urges us to remember that "each day should be devoted to miracles" (T-1.I.15:1).

Conclusion

The attitude the Course would have us adopt toward time is a paradoxical blend of patience and urgency. On the one hand, the Course wants us to remember that no matter how much resistance we have to awakening and how long our journey through time seems to take, all is well. It must be, because time is only an illusion, with no effect whatsoever on our true Self, which abides forever in our eternal Heavenly home: "Both time and delay are meaningless in eternity" (T-5.III.5:2).

But on the other hand, the Course does not counsel complacency: "Delay does not matter in eternity, but it is tragic in time" (T-5.VI.1:3). The time we spend delaying our homecoming is truly exhausting, bringing bitter and totally unnecessary pain to everyone who refuses to accept the fact that this dream of separation is over. One need only look at the state of our world to see what tragedy our delay has wrought. In light of this tragedy, Jesus implores each and every one of us to "save time, my brother; learn what time is for" (T-29.VII.9:3). Time is for extending the miracle of forgiveness to all our brothers.

Greg Mackie

Time is for bringing about the *end* of time. When we learn to use time only for this purpose, we will at last awaken to eternity.

4

The Course tells us that we are responsible for all the circumstances of our lives, as well as for how we perceive those circumstances. Does this apply to children who are suffering from painful circumstances like sickness, starvation, and child abuse?

Short Answer

Yes, I believe it does. The Course says that both our perception of the events in our lives *and* the events themselves come from our choices. This must apply to children as well as to adults. That being said, the best way to help children heal (and to help adults who have suffered from childhood trauma heal) is not to focus on their responsibility, but simply to extend love, kindness, and forgiveness to them.

☾☾☾

The idea that children, like adults, are responsible for all the events of their lives as well as their perception of those events probably arouses more anger and distress, among Course students and Course detractors alike, than any other idea in the Course material. I can understand why people get angry, because this idea seems at first glance to be a cruel and heartless teaching. However, I believe that on closer inspection it is by far the most benevolent, compassionate, and hopeful explanation for what happens to children. If children *weren't* responsible, they would be helpless victims of a cruel world, absolutely powerless in the face of the pain inflicted upon them. But if they *are* responsible, then they have the power to heal the pain of their circumstances by changing their minds.

Because I think this idea is ultimately so kind and liberating, I urge you to bear with me even if parts of my answer here arouse anger and distress in you. In this answer, I will first present Course evidence for the idea that we choose all of the events in our lives as well as how we perceive them. Then, given the strong negative feelings it arouses, I will address the various objections I have heard to applying this idea to children. Finally, I will offer some ideas on how we can be truly helpful to suffering children and adults recovering from childhood trauma.

The Course says that both our perception of the events in our lives *and* the events themselves come from our choices. This must apply to children as well as to adults.

Here is the Course's most direct statement that we are responsible for all of the events of our lives as well as for our perception of them:

> *I **am** responsible for what I see.*
> *I choose the feelings I experience, and*
> *I decide upon the goal I would achieve.*
> *And everything that seems to happen to me*
> *I ask for, and receive as I have asked.*

> Deceive yourself no longer that you are helpless in the face of what is done to you. Acknowledge but that you have been mistaken, and all effects of your mistakes will disappear.

> It is impossible the Son of God be merely driven by events outside of him. It is impossible that happenings that come to him were not his choice. His power of decision is the determiner of every situation in which he seems to find himself by chance or accident.
> (T-21.II.2:3-3:3)

To me, the message of this passage is unequivocal: We choose everything—both our perception of the events in our lives ("the feelings I experience," which are rooted in my perception of events) and the events themselves ("everything that seems to happen to me").

Greg Mackie

A later passage calls the recognition that we are responsible for all of the suffering that we experience "the secret of salvation":

> The secret of salvation is but this: that you are doing this unto yourself. No matter what the form of the attack, this still is true. Whoever takes the role of enemy and of attacker, still is this the truth. Whatever seems to be the cause of any pain and suffering you feel, this is still true.
> (T-27.VIII.10:1-4)

Again, the message is unequivocal: When we suffer, it is always our responsibility, *however much it may appear otherwise*. Now, certainly it doesn't seem that way to us. Certainly many of our choices, especially the ones that have dreamed our particular life circumstances and events into place, come from a very deep level of mind, far below our current conscious awareness. But they are choices nonetheless.

Given the above passages and others like them throughout the Course, I see no way to squirm out of this conclusion. However unpalatable the idea may seem at first, I think we have to admit that the Course does teach it. Moreover, I see absolutely no evidence in the Course that this idea does not apply to children, and plenty of evidence (which we will examine below) which suggests that it does. If this is the case, the inevitable conclusion is that all suffering that a child experiences—whether it takes the form of starvation, sickness, child abuse, or anything else—is ultimately caused, at some level, by the child's own choices. (I should note that all of the *positive* things a child experiences are a result of the child's own choices too—it's not all dark.)

Objections to applying this idea to children

As I've said, I have found that the idea that children choose their experiences (both perceptions and events) is a lightning rod for anger and distress. People ask, "How could this be?" and offer up all sorts of reasons why it can't be. I think "How could this be?" is a very reasonable question, and I think it is important to face the objections to this radical idea squarely. The following, then, are some of the major objections I have heard to the idea that children choose their experiences, and my answers to those objections.

1. Children are innocent.

This is probably the primary objection. It is a truism that children are innocent—that is, pure beings who come into this world as pristine blank slates, who over the course of time "lose their innocence" as they are shaped and molded by parents and the world around them. The idea that children are innocent is coupled with the idea that they are not responsible for their thoughts and actions, because they are not mature enough to be capable of real choice. In a nutshell, the idea of childhood innocence says that children come into the world without egos, and don't develop egos until they've spent some time in the "school of hard knocks" we call life.

Of course, children *are* innocent in the same sense that all of us are innocent: We are innocent Sons of God, who have not sinned no matter how mistaken our choices may have been. But if we read the Course carefully, it becomes clear that children are *not* innocent in the sense of being egoless. Lines like the following strongly suggest that we have egos (in the Course's sense of the term) before we ever enter this world:

> No one who comes here [to the world] but must still have hope, some lingering illusion, or some dream that there is something outside of himself that will bring happiness and peace to him. (T-29.VII.2:1)

This line tells us that our purpose for coming into this world is to find happiness in external things—the ego's endless search for idols. It seems pretty clear to me that if our very purpose for coming into the world is the ego's purpose of seeking idols, then we must have egos before we are born. We don't enter the world egoless. Children, then, are not innocent in the sense of being egoless. They, like all of us until we change our minds, identify with the ego and make decisions based on its dictates. Following the ego is the very reason they come to this world. And if the world the ego made is indeed "the symbol of punishment" (T-13.In.2:4), then children, identifying with their egos like the rest of us, choose to come to the world to be punished. This punishment takes the form of suffering at the hands of the external world.

2. Children are helpless.

This, of course, is related to the idea of childhood innocence: We think that children are weak and powerless, so how can they be responsible for anything? But we've already seen that as far as the Course is concerned, *no one* is weak and powerless. We have powerful egos that predate our entry into this world, and influenced by our egos, we choose the circumstances of our lives before we are born. Once in this world, our choices continue to affect our circumstances, as well as our perception of our circumstances.

That this applies to children (at the very least, the part about our perception of our circumstances) is made abundantly clear in personal comments Jesus made to Helen Schucman and Bill Thetford, recorded in Ken Wapnick's *Absence from Felicity*. These comments were specifically directed to Bill, who resented his parents for what he felt they did to him, and blamed them for many of his current problems. In these comments, Jesus directly refuted Bill's belief that as a child he was helpless and therefore had no choice but to be molded by the authority of his parents:

> Children have an authority problem *only* if they believe that their image is influenced *by* the authority. This is an act of will on their part, because they are electing to misperceive the authority and *give* him this power.
>
> (*Absence from Felicity,* p. 273)

There is little doubt that external factors like parental attitudes and societal influences play a role in molding a child's self-image. But according to this passage, this only happens because the child has chosen to allow this. The child is not helpless in the face of powerful external forces; rather, the child chooses to believe that external forces have such power. This choice is an "act of will," something the child is actively choosing to believe.

Jesus provides further evidence for this idea in the following comment to Helen about Bill:

> As you [Helen] have so often said, no one has adopted *all* of his parents' attitudes as his own. In every case, there has been a long process of choice, in which the individual has escaped from those he himself vetoed, while retaining those he voted *for*....
>
> There must be some acute problem *of his own* that

would make [Bill] so eager to accept [his parents']
misperception of his own worth. This tendency can
always be regarded as punitive. It cannot be justified by
the inequality of the strengths of parents and children.
This is never more than temporary, and is largely a matter
of maturational and thus physical difference. It does not
last unless it is held onto. (*Absence from Felicity,* p. 269)

The first paragraph here presents a persuasive argument against the
idea that children are totally at the mercy of their parents (or the larger
world): If this were so, then children's beliefs would simply be carbon
copies of their parents' beliefs, and it is clear that this is rarely the case.
Indeed, children are often quite rebellious. Therefore, children are not
simply blank slates on which parents write their beliefs, but free agents
who are constantly making choices as they interact with their parents'
attitudes and beliefs.

To me, this idea helps to explain why different people can emerge
from virtually identical childhood experiences with vastly different
perspectives on themselves and the world. Many of us, I'm sure, have
wondered at the fact that some children are so much more resilient than
others, even in the face of suffering. Why is it that some people are
horribly traumatized by childhood suffering, while others seem to
emerge from similar circumstances virtually unscathed? If Jesus is
correct, then the reason for this is that different children make different
choices about how to perceive their respective situations.

The second paragraph here directly refutes the common idea that
children are helpless because they are weaker and less mature than
parents. Here, Jesus says directly that children's tendency to adopt
their parents' misperceptions is a matter of choice, not of helplessness
(a choice that is "punitive," a means of punishing themselves). Jesus
acknowledges that a difference in strength and maturity does exist, at
least temporarily, and certainly this difference makes parents and the
surrounding world highly influential in molding the lives of children.
But an *influence* is not the same as a *cause*. A television commercial
may influence me to buy a product if I am open to being influenced,
but it is still my free decision that actually causes me to buy the
product. It is the same with parents' influence on children. The Course
refers to this idea that others can influence but not directly cause our
choices in the following passage:

Greg Mackie

> When you project [error] to others you imprison them, but only to the extent to which you reinforce errors they have already made. This makes them vulnerable to the distortions of others, since their own perception of themselves is distorted. (T-1.III.5:9-10)

Certainly children, as a result of their temporary weakness and immaturity, are highly susceptible to influence. But this does not make them helpless; their choices are still their own. And whatever choices they make under the influence of parents or the world at large can be unmade, especially as they grow up and come into their own strength and maturity.

3. This idea is "blaming the victim," which adds guilt onto the victim's suffering.

The way we normally perceive things, responsibility is inextricably fused with *guilt*. If you're responsible for something painful, you're guilty; if you're not responsible, you're innocent. We think that responsibility and innocence are mutually exclusive, and so we flip-flop between acknowledging responsibility (which seems to preserve personal power, but at the cost of innocence) and denying responsibility (which seems to preserve innocence, but at the cost of personal power). Applying this to children, we believe that the way to preserve their innocence is to deny their responsibility.

But the Course's idea of responsibility severs the connection between responsibility and guilt. In its system, we *are* responsible for our experiences within the illusion, but precisely because it *is* an illusion, we are *not* responsible for causing any real damage. Therefore, however mistaken our perception may be, we have not caused any actual damage to reality, and thus have no cause for guilt: "There is nothing [the Son of God] can do that would really change his reality in any way, nor make him really guilty" (T-19.II.3:3).

All of us, including children, are indeed responsible for what happens in our lives, but we are not guilty. Thus the Course's idea of responsibility is never about "blaming" anyone, a word that is filled with connotations of guilt. As Robert Perry puts it, we are *always responsible,* but *never to blame* (see Robert's article "Are We Responsible?" in Issue #3 of the Circle's newsletter, *A Better Way*). The Course's notion of responsibility has nothing to do with guilt and blame.

Now, certainly most people do associate responsibility with guilt, and for this reason I believe that we would be wise in the vast majority of cases not to tell a child (or anyone) who's currently experiencing a painful trauma that he or she is responsible for it. When people are suffering, they usually benefit far more from being reminded of their true innocence than being reminded of their responsibility. But, that being said, I think it is vitally important for us to learn that responsibility and guilt do not inevitably have to be connected. The idea that responsibility does not imply guilt is simply one of the most radical and liberating ideas in the Course. The Course disconnects the two in a marvelous way that preserves both the personal responsibility that can empower us to undo suffering, and our incorruptible innocence as Sons of God, which is the very thing that makes it possible for suffering to be undone.

4. In situations where a child is being abused by another person, this idea exonerates the abuser.

The Course's notion of responsibility does not deny the fact that people can and do abuse children, at least on a form level. And if it is true that our choices determine our lives, then it must be true that abusers' choices determine their own lives, just as children's choices determine theirs. If *both* parties are responsible for a situation, then their coming together must be a kind of unconscious agreement in which each person chooses to participate, an agreement that can be ended at any time by either party. In the case of Bill and his parents, Jesus recognized that while Bill was ultimately responsible for his difficult childhood, Bill's parents certainly didn't help matters. At one point, he told Bill plainly, "Bill, your parents did misperceive you in many ways" (*Absence from Felicity,* p. 271). While Bill's parents didn't cause his pain, their own attitudes were certainly a negative influence.

Thus, the idea that children are responsible for their experiences doesn't exonerate child abusers in the sense of denying the abusers' responsibility for their own experiences (and actions). Child abusers are fully responsible for their choices, just as children are fully responsible for theirs. Abusers will experience the painful effects of their decision to attack children, just as children will experience the painful effects of their decision to be attacked. But, as discussed above, while everyone involved is making mistakes which have painful consequences, no one involved is guilty. This acknowledges that both abuser and child are responsible for their mistakes, but also affirms that both are innocent in truth.

5. Accepting this idea means that we would do nothing to change painful external situations, since any suffering a child experiences is the child's fault.

As I said above, acknowledging the responsibility of children (which is quite different than "fault") does not mean denying the responsibility of abusers. Nor does it deny that, at least on the level of everyday experience, external conditions do affect children, and those external conditions need to be addressed. The question of how we should address them is a behavioral question, and the Course tells us that we should refer all such questions to the Holy Spirit. As I've said in other Q & A's, I believe that the Holy Spirit will guide us to do the most loving thing possible, given our level of development. Applying this to the suffering of children, I am certain that He would guide us to feed starving children, nurse sick children, and protect children from abusers. What else would love do? The question of how to solve the larger problems facing children is fraught with controversy, and I certainly do not have all the answers. But I doubt very much that the Holy Spirit would guide us to do nothing externally to alleviate children's suffering, since that would hardly be the loving thing to do.

The best way to help children heal (and to help adults who have suffered from childhood trauma heal) is not to focus on their responsibility, but simply to extend love, kindness, and forgiveness to them.

This, I think, would be the Course's short answer to the question of how to help suffering children, as well as adults recovering from childhood trauma. What does this look like in specific, concrete terms? Again, guidance on specifics should come from the Holy Spirit. But I do think there are some basic guidelines we can follow. (I think these guidelines can be applied to any situation in which we are working with a suffering person.) First, I think we simply need to do whatever can be done behaviorally to get children out of harm's way—again, we feed the starving, nurse the sick, and protect the abused. This is simply good old-fashioned human kindness.

Second, once they are out of harm's way, we can "reassure them that they are safe *now*" (T-6.V.2:3). This, I think, applies equally to working with adults recovering from childhood trauma. Before they can really do any deeper work on healing childhood issues, they need to feel safe. Only in an atmosphere of safety and love can real healing take place.

Third, as I mentioned above, I think that in working with children and adults recovering from childhood trauma, we should primarily emphasize their true innocence rather than their responsibility; we should focus on the fact that they're not to blame, rather than the fact that they're always responsible. Most people simply are not ready to accept the radical idea that their own decisions cause their suffering. Given the inevitable association between responsibility and guilt that most people (especially children) make, telling them they are responsible will most likely just exacerbate their guilt, which is the last thing that frightened, suffering people need.

Therefore, rather than focusing on a person's responsibility, we should focus on a person's innocence. This emphasis is apparent in the following Course line, which describes how the advanced teacher of God facilitates the healing of the sick:

> He overlooks the mind *and* body, seeing only the face of
> Christ shining in front of him, correcting all mistakes and
> healing all perception. (M-22.4:5)

When the advanced teacher of God beholds a sick and suffering person, he looks past the sick body *and* the faulty decisions that brought the sickness about, and sees only the innocent Christ in this person. In short, he forgives his patient, and his behavior toward the patient then becomes a means of communicating his love for the patient. It is this—seeing the patient's innocence and loving her—which heals the patient's mind, including the patient's mistaken belief that she is not responsible for her sickness. Ironically, it is through emphasizing the patient's innocence that the teacher of God helps the patient to accept her responsibility. This is how mistakes are corrected. This is how healing occurs. This is the best thing we can do for children and those who have suffered from childhood trauma.

Unfortunately, I've seen all too many Course students (myself included), in their well-intentioned efforts to help others, emphasize responsibility at the expense of innocence. I'm sure that most of us, when discussing a painful situation with fellow Course students, have had someone offer up some version of the classic New Age line, "What did you do to create that?" Has that ever really felt loving to you? The personal responsibility idea is challenging enough when it comes from an egoless Jesus; when it comes from another ego-bound person, however well intentioned, it usually ends up being a judgmental attack, which just reinforces the problem. For that reason, I think we are best off refraining from this for the most part. The Course itself says as much when it tells us what the teacher of God should *not* do in responding to his pupil's magic thoughts:

> If he argues with his pupil about a magic thought, attacks it, tries to establish its error or demonstrate its falsity, he is but witnessing to its reality. (M-18.1:2)

I don't think this means that we should never teach people that they are responsible for their experiences. Certainly the Course itself does so all the time, and as we've seen, the Course considers learning this lesson "the secret of salvation." I myself am obviously teaching it in this Q & A. Children, especially as they get older, can certainly benefit from learning that they can choose how to perceive a situation and that they have real power over the circumstances of their lives. And teaching adult survivors of childhood trauma that they can make new choices in the present that will help them to reclaim their lives is an important aspect of many successful therapies.

However, I simply believe we should exercise caution with this, especially with the Course's radical idea that we are responsible for *all* of our experiences. We should discuss it with another person—especially a suffering person—only when we truly feel prompted by the Holy Spirit (we need to exercise careful discernment in determining whether we are truly prompted), and only when the other person expresses some willingness and desire to explore the idea. Personally, I generally don't talk about this idea unless the person asks me about it directly. Above all, our teaching of personal responsibility should be rooted in the deeper truth that we are all innocent. People who are suffering don't want to be tersely reminded of their responsibility; they just want to be loved. Everything else must flow from that.

Conclusion

The idea that all of us, including children, choose all of our experiences does seem cruel at first. But I truly believe that it is an incredibly benevolent, compassionate, hopeful, and liberating idea if it is rightly understood. It frees us from the shackles of victimhood, and empowers us to be as God created us. It does not imply guilt, however much we may believe it does. It is not a license to ignore the external conditions that contribute to suffering, nor is it a license to callously remind suffering people of their responsibility when what they really need is love. Placed in the deeper context of our absolute innocence as Sons of God, this idea frees us from guilt, and thus opens the door to true healing. For if we are responsible for our suffering, the key to salvation is also in our hands. If our choices crucify us, then they can also save us. Let us, then, see this idea for the blessing that it is:

> How kind and merciful is the idea we practice! Give it welcome, as you should, for it is your release. It is indeed but you your mind can try to crucify. Yet your redemption, too, will come from you. (W-pI.196.12:3-6)

Greg Mackie

5

What happens to the ego after the death of the body? Does the ego have less "reality" after bodily death?

Short Answer

Bodily death does not end the ego nor give it less "reality" in our minds because the mind's *belief* in it, not the body, is responsible for making it seem real. Therefore, as long as the mind is unhealed, the ego must continue on in some form when the body dies, presumably in another body of some sort. However, when the mind is healed through letting go of its belief in the ego, bodily death can become a final release from the limitations of the body.

ෆෆෆ

Bodily death does not make the ego less "real" in our minds because the mind's *belief* in it, not the body, is responsible for making it seem real.

It is a common human belief, however that belief might be expressed, that the ego (the sense of separate selfhood) is born when the body is born, and dies when the body dies. In short, we believe we *are* our bodies. This becomes apparent if we simply consider how we identify ourselves. When I say, "I am Greg Mackie," "Greg Mackie" refers to a body that was born on a particular date in the past, and will die on a particular date in the future. In other words, my individual selfhood is defined by the lifespan of my body; one could say that my body *causes* my individual selfhood—my ego—to exist. When my body was born, *I* was born; when my body dies, *I* will die.

But according to the Course, the ego is not the result of the body; on the contrary, the body is the result of the ego (see W-pI.72.2:1-3). Our belief in separate selfhood is what causes us to manifest a body to house that separate self. As contrary as this is to our usual way of seeing things, the Course tells us that both the body and the ego (and death too, for that matter) are caused solely by the mind's belief in them.

The mind that has placed its faith in these things is not the body's brain, which does die when the body dies, but the eternal mind of the Son of God, our true Identity. "The ego is the mind's belief that it is completely on its own" (T-4.II.8:4), the erroneous conviction that we have somehow separated from our eternal life in God and become solitary, separate bodies, born into a cruel world and doomed to die at the hands of that cruel world. The implication here is clear: Since the ego's cause is a belief of the mind, it cannot be undone or even weakened by the death of the body. How could it be undone by the death of the body, since the birth of the body didn't cause it to begin with?

Ironically, the very belief that we are separate bodies trapped in a cruel world leads to the belief that the ego *can* be overcome by bodily death, an idea which the ego itself endorses. The belief that death can overcome the pain wrought by the ego is extremely common; many of us really do think that death brings peace and respite from the slings and arrows of the ego and its world. This idea is reflected in the common tombstone inscription "Rest in peace" (which the Course refers to and reinterprets; see T-8.IX.3:5); in the suicidal lament "Goodbye, cruel world!"; and in the way we often console the grieving by saying that the dead loved one is no longer in pain but has "gone on to a better place."

But as common as the belief that death brings peace is, the Course considers it an error and cautions against it (though I would not try to talk the grieving out of the idea if it brings them comfort, nor do I deny that death can be a *temporary* release from pain). The Course tells us that "there is a risk in thinking death is peace" (T-27.VII.10:2). Why is this risky? Because this thought is an ego ploy designed to get us to

Greg Mackie

seek death, either through suicide or through other "causes" of death, such as accidents, murder, sickness, or old age. Of course, with the exception of suicide, the causes of death that I've listed are normally regarded as things that happen to us against our will, but the Course is clear that death is always the result of our decision (see W-pI.152.1:4). Obviously, this decision is made at a very deep level of mind that we're not usually consciously aware of, but it is still a decision. Thus, as long as the ego is governing our lives, all death is suicide. We "see in death escape from what [we] made" (M-20.5:2), and so we seek it to escape the pain of human life.

But underneath the tempting thought that death is peace lies the ego's real payoff: Thinking that the pain of human life can be escaped through death actually reinforces our belief that life—the life of our body, beset by the cruelties of the world—is the cause of our pain. On the contrary, says the Course, "death cannot be escape, because it is not life in which the problem lies" (M-20.5:4). The problem has nothing to do with life, which is of God and is eternal, but instead stems from the mind's belief that life is limited to the "life" of a separate ego encased in a frail, mortal body. Since this is a belief of the mind, it is a *change of mind*, not death, that brings us peace. And this change of mind is, in essence, a turning away from the "life" of the ego, which is really death, and an affirmation of true life, the eternal life of the mind, which we share with God:

> When your body and your ego and your dreams are gone, you will know that you will last forever. Perhaps you think this is accomplished through death, but nothing is accomplished through death, because death is nothing. Everything is accomplished through life, and life is of the mind and in the mind. (T-6.V(A).1:1-3)

Thus, the ego is not undone or weakened by bodily death; in fact, the ego uses bodily death to *strengthen* our belief in it. To the ego, death "proves" that we really are separate beings bound by bodies, forever cut off from God. The death penalty, in the ego's view, is God's ultimate punishment for the "sin" of separating from Him. Death, then, cannot undo the ego; only the mind's decision can undo the ego: "As you made it by believing in it, so you can dispel it by withdrawing belief from it" (T-7.VIII.5:2). The only way to make the ego less "real" in our minds is to recognize that the ego is in fact unreal, and reaffirm our true Identity as Sons of God, rightful heirs to God's Kingdom. "The world is not left by death but by truth, and truth can be known by all those for whom the Kingdom was created, and for whom it waits" (T-3.VII.6:11).

As long as the mind is unhealed, the ego continues on in some form after bodily death.

This point—that the ego continues on after bodily death—is the clear implication of the idea that the ego cannot be undone by bodily death. It is a matter of simple logic: If the ego is not undone by bodily death but only by a change of mind, then when a person dies without making that change of mind, that person's ego *must* continue on after death. I, for one, certainly wish at times that it were otherwise, because the idea that death ends the ego has a definite appeal. If it were true, then all we would have to do is wait until we die, and *poof*—the ego would be gone! Alas, it's not that simple. The truth of the matter, according to the Course, is that as long as the mental decision that made the ego remains in force, the ego will continue in some form.

What form might the ego take? It's hard to say, since the Course really doesn't talk about this, but I think it's safe to say that the ego would have to manifest some sort of form in which to "live": "All thinking produces form at some level" (T-2.VI.9:14). Personally, I think that the ego simply manifests another "body" of one sort or another after we die. What kind of body? I don't know, but I suppose it could be anything from another earthly body (if one believes in reincarnation) to some sort of ethereal body. There are all sorts of theories about different kinds of bodies in various realms, but I don't think we really need to know anything about that. As Section 24 of the Manual tells us, "All that must be recognized...is that birth was not the beginning, and death is not the end" (M-24.5:7). This is the recognition of the eternal nature of life, which ultimately undoes the ego, whatever form it takes.

When the mind is healed through letting go of its belief in the ego, bodily death can become a final release from the limitations of the body.

Even though the ego uses death to confirm its existence, bodily death is neutral in itself. The *idea* of death is definitely of the ego, but

Greg Mackie

the *form* of bodily death can be used by either the ego or the Holy Spirit. How might the Holy Spirit use death? Well, certainly, even the ego-based death described above can be transformed into an opportunity to give and receive love, if His perception of it is allowed to enter. Seen with His vision, even a painful death can be a time for friends and family to join together in love, compassion, and gratitude for one another and for the one who is passing on.

But perhaps the best example in the Course material of death as He sees and uses it is the beautiful depiction of death in a section of *The Song of Prayer* entitled "False versus True Healing" (S-3.II). This section describes what bodily death is like for a person whose mind is completely healed, a person whose ego has been completely undone *before* bodily death through a change of mind. (I recommend reading the entire section.)

The section starkly contrasts death as it is normally experienced by the unhealed mind with death as it is experienced by the healed mind. For those of us with unhealed minds, who still identify with the ego, death comes "in forms that seem to be thrust down in pain upon unwilling flesh" (S-3.II.3:2)—the "causes" of death I mentioned above. Isn't this how death is for most of us? Whether a person dies suddenly in a car accident or slowly from the ravages of sickness or old age, death is usually painful and rarely welcomed (except, as discussed above, as an escape from pain to "peace"). We certainly don't see it as something we choose, however much the Course may tell us that death is always our decision. To us, death is the Grim Reaper, a dark angel who comes when we least expect him, whether we want him to or not.

But for a person whose mind is healed, death is something else entirely. For such a person, death is not a Grim Reaper that seems to cut him down against his will, but rather a conscious, peaceful decision to let the body go because it is no longer needed. The healed person uses the body only for the Holy Spirit's purpose of extending healing to others, and when its purpose is done, "it is discarded as a choice, as one lays by a garment now outworn" (S-3.II.1:11).

This may sound hard to believe, but spiritual literature is full of accounts of enlightened masters (including some fairly recent ones) who apparently chose consciously when to leave their bodies, and quietly did so when the proper time came. Certainly this represents an extremely high state of spiritual development, one that will take most of us a long time to achieve. But even if we aren't there yet, we can read *The Song of Prayer*'s account of "what death should be" (S-3.II.2:1) as an inspiring foretaste of what awaits us when we finally let go of the ego. When we do so, bodily death is transformed from the ego's *proof* of limitation to the Holy Spirit's *release* from limitation. Death will not free us from the ego, but freeing ourselves from the ego through changing our minds can transform bodily death from the grim witness to separation into "a gentle welcome to release" (S-3.II.3:2). What was once the ultimate bondage can become the gateway to liberation:

> We call it death, but it is liberty....If there has been true healing, this can be the form in which death comes when it is time to rest a while from labor gladly done and gladly ended....For Christ is clearer now; His vision more sustained in us; His Voice, the Word of God, more certainly our own.   (S-3.II.3:1,3,5)

6

Does the Sonship consist only of human beings, or does it include other earthly entities like animals?

Short Answer

The Course strongly implies that the Sonship includes *everything* in this world: animals, plants, and even what we normally regard as "inanimate" things. Therefore, behind every illusory form in the world, there is a part of the Son of God's mind that is dreaming it is that form. Our function, then, is to extend love and healing to all of our brothers, including our nonhuman ones. This not only heals our non-human brothers (and ourselves), but also enables them to heal others by bearing witness to the healing of the mind of the Sonship.

☺☺☺

Note: I am indebted to Robert Perry for his article "The Course and Mother Nature," which has inspired much of what I have written here. This article appears on the Circle of Atonement's website, and also in Issue #6 of the Circle's newsletter, *A Better Way*. It addresses the topic of how Course students should regard nature, and I highly recommend reading it.

The Course strongly implies that the Sonship includes *everything* in this world: animals, plants, and even what we normally regard as "inanimate" things.

The Course's focus is on human beings and their relationships, and so it has very little to say about the nonhuman inhabitants of the earth. Yet what little it does say about them is enough, in my opinion, to support the conclusion that they are part of the Sonship, just as human beings are.

Our first clue lies in the fact that the Course tells us we are joined not only with other human beings, but with "all living things" (see, for instance, W-pI.57.5:6; W-pI.163.9:6; and W-pI.188.10:1). Since true joining can only take place between eternal, nonphysical minds, this certainly suggests that non-human living things have such minds.

This point is further reinforced by the fact that the word "living," as the Course uses it, doesn't refer to the temporary and illusory "life" of the body, which "neither lives nor dies" (T-6.V(A).1:4), but to eternal life, which is "of the mind and in the mind" (T-6.V(A).1:3). Thus the Course term "living things" refers not so much to things that have biological "life," but to things that have *true* life, which resides only in the mind. The implication of this is clear: If true life resides only in the mind, and the Course speaks of nonhuman living things, then the logical conclusion is that these nonhuman living things have minds. (Remember, we are speaking of eternal, nonphysical minds here.) If this is so, these nonhuman living things must be part of the Sonship.

What specific nonhuman things are part of the Sonship? Certainly plants and animals seem to qualify, as suggested by the following line: "Forgiveness shines its merciful reprieve upon each blade of grass and feathered wing and all the living things upon the earth" (S-3.IV.2:3). If plants (like blades of grass) and animals (like birds) are considered to be "living things" in the Course sense, then certainly they are part of the Sonship.

Surprisingly, however, the Course suggests that even things we normally don't consider to be alive at all are part of the Sonship. At one point in the Text, for instance, it clearly puts grains of sand in this category: "How holy is the smallest grain of sand, when it is recognized as being part of the completed picture of God's Son!" (T-28.IV.9:4). If grains of sand are part of the Sonship, then the most reasonable conclusion in my mind is that all physical objects fall into this category (even man-made objects, since I can find no compelling reason to exclude them). But the category of things that are part of the Sonship seems to be even broader than that. Lesson 156 of the Workbook indicates that not only flowers and trees, but even waves and wind share the life of God (see W-pI.156.3-5). Thus, amazingly, even physical *processes* such as waves and wind are part of the Sonship.

All of this points to a single, startling idea, which I have already stated: *Everything* in this world (and presumably, in the entire physical universe) is part of the Sonship. Everything we see, whether it takes the form of a human being, a dog, a cockroach, a tree, a virus, a star, a hurricane, a refrigerator, or a dust bunny under that refrigerator, is in a very real sense our brother. I will say more about what this means in my next point.

Therefore, behind every illusory form in the world, there is a part of the Son of God's mind that is dreaming it is that form.

I said above that everything in this world is part of the Sonship, but that idea has a crucial qualifier: The *form* of everything in this world is *not* part of the Sonship. Form is pure illusion, and God did not create it. So, although the line quoted above told us that grains of sand are part of the Sonship, the line immediately following that one says, "The forms the broken pieces [of God's Son] seem to take mean nothing" (T-28.IV.9:5). The idea that everything is part of the Sonship, then, is not pantheism, a philosophy which says that the physical universe is God. Nor is it panentheism, a philosophy which says that the physical universe is *in* God. The things we see are not part of God's creation, the Sonship, in that sense.

In what sense, then, is everything part of the Sonship? Quite simply, the physical forms of things are not part of the Sonship, but the minds behind the forms are. What this means to me is that things in the physical universe are no different in their basic nature than human beings. In the Course's view, each human being consists of both an illusory form and a real, eternal mind in Heaven that is dreaming up that form. What I gather from all of the clues discussed above is that the same basic principle holds true for animals, plants, and even "inanimate" things. As Robert Perry succinctly put it in the article I cited above, "Behind every form is a part of God." This idea has some very powerful implications for how we relate to the world, as we shall see.

Our function, then, is to extend love and healing to all of our brothers, including our nonhuman ones.

If the Sonship is everywhere, then clearly the Course would have us love not only human beings, but also animals, plants, grains of sand—in short, everything we look upon. While the Course's emphasis is definitely on human relationships, its teaching is not confined to them.

This is something I like to keep in mind when I'm interacting with the nonhuman world. When I'm relating with my cats, for instance, I remind myself that they aren't just projections of my own mind, but beloved brothers whose holy minds are joined with mine (no matter how much they refuse to do what I ask them). Their forms, like mine, are illusions, but their true Identity, like mine, is the glorious Son of God. They are thus worthy of infinite love.

The idea that the Sonship includes everything in the world is, in my opinion, a strong rationale for a truly Course-based environmentalism. Personally, I've always been drawn to the idea of "walking gently on the earth," but as a Course student, I've long found it difficult to relate to the environmental movement. Most environmentalists seem to stress the idea that we should love (or even worship) the earth because it is our home, and if we don't change our ways soon, life will be destroyed forever. This way of seeing things is totally alien to the Course, which stresses that the earth is *not* our home, and that true life resides only in Heaven and cannot *be* destroyed. Conventional environmentalism is simply incompatible with the thought system of the Course. How, then, can we as Course students love the earth? And even if we can find a way to do so, should we?

Recognizing the earth and its inhabitants as part of the Sonship is, in my mind, the key to answering these questions. The earth is not our mother, but it and its inhabitants are our brothers. Because of this, I personally believe that we Course students can love the earth in a way that is true to our own path.

Not only *can* we do so, but I believe the Course is clear that we *should* do so. Extending love and healing to our brothers is at the heart of the Course's path. And one way in which this extension takes place

Greg Mackie

is through treating our brothers' physical forms with kindness. Even though those forms are illusory, we don't express love to our nonhuman brothers by wantonly destroying their forms, any more than we express love to our human brothers by punching them in the nose. Healed minds lead inevitably to healed external forms, and so I truly believe that following the path of the Course has the potential to bring great healing to our earthly environment.

This not only heals our nonhuman brothers (and ourselves), but also enables them to heal others by bearing witness to the healing of the mind of the Sonship.

I believe that the greatest gift we human beings can offer the world is to follow a healing path like the Course. This, I think, is the primary way in which the minds of nonhuman members of the Sonship are healed. Obviously, things like birds, blades of grass, and grains of sand can't read the Course or follow any other spiritual path for themselves. Therefore, our job as human beings is to lead the way. By extending love to our nonhuman brothers, we heal them. In so doing, of course, we also heal ourselves.

But the healing doesn't stop there. Once our nonhuman brothers are healed, they extend the healing we have given them to others. They do this not by consciously extending healing the way human beings do, but simply by serving as living witnesses that a healing in the mind of the Sonship has taken place. This, at least, is what Lesson 109 of the Workbook seems to suggest. This lesson describes a healing process that begins with the healing that extends from our minds to others whenever we do our spiritual practice (in this case, an hourly meditation practice in which we "rest in God"):

> Each hour that you take your rest today, a tired mind is suddenly made glad, a bird with broken wings begins to sing, a stream long dry begins to flow again. The world is born again each time you rest. (W-pI.109.6:1-2)

How literally are we to take this poetic description? Well, I don't think it literally means that every single time we do our practice, a dry riverbed somewhere is filled with water, and a bird starts singing because its wings are suddenly healed. However, I do think it literally means that whenever we truly enter the peace of God, minds in the

Sonship (human and nonhuman) are healed, and this healing can express itself in healed physical forms. In a nutshell, our spiritual practice can and sometimes does literally lead to physical healing in the world—including, in some cases, revitalized streams and restored birds.

This leads to the next step in the process. Lesson 109 goes on to describe what happens to those with "worn and tired minds" (W-pI.109.7:2) who encounter the brothers in the natural world whom our spiritual practice has healed:

> And they will hear the bird begin to sing and see the stream begin to flow again, with hope reborn and energy restored to walk with lightened steps along the road that suddenly seems easy as they go. (W-pI.109.7:3)

Again, this is a poetic description, but I think it points to a very real phenomenon: As a result of healing our nonhuman brothers through our practice, they bear physical witness to the healing that has taken place, and thus heal the minds of all who encounter them. Our practice leads to the world's rebirth; the world's rebirth leads, in turn, to the rebirth of all who walk the world in need of healing. The gift we gave is given everyone. In this way, the entire mind of the Sonship will ultimately be healed.

Conclusion

I find the idea that everything in the world is part of the Sonship to be profoundly beautiful. I also see in it a Course explanation for the spiritual experiences so many of us have in nature. For ages, human beings have been refreshed and renewed by encounters with nature— in particular, encounters with vibrant, healthy nature. It is this experience of renewal that has led some to conclude that the forms of nature are inherently holy, and so nature should be worshiped.

But I think that the real source of renewal is not the forms of nature, but a vision of the radiant Sonship *behind* the forms of nature: a Sonship that shouldn't be worshiped, but should certainly be treated with brotherly love. In this vision (which can be extended to man-made things as well), we commune with the minds that animate the forms we see, and recognize our oneness with those minds. This recognition heals those minds, along with our own.

And with this recognition, even the forms take on new beauty. They are not holy in themselves, but they can be infused with the holiness of the minds that made them. In addition, as we've seen, the healing of those forms can serve as a powerful witness to the healing of the mind of the Sonship. This is a deeply spiritual vision, and one I think the Course would have us cultivate. Let us, then, cultivate this vision of all our brothers who share the earth with us, the vision of Christ in which "the smallest leaf becomes a thing of wonder, and a blade of grass a sign of God's perfection" (T-17.II.6:3).

7

Workbook Lesson 76 says that we have made up the "laws" we think we live by, and we are really under no laws but God's. What are the "laws" we think we live by, what are God's laws, and how do we come to recognize God's laws?

Short Answer

The "laws" we think we live by are the ego's illusory laws of taking, which reinforce our belief that we are limited, lacking bodies at the mercy of an external world. The laws of God as He created them are Heaven's laws of giving, which affirm the truth that we are limitless Sons of God who both *have* everything and *are* everything. We come to recognize God's laws by repeatedly denying the reality of the "laws" we think we live by and affirming the reality of God's laws. We also come to recognize God's laws by consciously using them as they function in this world: We give to others what we have received from God, and thus come to recognize what God has given us.

ඏඏඏ

The "laws" we think we live by are the ego's illusory laws of taking, which reinforce our belief that we are limited, lacking bodies at the mercy of an external world.

All of us believe that we are bodies living in an external physical world. This is so obvious to us that we usually don't consider it a belief, but a fact; after all, our physical senses "prove" it to us every day. As bodies, we are constantly engaged in the fight for survival in this dog-eat-dog world, a never-ending war that requires us both to take things from the world to sustain our bodies, and to protect our bodies from those forces in the world that are trying to take from us.

Fortunately, however, there seem to be some rules of engagement in this war, laws that bring some semblance of order to the chaos. What's more, we can learn what these laws are, and how to live in harmony with them. To do so, it seems to us, is just common sense. It enables us to become more skilled in the game of acquiring and protecting that ensures our survival, at least for a little while. And learning the "higher" human laws that govern our society and our religious life gives us some added benefits. This learning enables us to acquire the more intangible things that we believe are essential to human happiness, such as special love, respect, self-esteem, moral uprightness, and right relationship with God. It also has the effect of mitigating the war to some extent, replacing the raw laws of the jungle with what at least appears to be a kinder, more "civilized" way of living.

Lesson 76 gives us a good sampling of some of the laws that we believe we must live by in order to make it in this world. (Since I will be citing Lesson 76 frequently, I will give only paragraph and sentence numbers when referring to this lesson.) Among these laws are the following:

- *Physical* laws, such as the laws of bodily health and medicine (3:3; 4:3; 8:2), and the laws of physical supply and demand that we call the laws of economics (3:2; 4:3). We believe that obeying these laws will help us to acquire for ourselves the things our bodies need to make it in this world, and protect ourselves from the things that threaten them.

- *Social* laws, such as the laws of fairness, self-sacrifice, and mutual give-and-take that we think are vital to happy and harmonious human relationships (8:3). We believe that

Greg Mackie

obeying these laws will help us to acquire for ourselves friends and companions in our struggle to make it in this world, and protect ourselves from enemies who threaten us by plotting to unfairly take from us what is rightfully ours.

- *Religious* laws, such as the "laws which set forth what is God's and what is yours" (8:4). We believe (or at least some of us believe) that obeying these laws will help us to acquire for ourselves the favor of God (Whom we see as the Creator of this world and the laws that govern it), and protect ourselves from His wrath. We hope that by gaining His approval, we can get Him to help us acquire the things we need to make it in this world, and protect us from the things that threaten us. And if we are really good at obeying His laws, perhaps He will even give us a juicy reward in the afterlife when our time in the world is done.

Throughout the Course, we find many other examples of worldly laws that we believe command our obedience. Among them are the basic laws of physics, such as those of time, space, magnitude, and mass (T-12.VII.3:3), and the basic laws of bodily survival, such as those that dictate that the body requires food, water, sleep, and protection from the elements (W-pI.136.18:3). Who would question that we need to live by these laws? They seem to be the very foundation of reality, and so we simply *must* live by them, or else we are bound to *die* by them. Right?

Wrong, says the Course. Even though these laws seem to be the very foundation of reality, the Course unequivocally dismisses them all as "foolish magical beliefs" (9:2). We may think that adhering to them is the very essence of sanity, but in the Course's view, "it is insanity that thinks these things" (4:1). Shocking as it may seem, the Course is saying that what we regard as the laws of reality are in fact the laws of illusion. As such, the laws themselves are pure illusion.

What is the essence of these illusory laws? In a nutshell, they are laws of *taking*. We can easily see this in the examples of physical, social, and religious laws presented above; all of them are laws that enable us to take things from others and avoid being taken from. Of course, it appears to us that these are laws of giving as well as taking, since they seem to govern a kind of give-and-take relationship between us and the world. However, the "giving" here is not really giving. It is simply a bargain in which the giver gives something in payment in order to get something better in exchange for what he gives; in other words, the ego's law of "giving to get" (T-4.II.6:5). Whatever giving that happens under the auspices of these laws is really just another means of taking. These laws, then, are the perfect expression of what T-23.II calls the fourth law of chaos: "You have what you have taken" (T-23.II.9:3). Indeed, in a war in which all participants are fighting for their own survival, how could you possibly have anything except by taking it?

These "laws" that we seem to live by are the ego's laws, and the ego's purpose for them is to reinforce our belief in the very situation that seems to make the laws necessary: that we are limited, lacking bodies at the mercy of an external world. Lesson 76 calls them "the strange and twisted laws you have set up to save you" (3:1). What they are designed to "save" us from is the recognition that the real cause of our suffering is not the external world's attack on us, but our attack on *ourselves* for our "sin" of separating from God. (This, I think, is the idea behind 5:2-7.) The mind's own self-punishment for its seeming sins is the real cause of our entire sense of limitation and lack. But the laws of taking that seem to govern the world "prove" to us that the cause of our limitation and lack is really the body, and the external world it lives in. These laws convince us that we truly are frail, vulnerable, lacking bodies who must take from the world in order to survive. (The ultimate cause of our suffering, in this view, is God, Whom we believe created the body and the external world. For a chilling description of the entire human life cycle as an expression of the laws of sin, guilt, and death, see T-13.In.2-3.)

Why does the ego want us to believe all this? Because as long as we do, we will not recognize the power we have to end the entire illusion—our belief that we separated from God, our belief in sin, our suffering, the world, and the ego itself—simply by changing our minds. As long as we follow the "laws" of the ego instead of the laws of God, we will believe that we *are* the ego instead of the Son of God, and the ego's survival is thus assured.

The laws of God as He created them are Heaven's laws of giving, which affirm the truth that we are limitless Sons of God who both *have* everything and *are* everything.

The laws of God as they operate in Heaven stand in stark contrast to the "laws" we think we live by in this world. (Actually, God's laws operate in this world as well, in a form adapted to this world. I will discuss this in more detail below.) God's laws are not rules of engagement set up to bring some semblance of order to a war of bodies, but "laws of love" (T-13.VI.13:1), created to ensure the peaceful communion of the Sonship and the loving increase of the Kingdom.

The Course has much to say about Heaven's laws, but they can basically be boiled down to the law of *creation*, or extension. This law says that thoughts naturally extend outward from the mind that thinks them, creating extensions of that mind that are reflections of its basic nature. Since God is Love and His Thoughts reflect His nature, the law of creation ensures that His Kingdom is a continual outpouring of love: "Love creates itself, and nothing but itself" (T-25.III.1:6). This continual outpouring of love by both God and His Son, who creates as His Father does, is the way in which each member of the Kingdom both keeps the love that was given to him in his own creation, and increases the love that everyone has to share. For in the Kingdom, it is fully understood that the way to have and keep the gifts we have received is not to hoard them to ourselves, but to give them away: "To have, give all to all" (T-6.V(A).5:13).

We can easily see that the essence of God's laws is the exact opposite of the illusory "laws" we think we live by: The ego's laws are laws of *taking*, but God's laws are laws of *giving*. The ego's laws are laws of gain and loss, but "there is no loss under the laws of God" (9:3). The ego's laws are laws of payment and exchange, but the laws of God proclaim that "payment is neither given nor received" (9:4), and "exchange cannot be made" (9:5). The ego's laws are laws of both "giving to get" *and* taking, but "God's laws forever give and never take" (9:6). Through God's laws "is creation endlessly increased" (11:2). And just as the ego's laws reinforce our belief that we are limited, lacking bodies at the mercy of an external world, so do the laws of God affirm the fact that we are eternal, limitless Sons of God who "both *have* everything and *are* everything" (T-4.III.9:5), forever extending love and joyfully increasing the Kingdom of Heaven.

We come to recognize God's laws by repeatedly denying the reality of the "laws" we think we live by, and affirming the reality of God's laws.

Speaking in general terms, we come to recognize God's laws by doing the Course. The Course's entire program is a program in how to let go of the "laws" of the ego and remember the laws of God. More specifically, one means the Course gives us for recognizing God's laws is simply to repeatedly deny the reality of the "laws" we think we live by, and affirm the reality of God's laws instead. This is the practice of Lesson 76. It has us mentally review the "laws" we think we live by, dismiss them with the thought "I am under no laws but God's," and then keep repeating this thought while waiting receptively for the Holy Spirit to reveal to us the laws of God.

Of course, denying the "laws" of the ego doesn't mean denying the fact that we *seem* to live by them. As long as our minds are unhealed, we will believe in these laws to some extent, and as long as we believe in them, we will live by them within the illusory world. We are not to deny this; instead, we are to deny the ultimate *reality* of these laws. The more we do this kind of denial, the closer our minds come to truly renouncing their belief in these laws. And it is when that belief is fully renounced on a deep level (a very long-term goal, I think) that we will finally be free of the laws that seem to rule our world.

We also come to recognize God's laws by consciously using them as they function in this world: We give to others what we have received from God, and thus come to recognize what God has given us.

To clarify this point, a discussion of how God's laws function in this world is necessary. The Course says that even though "the laws of God do not prevail in perfect form" (T-25.VI.5:1) in this world, they do prevail in adapted form, as I said above. Specifically, the Holy Spirit has taken God's Heavenly law of creation and translated it into the earthly law of *perception* (see T-7.II.2-4). Recall that in the Heavenly law of creation, the mind extends its thoughts outward and creates extensions that are reflections of what that mind is. In like manner, in the earthly law of perception, the mind projects its thoughts outward and makes a perceptual *experience* of what it *thinks* it is. Extension creates reality in Heaven, while "projection makes perception" (T-21.In.1:1) on earth.

Greg Mackie

Thus, we actually have no choice but to live by the laws of God, even here in this world; the law of perception that governs this world reflects "a fundamental law of the mind, and therefore one that always operates" (T-7.VIII.1:2). However, we do have a choice about how to use this law. If we choose the ego's interpretation of it, we will mistakenly believe that the law of perception enables us to rid our minds of undesirable thoughts by projecting them onto something outside ourselves. This distorted process is what produces the illusory "laws" we think we live by: As we saw above, the mind's self-attack (an undesirable thought) is projected onto the external world, making it seem that the external world and its "laws," not the mind, is the cause of our suffering.

But the truth is that projecting thoughts out of our minds, be they desirable or undesirable thoughts, is not the way to get rid of them, but the way to keep them. The ego wants to hide this fact in order to deceive us, but the Holy Spirit wants to reveal this fact in order to free us. Therefore, if we choose the Holy Spirit's interpretation of the law of perception, we will correctly see it as the law of earthly extension, "the fundamental law of sharing, by which you give what you value in order to keep it in your mind" (T-7.VIII.1:6). By sharing the Holy Spirit's perception, we will come to recognize that the world is not governed by the "laws" the ego made, but by the earthly reflection of the law of God I mentioned above: "To have, give all to all."

How do we come to recognize this law? By applying it to our lives in a conscious way, and thus discovering for ourselves that it really works. We must *give* in order to *have*; specifically, we must *give* to others what we have received from God, in order to recognize that we *have* what God has given us. This act of giving is absolutely vital to the Course's process of salvation, as the following passage makes clear:

> We will not recognize what we receive until we give
> it. You have heard this said a hundred ways, a hundred
> times, and yet belief is lacking still.   (W-pI.154.12:1-2)

The Course is filled with practices intended to help us learn just what this passage is teaching us. One of the best is the practice given in Workbook Lesson 108, "To give and to receive are one in truth." This lesson offers us a very simple practice, in which we mentally extend the gifts of God to our brothers and experience those gifts returning to us, which demonstrates to us that we have them. The Course considers this particular practice to be especially powerful, "because it can be tried so easily and seen as true" (W-pI.108.6:1). I have done it myself many times, and can vouch for that. The Course goes on to say that once we have tried this practice and seen the laws of God at work in this particular instance, "the thought behind it can be generalized to other areas of doubt and double vision" (W-pI.108.6:2). In other words, through this simple practice of giving in order to recognize what we have received from God, we come to recognize the laws of God at work in every aspect of our lives. (I should mention that this law of giving works even when we give material things; while we do lose the particular material thing we give, the thought behind our giving returns to us in some form and is reinforced in our minds—see W-pI.187.2.)

This all makes perfect sense, does it not? If we want to turn away from the ego's illusory laws of taking and recognize God's laws of pure giving, what better way is there than to give? Through giving as God gives, we learn that His laws are reflected everywhere, even in this world where other "laws" seem to rule. Not only that, but giving as God gives ultimately teaches us who we really are. For if, as I said above, the law of perception allows us to project our thoughts outward and thus experience what we think we are, then using it to extend love allows us to experience the fact that what we *really* are is *love*. Through extending love and healing to all of our brothers, an extension that "reflects creation" (T-7.II.2:3), we ultimately come to recognize the eternal inheritance that God has given us: our true Identity as His beloved Son. We will finally know that we are under no laws but God's, forever creating and extending the Kingdom of Heaven, forever living in perfect harmony with our Father's eternal laws of love.

8

Does the Holy Spirit actually *do* things in the world? Ken Wapnick says He does not, and I would like to know your view.

Short Answer

In my view, the Holy Spirit definitely does things in the world. I have two main reasons for this view:

1. The Course very clearly states that the Holy Spirit does things in the world.

2. The Course offers no reason to believe that it doesn't mean this literally.

Not only do I believe this view to be true, but I also find it very comforting, because it means that we are not cut off from God. He is aware of our seeming exile, and has actively sent us a Guide to help us find our way home.

ʊʊʊ

This is certainly a controversial topic in Course circles, with strong opinions on both sides of the issue. To me, the resolution of this issue comes down to one very simple question: What does the *Course* say about it? The two numbered points above represent my own interpretation of what the Course says on this subject.

Before we look at those points in more detail, I want to clarify how I understand the question being posed here, and what I mean by my answer. As I am understanding it, the question basically means this: "Does the Holy Spirit actively do things in the world in the same sense that we, the members of the Sonship, actively do things in the world?" This is what I think most people mean when they ask whether the Holy Spirit does things in the world. So, while I know the Course teaches that the world is an illusion and therefore no *real* acts occur in the world, the question I'm addressing here is whether or not the Holy Spirit acts *within the illusion*. My answer is that He does act within the illusion, in the same sense that we do. This is what I mean when I say that the Holy Spirit does things in the world.

1. The Course very clearly states that the Holy Spirit does things in the world.

While the Course tells us that the Holy Spirit's primary function is to teach us true perception—in other words, to help us change our minds, not our external world—it also tells us clearly that one means the Holy Spirit uses for changing our minds is working within the world of form. The Holy Spirit Himself has taken form to teach us in this world (see C-6.1:4), and He uses the forms of the world for this teaching purpose. Indeed, the Course itself—a form brought into the world by the Holy Spirit through Jesus—is a prime example of the Holy Spirit using form as a teaching tool.

Why does He use form as a teaching tool? Because we who are committed to the ego have a heavy investment in the world of form that the ego made. Form is what we believe in; it is a language we can understand. Therefore, in order to be an effective Teacher, the Holy Spirit needs "to use what the ego has made, to teach the opposite of what the ego has 'learned'" (T-7.IV.3:3). He needs to *use* the world of form as a means to teach us how to *transcend* the world of form.

If the Holy Spirit does indeed work within the world of form, what exactly does He do? The following italicized points are a list of some of the things the Course explicitly says the Holy Spirit does (or has done) in the world:

He has given us God's plan for salvation, which includes a script for our entire journey through the world.

The plan for salvation (also called the plan of the Atonement) is God's response to the separation, and we are told that the Holy Spirit has the function of "bringing the plan of the Atonement to us" (C-6.2:1). The content of that plan is forgiveness, the earthly reflection of the formless Love of God. Yet because we believe in a world of form, the plan has also taken form. In fact, we are told that the Holy Spirit has written the script (see W-pI.169.9:3) for every single thing that happens in the world. Absolutely nothing is left to chance. While this may seem painfully restrictive at first glance, ultimately it is deeply reassuring, as the following passage invites us to recognize:

> What could you not accept, if you but knew that everything that happens, all events, past, present and to come, are gently planned by One Whose only purpose is your good? (W-pI.135.18:1)

For more about the Holy Spirit's script and how it relates to the Course's idea that *we* are responsible for everything that happens to us in our lives, see Q & A #2, entitled "Are all the events and circumstances in our lives predetermined, or do we have free choice?"

He has given each of us a function in His plan for salvation: both a general function, and a special function in the world.

In addition to giving us God's plan for salvation, the Holy Spirit has the function of "establishing our particular part in it and showing us exactly what it is" (C-6.2:1). Since the content of the plan is forgiveness, our general function in that plan is also forgiveness— primarily, extending forgiveness to others. Yet because each of us is different on the level of form, the Holy Spirit has given each of us a particular form in which we are to fulfill our function of forgiveness:

> Such is the Holy Spirit's kind perception of specialness; His use of what you made, to heal instead of harm. To each He gives a special function in salvation he alone can fill; a part for only him. (T-25.VI.4:1-2)

Our special function is the specific form our forgiveness takes in the world, a form that is uniquely suited to our individual personalities, talents, and life circumstances (see T-25.VII.7:1-3 and W-pI.154.2:1-2). In short, it is the particular part each of us has been assigned in God's plan for salvation.

He gives us all the physical things and circumstances we need to fulfill our special function in the world.

To some Course students, it may seem almost sacrilegious to suggest that the Holy Spirit literally gives us *things*. Yet the Course unequivocally states that He supplies us with material possessions (see T-13.VII.12-13) and money (see P-3.III.1,4-6). In addition, He takes care of the circumstances of our lives, including bringing about meetings with specific people (see M-2.1:1) and arranging our life situations (see T-20.IV.8:1-8).

Of course, He does not do this to serve our ego needs; He is not a divine butler at our beck and call, Who delivers worldly goodies to keep our egos fat and happy. Rather, He gives us things only to enable us to fulfill our special function in God's plan for salvation. Thus, the surprising answer to the often-asked question of whether the Holy Spirit manifests parking spaces is "Yes, He does manifest parking spaces, *if* doing so serves God's plan."

He gives us detailed guidance for all of our decisions and all of our actions in the world.

In the Course's view, we are utterly incapable of making sound decisions on our own. Our limited human judgment is simply not adequate to the task. Therefore, we need a Guide Whose judgment is unlimited, a Guide Who can make decisions *for* us. That Guide, of course, is the Holy Spirit.

Again and again, we are told to let go of our judgment and allow the Holy Spirit's judgment to replace it. An entire section of the Manual for Teachers (M-10) is devoted to this topic. And while the Holy Spirit's most important role is to guide our perception of the world, the Course is clear that He is to specifically guide our actions in the world as well. We are told very explicitly that if we turn to Him, the Holy Spirit will tell us "what to do and where to go; to whom to speak and what to say to him, what thoughts to think, what words to give the world" (W-pII.275.2:3; see also T-2.V(A).18:4-5; W-pI.71.9:3-5; and W-pI.rVI.In.7:2). Not only will He tell us what to do, but He will even "do it for [us]" (T-14.IV.6:6). It can't get any clearer than that. There is simply no doubt that the Course depicts the Holy Spirit doing things in the world.

2. The Course offers no reason to believe that it doesn't mean this literally.

Even those who believe the Holy Spirit doesn't do things in the world don't deny that the Course depicts Him doing things in the world. What they do deny is that those depictions are to be taken literally. They offer various reasons for why the Course doesn't literally mean the things it says about the Holy Spirit. Usually, these reasons are based on the underlying assumption that the Course can't possibly mean these things, given its overall thought system.

As I've already made clear, I disagree with this view. I can find no evidence whatsoever in the Course to support it. I can find nothing in its overall thought system that precludes the possibility of the Holy Spirit acting in the world. In fact, the thought system I see in the Course makes the Holy Spirit's activity in the world absolutely indispensable to our salvation.

Given the pervasiveness of the view that the Holy Spirit doesn't do things in the world, I'd like to address some of the specific reasons offered for this view. The following italicized points present some of the main arguments I have heard in support of this view, along with my response to those arguments. I have heard these arguments from many Course students, but the main source from which I will draw most of them is the highly influential works of Ken Wapnick. Since Wapnick is by far the most prominent proponent of this view, I think it will be beneficial, in the spirit of scholarly dialogue, to address his ideas directly. Therefore, I will do so in a number of places, and I will include references to his works for people who wish to consult the original sources.

The Holy Spirit doesn't do things in the world because the world is an illusion.

People who present this argument say something like the following: "The Holy Spirit can't really act in the world, because there is no world to act *in*. If the world is an illusion, then the Holy Spirit's 'acts' in the world must be illusions too." This point is perfectly logical, and I have no argument with it. From the Course's standpoint, all acts in the illusory world, whether they are ours or the Holy Spirit's, are illusions. Given this, I wholeheartedly agree that the Holy Spirit doesn't do *real* things in the world, just as *we* don't do real things in the world.

But this valid point doesn't really address the question I think most people have in mind when they ask if the Holy Spirit does things in the world. As I framed it above, the question isn't whether or not the Holy Spirit's acts within the illusion are real, but whether or not He does act within the illusion. In other words, to repeat the version of the question I presented earlier: Does the Holy Spirit actively do things in the world in the same sense that we, the members of the Sonship, actively do things in the world? The ultimate reality-status of those things and of that world is not really relevant to this question. Therefore, the world's illusory nature can't really be used to refute the idea that the Holy Spirit does things in the world.

The Holy Spirit doesn't do things in the world because if He did, that would make the error real.

This is a major argument of Ken Wapnick, who says that if God or His agents were to act in the world, they "would be violating the Course's 'prime directive' (to borrow a term from *Star Trek*), which is not to make the error real" (*The Most Commonly Asked Questions about 'A Course in Miracles,'* p. 90). But would such action in the world really be an automatic violation of that "prime directive"? The author of the Course doesn't seem to think so. There is no explicit statement in the Course that says so, and as we've seen, there are plenty of explicit statements that say the Holy Spirit does act in the world. This certainly suggests that His doing so doesn't make the error real.

In fact, there are places in the Course that indicate that He acts in the world to prove the error *unreal*. One example is in Chapter 30, Section VIII of the Text. The second paragraph of that section discusses a miracle that brings about a positive external change in your brother's life situation. According to that paragraph, one powerful effect of that miracle and the external change it brings about is the following:

> The miracle attests salvation from appearances by showing they can change....The miracle is proof [your brother] is not bound by loss or suffering in any form,

Greg Mackie

because it can so easily be changed. This demonstrates that it was never real, and could not stem from his reality.
(T-30.VIII.2:2,6-7)

In other words, the miracle changes external situations, and in so doing proves that those external situations are only illusory appearances, not reality. We are thus saved from those appearances.

Think about the implications of that. Miracles come from the Holy Spirit, "Who gives all miracles" (T-30.VIII.4:7). Their primary result is a change of mind, but they also produce positive external effects. And these external effects are not simply pleasant by-products of miracles, but actually perform a vital role in reinforcing that change of mind: They prove the unreality of appearances. Therefore, the result of the Holy Spirit's intervention in the world (through the external effects of the miracles He gives) is that the error is made unreal. This is reason enough to dismiss the idea that the Holy Spirit cannot do things in the world because that would automatically make the error real.

The Holy Spirit doesn't do things in the world because God does not even know about the separation.

This, too, is a major argument of Ken Wapnick: "This God [the God of the Course] does not even know about the separation...and thus does not and cannot respond to it" (*Commonly Asked Questions*, p. 4). Therefore, God could not possibly have literally created a Being like the Holy Spirit in response to the separation. Given this, it goes without saying that He didn't create a Being Who could actually *act* within the illusory world of separation.

But the Course never actually says that God doesn't know about the separation. In fact, there are two passages that directly say otherwise. One is T-6.V.1:5-8; the other is the following:

Unless you take your part in the creation, [God's] joy is not complete because yours is incomplete. *And this He does know. He knows it in His Own Being and its experience of His Son's experience.* The constant going out of His Love is blocked when His channels are closed, and He is lonely when the minds He created do not communicate fully with Him.   (T-4.VII.6:4-7, emphasis mine)

Clearly, this passage tells us that God knows we have somehow cut off our minds from Him—or at least cut off our awareness of Him. Some may dismiss this passage as metaphor, but I personally find that very hard to do. The part I emphasized, in particular, looks a lot more like the technical language of abstract philosophy than the colorful language of vivid, concrete imagery; it is more metaphysics than metaphor. In my opinion, this passage (along with the second passage that I've cited) is strong evidence that God knows about the separation, and could therefore respond to it by creating a Being capable of acting within the illusion of separation. Indeed, the second passage goes on to say that God did respond to it: "So He thought, 'My children sleep and must be awakened'" (T-6.V.1:8).

For more on the topic of whether God knows about the separation, see Robert Perry's article entitled "Does God Know We Are Here?" This article is available in Issue #21 of the Circle of Atonement's newsletter, *A Better Way*, or on the Circle's website.

The Holy Spirit doesn't do things in the world because He is only the memory of God.

This point follows from the previous one. For if the Holy Spirit is not a Being created in response to the separation, then just what is He? Clearly, He can't really be anything substantial. Ken Wapnick, in fact, says point-blank that "the Holy Spirit is an illusion" (*Duality as Metaphor in 'A Course in Miracles'* tape set). What is the nature of this illusion? According to Wapnick, the Holy Spirit is simply "the memory of God's Love and the Son's true Identity as Christ that he carried with him into his dream" (*Commonly Asked Questions*, p. 103). He is "a distant memory of our Source" (*The Message of 'A Course in Miracles,' Volume One: All Are Called*, p. 33), a memory that comforts us within the dream of separation just as the memory of a human loved one comforts us when we feel lonely and cut off from our home.

But there are at least two problems with this definition. First, the Course itself never uses anything like this definition. The closest it ever comes is to say that the Holy Spirit *reminds* us of God (see, for instance, T-5.II.7:1-5), but saying that He reminds us of God is quite different than saying that He is actually the *memory* of God. That would be like saying that when my wife reminds me of the trip to San Francisco we took ten years ago, she herself *is* my memory of that trip.

Second, the term "memory of God" has a specific, technical meaning in the Course, and it is not synonymous with the Holy Spirit. Rather, the term "memory of God" refers to our final awakening in Heaven, accomplished by God in His last step (see, for instance, W-pII.8.5 and C-3.4). One passage, in fact, spells out the relationship *between* the memory of God and the Holy Spirit: "I have within me both the memory of You [God], *and* One [the Holy Spirit] Who leads me to it" (W-pII.352.1:7, emphasis mine). Here, the memory of God and the Holy Spirit are clearly depicted as different things. Thus, rather than defining the Holy Spirit as the memory of God, I think we are wiser to adhere to the definition of the Holy Spirit that the Course itself gives us: a Being Whom God created in response to the separation, a Being Who can and does do things in the world to carry out God's plan of salvation.

The Holy Spirit doesn't do things in the world; if we believe He does, we are falling into the trap of "spiritual specialness."

According to Ken Wapnick, the belief that the Holy Spirit does things in the world is not only incorrect, but is actually a sneaky ego ploy to get us to engage in what he calls "spiritual specialness." (See the discussion on pp. 137-142 of *The Message of 'A Course in Miracles,' Volume Two: Few Choose to Listen.*) In his view, the belief that the Holy Spirit does things in the world is simply the ego's insatiable drive for specialness masquerading in a "spiritualized" form. In particular, seeing the Holy Spirit as a personal Being Who has "specially chosen [us] to do *holy, special, and very important work* in this world" (*Few Choose to Listen*, p. 137, emphasis Wapnick's) is nothing more than the ego's last-ditch effort to make the error real, to defend its specialness against the threat posed by the ego-undoing message of *A Course in Miracles.*

Certainly, the idea that we have a special function in the world can be a fertile ground for ego-based specialness. But to say that this idea is *inherently* ego-based is a classic case of throwing out the baby with the bathwater. As we saw above, the Course clearly says that the Holy Spirit has indeed given us a special function in the world. Rather than being an ego trap, this special function is, in the words I quoted earlier, "the Holy Spirit's kind perception of specialness; His use of what you made, to heal instead of harm" (T-25.VI.4:1). It is the Holy Spirit's reinterpretation of our desire for specialness, in which He converts it from an ego trap to a means to serve God's plan.

Far from discouraging the idea, then, Jesus really wants us to know that we do have a special function, because "[our] part is essential to God's plan for salvation" (W-pI.100.Heading). If we totally reject the idea that the Holy Spirit has given us a special function and does things in the world to help us fulfill that function, it will have the devastating effect of causing us to reject our part in God's plan. Ironically, in trying to escape "spiritual specialness," we will end up playing right into the ego's hands.

The Holy Spirit doesn't do things in the world because pure, non-dualistic spirit simply cannot interact with a dualistic world without compromising spirit's non-dualistic nature.

This, I believe, is the fundamental assumption underlying all of the arguments presented above against the idea of the Holy Spirit doing things in the world. It also seems to be at the core of Ken Wapnick's view of the Course's thought system, which he explains in a section of *Few Choose to Listen* entitled "An Uncompromising Non-Dualism" (*Few Choose to Listen*, p. 94). In that section, one way in which he expresses his basic rule of Course interpretation is to paraphrase M-27.7:1, replacing the word "death" with "duality," as follows: "*Accept no compromise in which **duality** plays a part*" (*Few Choose to Listen*, p. 94, emphasis Wapnick's).

In this view, God's Heaven is so purely non-dualistic, so absolutely One, that nothing within it can possibly reach down and interact with a dualistic, separated world in any way, shape, or form. If anything in this realm of pure spirit were to do so, its purity and Oneness would be impossibly compromised. Therefore, whenever the Course talks about spirit interacting with the world (as when it describes the Holy Spirit doing things in the world), it simply can't be taken literally.

Why, then, does the Course talk this way? According to Wapnick, Jesus' only purpose for this "metaphorical" dualistic language is to comfort beginners on the path by "couch[ing] his teachings in words that his students—always referred to as children (or sometimes even younger)—can understand without fear" (*Commonly Asked Questions*, pp. 85-86). Taking this language literally is fine for beginners, but once we have progressed beyond the beginning stage, we should give up childish notions like the idea of spirit interacting with the world.

But how do we know that the assumption that spirit cannot interact with the world is correct? The Course itself never states this once; it is only a logical inference based on a particular interpretation of certain passages. Not only does the Course not state this, but it states the opposite—that spirit can and does interact with the world—countless times. How do we know that it does not mean what it says? If the choice is between a questionable logical inference never stated in the Course and a teaching stated again and again in the Course, which should we choose?

In my opinion, the clear choice is the latter. Whenever we are trying to determine what the Course teaches, I think we are on much firmer ground when we stick to what the Course itself actually says, rather than taking unwarranted logical leaps. And besides, we actually have a very obvious, irrefutable example of non-dualistic spirit interacting with a dualistic world without compromising spirit's non-dualistic nature. That example is *us*: the Sonship.

Think about the current situation of the Sonship as the Course describes it. Our true nature is non-dualistic spirit. Our home is the absolute Oneness of Heaven. Yet somehow, in a way that the Course says is unexplainable, we managed to convince ourselves that we are something other than spirit. Out of this mental error, we managed to project a dualistic, illusory world with which we interact. But in spite of this, we are told, we have not really compromised our non-dualistic spiritual nature. We remain in the Oneness of Heaven, which we never really left.

Clearly, then, it is possible for a non-dualistic Sonship to somehow mentally separate from God, make an illusory, dualistic world, and interact with that world without compromising the Sonship's non-dualistic nature. Now, here's the punch line: If this is so, then why can't a non-dualistic God *respond* to the separation by sending a Teacher and Comforter Who can and does interact with the illusory, dualistic world without compromising God's non-dualistic nature? Personally, I see no reason why He cannot.

Conclusion

I have every reason to believe that the Course literally "means exactly what it says" (T-8.IX.8:1) when it tells us that the Holy Spirit does things in the world. I have no reason to believe otherwise. Personally, I am immensely comforted by this, because it means that we are not cut off from God, all alone in a nightmare world that our remote Father does not even know about. Instead, He knows in His Own Being that we are suffering in seeming exile. And so, out of His Love for us, He created the Holy Spirit, a Guide Who leads us home using every means at His disposal. Nothing is too "impure" for our Guide to use; He even uses the illusory world that we made to imprison ourselves as a means to set us free. In the pages of the Course, Jesus assures us that we have Help in this world. Why not take him at his word?

9

Why does the Course always use masculine terms when referring to God, the Holy Spirit, and the beings that God created?

Short Answer

In my opinion, the Course uses masculine terms in order to heal the wounds that stem from our conventional understanding of those terms, an understanding which has often been used as a means of exclusion. The Course brings about this healing by giving masculine terms a meaning that is nonphysical and all-encompassing, thus transforming them into a means of inclusion. The Course does use the traditional Christian terms "Father" and "Son" and the earthly father-son relationship as metaphors, but it applies these metaphors to everyone in a totally inclusive way. As we read and practice the Course over time, the old negative meanings we have assigned to these masculine terms are gradually replaced by the Course's new positive meanings, and it is this that heals our wounds.

ϾϾϾ

The Course's use of masculine terms for God, the Holy Spirit, and the beings God created (us) has been a source of controversy from the time it was first published. Since the Course emerged in a time of women's liberation, this language has struck a number of people as anachronistic and exclusionary. (It is ironic that all of this masculine language was scribed by a woman!) I know of some Course students who were so offended by this language that they crossed the masculine terms out wherever those terms appeared in the Course, and replaced them with gender-free equivalents.

All of this has led many people to wonder: Why did Jesus, the teacher of radical inclusion, use language that seems to exclude fifty percent of the human race? Is Jesus sexist? Or was the masculine language in the Course a mistake, a distortion that reflected Helen Schucman's own writing style rather than the words of Jesus?

In my opinion, the masculine terms in the Course did indeed come from Jesus. I believe that he chose the words he used in the Course very carefully, and the words he used for God and His creations are no exception. He is certainly not sexist. Why, then, did he use the masculine terms? The Course never gives us a specific answer, but my own opinion is that he used them for the same purpose that he used every word in the Course: the purpose of healing. Just as he did with so many words—especially those from the Christian tradition—he radically redefined the masculine terminology that he used, transforming it from a means of exclusion into a means of inclusion, and thus from a means of wounding to a means of healing.

To show how the Course does this, I will expand on my short answer in the points below. But before I do, I want to add an important note concerning the scope of this inquiry. In this Q & A, I am not addressing the wider issue of how human beings in general should deal with gender-specific language for God and collective humanity; rather, I'm addressing the much narrower issue of why the author of the Course used the language that he did. I think there are many valid approaches to the issue of gender-specific language, and different traditions deal with it in different ways. Here, I'm simply presenting what I believe to be Jesus' particular way of using such language in the Course.

The Course gives masculine terms a meaning that is nonphysical and all-encompassing, thus transforming them into a means of inclusion.

Normally, of course, masculine terms bring to mind an image of beings who are physically male. There is nothing exclusionary or wounding about this if one is referring to specific beings who are definitely physically male. The problem comes when we use masculine terms to refer to collective humanity, or to beings whose gender (if any) we cannot readily determine, such as God.

When we use such terms to refer to collective humanity—as we do when we use "he" and "him" as generic pronouns, or use words like "man" to refer to the entire human race—we imply that humanity is primarily defined as male, and the female is secondary. When we use such terms to refer to God, we imply that *divinity* is primarily (or exclusively) male as well. It is men, not women, who are created in the image and likeness of God. In general, the use of masculine language tends to suggest that men and maleness are first and foremost in the hierarchy of things, and women are, to borrow the title of Simone de Beauvoir's feminist classic, "the second sex." Historically, the outward social, political, and religious dominance of men reflected in this masculine language has been a source of great pain in our world, both for women and for men. Such language has tended to exclude women, to the detriment of both sexes.

However, that being said, a crucial point must be made: Masculine terms are not *inherently* exclusionary, because words are neutral in themselves, and only have the meanings we choose to assign to them. The implications discussed above are thus not in the words themselves; sexism isn't in words, but in people. And the sexism in people—simply another expression of the belief in separation that divides us all—isn't going to magically go away just by changing the words we use. Of course, I'm not saying that we should never change the words we use; such a change can be truly healing if it is the expression of a healed mind. I'm simply saying that if the content of our minds is still sexist, then just changing the form of our words, in and of itself, will not make a difference.

And just as we can still be sexist at heart even while using "inclusive" terms, we can also be nonsexist at heart while using masculine (or feminine) terms for God and humanity. I think masculine terms have often been used without the intent (conscious or unconscious) to exclude anyone. While the terms may have originally arisen from the exclusion of women, eventually these terms simply became conventions of our language, and have been used even by people who unequivocally support the equality of women. Great advocates of inclusion like Gandhi and Martin Luther King, Jr. used such terms. Indeed, numerous women have used them, including feminist icons such as the early women's rights advocate Elizabeth Cady Stanton. Many people today, especially older people, use them simply because these were the terms used when they were growing up, just as some older black people in America use "colored" or "Negro" (the word King usually used to refer to black people) instead of "African-American." Thus, as with all words, masculine terms are only as exclusionary as we choose to make them.

This inherent neutrality of words makes possible the Course's radical redefinition of the masculine terms it uses. How does it redefine them? Essentially, by stripping them of their conventional association with physical maleness, and the exclusion that implies. The Course makes it abundantly clear that the beings it refers to as "he" and "him" and "Father" and "Son" and "brother" are all *nonphysical* beings. God, the Holy Spirit, and our true Self are all formless, bodiless realities beyond the usual categories of this world, including the category of gender.

Indeed, some of the terms used to refer to God, such as "Formlessness Itself" (W-pI.186.14:1) and "Divine Abstraction" (T-4.VII.5:4), strongly emphasize God's nonphysicality. And God's creation, being an extension of Him, is as nonphysical as He is. Thus, the Course's masculine terms refer to beings that, whatever their surface appearance, are neither male nor female. These terms encompass literally everyone and everything, and so what was once exclusive has been transformed into something radically inclusive.

This inclusiveness is apparent in the Course's use of three traditional Christian terms: "Father," "Son," and "brother." In all three cases, a term that has traditionally been used to exclude is transformed by the Course into a term that includes. God the Father, Who is traditionally regarded as totally Other and commonly pictured as a bearded old man in the sky, is transformed by the Course into a formless, bodiless reality Whose Being literally includes everyone and everything. God the Son, who is traditionally regarded to be Jesus (a man) and no one else, is transformed by the Course into the Sonship, our true Self, an Identity that, as part of God, also literally includes everyone and everything. And the term "brother," which traditionally has been used to refer only to fellow male Christians, is transformed by the Course into a term that refers to every member of the Sonship. This term therefore includes men, women, children, and even (in my opinion) nonhuman aspects of the Sonship like animals, plants, and grains of sand. You can't get much more inclusive than that.

The Course does use the traditional Christian terms "Father" and "Son" and the earthly father-son relationship as metaphors, but it applies these metaphors to everyone in a totally inclusive way.

To slightly qualify what I said in the last point, in the case of the terms "Father" and "Son" (and perhaps "brother" as well), I don't think *all* gender associations have been removed. Even though the Course has stripped these terms of their literal gender-based meaning, I do think the Course has retained some of their metaphorical gender-based meanings. This is in keeping with the Course's *modus operandi* of retaining the loving connotations of the Christian terms it uses, while removing the fearful ones.

So, the Course does draw upon the positive aspects of the metaphor of God the Father: His love, strength, protection, majesty, generosity, etc. It also draws upon the positive aspects of the metaphor of God the Son: his holiness, power, compassion, his intimate relationship with the Father, etc. But at the same time, it drops the negative aspects of these metaphors as traditionally used: things such as the vengeful, punishing Father Who commands us to fear Him, and the fiercely condemning Son whom the Father sacrificed for our sins and who will judge us at the end of time. In particular, the Course drops the implication that we are *separate* from the Father and the Son. Since in truth we are all—men and women—included in both the Father and the Son, we share in all of Their wholly benevolent and loving characteristics.

The Course also uses the metaphor of an earthly father and his son to illustrate our relationship with God. It says that God is like the father in Jesus' parable of the Prodigal Son, welcoming his son (us) back with open arms even after the son had seemingly squandered his inheritance (as we have seemingly done by separating from God). It says that God is like a loving father who leaves his entire inheritance—including his very name—to his son, because he loves his son and the son carries on the father's lineage. In these metaphors, the Course uses the ideal father-son relationship as a means of illustrating what the relationship between God and us is like.

But even here, the Course is inclusive. It takes these father-son images and applies them to the relationship that all of us have with God. And none of the qualities illustrated in the father-son metaphor are exclusively male qualities. The qualities exemplified in the ideal father-son relationship are equally qualities of an ideal mother-daughter relationship (or mother-son, or father-daughter).

In fact, the Course material does use some feminine imagery to describe God and His relationship with His children. The "Clarification of Terms" depicts the miracle (which comes from God) as a healing balm which "corrects as gently as a loving mother sings her child to rest" (C-2.8:2). In *The Gifts of God*, the last work Jesus dictated to Helen Schucman, we read this beautiful description of God's Love: "He loves you as a mother loves her child; her only one, the only love she has, her all-in-all, extension of herself, as much a part of her as breath itself" (*The Gifts of God*, p. 126). This feminine imagery is extremely rare in the Course material, but the very fact that Jesus uses it at all shows us that he doesn't see God as exclusively male. The loving traits he assigns to God are as much feminine as masculine—or better, they are neither feminine nor masculine. Whatever metaphors the Course uses, whether they be the masculine terms it usually uses or the feminine terms I've cited here, they are meant to include everyone.

As we read and practice the Course over time, the old negative meanings we have assigned to these masculine terms are gradually replaced by the Course's new positive meanings, and it is this that heals our wounds.

As we've seen, the use of masculine terms for collective humanity and for God, while not inherently negative, has led to a lot of pain for many people. In response to this pain, many people have simply stopped using the traditional terms entirely, either using neutral terms or using masculine and feminine terms together, as in "he or she" or "Father-Mother God." I certainly think this can be a very positive approach; I often do it myself. Yet I think this method of dealing with the problem of gender-specific language, though it can be a positive statement of inclusion, has a potential downside: It can often leave the wounds associated with the masculine terms unhealed. The wounds are still there; they've just been pushed out of awareness by avoiding the words associated with them. And so those wounds fester in darkness, instead of being healed by the light.

I think that the Course's way of using masculine terms is its solution to this problem. Rather than avoiding these terms, it transforms them, as we've seen above. It takes these familiar words, pours out all of the negative meanings that they have accumulated over the years, and fills them up with its own meanings, meanings that are wholly positive, loving, and healing. As we read the Course over time, slowly but surely our old associations are leached out, and we begin to make new associations based on the Course's reinterpretation. We begin to think about these terms in a new way. And since emotions come from thoughts, as our thoughts about these terms change, our emotional response to them changes as well. Every page of the Course is so drenched with inclusion that eventually the masculine terms just get absorbed into that inclusion. As this happens, the wounds that have resulted from our old associations are not just buried by denial; they are truly healed.

Some may argue that it is impossible to redefine masculine terms in a truly inclusive way, and what I'm proposing here is just a convenient justification for holding on to them. But I think that given the inherent neutrality of words, it *can* be done. Moreover, this approach to masculine terms is not unique to the Course, but is used by people in other spiritual traditions as well. One example of this appears in Huston Smith's classic book on comparative religion, *The World's Religions*.[1] Apparently, in the Navajo tradition there is no name for God, which has led some people outside that tradition to conclude that it *has* no supreme God. A Navajo artist named Carl Gorman gives the following response to this claim:

> Some researchers into Navajo religion say that we have no supreme God because he is not named. This is not so. The Supreme Being is not named because he is unknowable. He is simply the Unknown Power.
>
> (*The World's Religions*, p. 378)

Notice that Gorman refers to God as "he." But clearly this "he" is not literally a male God, nor even a God with male qualities, because this "he" points to a nameless "Unknown Power" beyond any earthly categories. This strikes me as very similar to the Course using "He" to point to a God Who is "Formlessness Itself." It seems clear to me that Gorman, like the Course, has redefined his masculine terms for God in a way that takes them beyond their literal masculine meaning.

Based on my own experience, I can personally vouch for the efficacy of this redefining process and the healing it brings. Through reading and practicing the Course over a period of years, I have come to the point that when I use masculine terms in a Course context, they have little to no gender-association for me. So, for instance, if I'm working on mentally extending forgiveness to a particular woman, I can use a practice like "Because I will to know myself, I see you as God's Son and my brother" (T-9.II.12:6) without changing the words at all. And there is something curiously liberating about this. Since I now associate those words with our shared, gender-neutral Identity, they seem to lead me into a deeper joining with the woman to whom I'm mentally addressing them. Surprisingly, applying the redefined masculine terms to everyone (silently in my mind, not verbally in the presence of the individual) actually feels more inclusive to me than anything else. Since everyone is included in them, they have become in my mind a statement of inclusion. And I think this is exactly what the author of the Course is trying to accomplish.

Because of my experience (an experience shared by other Course students I've known, including women), and because I think Jesus is intentionally trying to facilitate such an experience, I recommend that Course students refrain from changing the Course's masculine terms to something else. Certainly people are free to do as they wish, and one should go ahead and change the terms if strongly guided to do so. But I believe we should think carefully before doing so, because changing the terms may rob us of the healing that Jesus intends to bring about through his use of language. Therefore, my suggestion is that we as Course students allow Jesus' own choice of words to bring about the healing he intended.

Conclusion

The relationship between men and women, and the masculine and feminine in general, is one of the thorniest and most divisive issues in our world. The "battle of the sexes" has been raging from time immemorial on many fronts. It is one of our most profound forms of separation—so profound that at least one best-selling author, John Gray of *Men Are from Mars, Women Are from Venus* fame, has made a career out of the observation that men and women seem to come from entirely different planets.

Yet what is striking about the Course is that it says *nothing* about this battle. There are no instructions for how Martians and Venusians can get along, no discussions of yin and yang, no discourses on the masculine and feminine faces of God. I think the reason for this is quite simple, and has already been stated above: Our gender difference is just one more form of *separation*. As an expression of separation, this difference is wholly illusory, and thus ultimately unimportant. The Course's focus is on teaching us about the difference between illusions and the truth, not about a meaningless difference between illusory bodies.

I think it is because of this focus, coupled with the fact that the Course addresses itself to a culture steeped in the Judeo-Christian tradition, that the Course uses masculine terms as it does. If it constantly said "he and she" and referred to "Father-Mother God," it would tend to lend reality to the illusory difference between the masculine and the feminine. If it constantly used totally gender-neutral terms instead, it would lack the emotional resonance that the traditional gender-specific terms have acquired in the Judeo-Christian culture to which the Course is addressed. But by taking traditional masculine forms of referring to God and humanity and transforming them into all-encompassing forms, it gives us the best of both worlds: It de-emphasizes the separation yet retains the positive emotional impact of tradition.

There is no doubt that these words are loaded, but the Course's goal is to *unload* them, and this is exactly what it does. By retaining traditional terms, Jesus is able to draw from the deep well of positive emotional associations we have with them; by redefining these traditional terms, he is able to undo the negative emotional associations we have with them by removing the fearful and exclusionary elements that have corrupted them. His usage strips them of their power as tools of separation, and points to a reality that is totally non-separate and all-inclusive. Therefore, let us allow the

Course's language to do its work. Let us allow the Course's inclusive use of masculine terms to heal the wounds that the illusory distinction between "masculine" and "feminine" has wrought.

---

[1] Huston Smith, *The World's Religions.* New York: HarperCollins, 1991.

Living the Course

10

Why are some judgments more difficult to give up than others? For example, why is it easy for me not to judge people for the color of their skin, but difficult not to judge them for their behavior or character?

Short Answer

The whole idea that some things are more difficult to overcome than others is based on the illusion of differences, an illusion which seems real only because our minds *prefer* illusions to the truth. Some illusions (such as particular judgments) seem more difficult to give up than others only because we prefer those particular illusions—they rank higher in our personal hierarchy of illusions. The solution to this problem is first to open our minds to the idea that all illusions are equally unreal and equally undesirable, and then to ask for a miracle to heal them. The miracle undoes all illusions regardless of seeming difficulty because "there is no order of difficulty in miracles" (T-1.I.1:1).

☼☼☼

In the following answer, I will be drawing heavily from Section 8 of the Manual, "How Can Perception of Order of Difficulties Be Avoided?" I recommend reading this section in its entirety, because it deals quite specifically with the very issue raised by this question. The section explains how the whole idea of order of difficulty (the belief that some things are more difficult to accomplish than others) arises, and how to overcome that belief. While the section deals specifically with the issue of how healers can overcome their belief that some sicknesses are harder to heal than others, it can certainly be applied to all order-of-difficulty issues.

The whole idea that some things are more difficult to overcome than others is based on the illusion of differences.

"Illusions are always illusions of differences" (M-8.2:1). Indeed, the entire world we see—the world which the Course tells us is an illusion—is literally defined by differences, by "thousands of contrasts in which each thing seen competes with every other in order to be recognized" (M-8.1:2). It is only through contrast, through noticing differences of height, weight, volume, texture, brightness, color, etc., that we are able to distinguish one object from another. Our inner world too, the world of ideas in our minds, is defined by differences. We distinguish one idea from another by noting the differences between them, such as differences of content, validity, and desirability.

Precisely because we see a world of differences, the world seems to present us with different problems, some of which seem more difficult to solve than others. Indeed, the Course tells us that "the belief in order of difficulties is the basis for the world's perception" (M-8.1:1). I don't think we need to look too hard to see that this is the case. The way we perceive things, Mount Everest is more difficult to climb than the jungle gym in our backyard. Beating Tiger Woods on the golf course is more difficult than beating our Uncle Louie. Cancer is more difficult to cure than a cold. Solving an advanced calculus problem is more difficult than solving an elementary arithmetic problem. Rage at Osama bin Laden is more difficult to heal than annoyance at drivers who use cell phones. And (at least for some of us) judgments based on behavior are more difficult to overcome than judgments based on skin color. Or so it seems.

The illusion of differences seems real only because our minds *prefer* illusions to the truth.

This is the Course's startling answer to the question of why we see the illusion of differences. As real as order of difficulty based on differences seems to be, the only reason it seems real is that we *want* it to be real. We see illusions because we want illusions to replace the truth, and thus become true themselves; "finding truth unacceptable" (M-8.2:6), we weave illusions in an attempt "to bring truth to lies" (M-8.2:5).

Why do we do this? Because we identify with the ego, and truth is the ego's ultimate enemy, the thing that would dispel it. Illusions are what keep the ego going; therefore, as long as we identify with the ego we will crave illusions, even though illusions are ultimately painful to us. Thus when the Course speaks of preferring and desiring illusions, it is referring not so much to things we consciously desire but to things the ego desires to keep itself going. Some of these things—such as physical pleasure and special relationships—we may well desire consciously, but others—such as sickness and guilt—we most likely don't desire consciously at all.

The idea that we see illusions because we want them to be true is a real reversal of how we normally regard the phenomenon of illusion. Normally, we think of illusions as things that deceive us against our will, like a mirage in the desert. The mirage fools us, but not because we wanted it to fool us. The Course, however, turns this reasoning on its ear:

> By definition, an illusion is an attempt to make something real that is regarded as of major importance, but is recognized as being untrue. The mind therefore seeks to make it true out of its intensity of desire to have it for itself.
> (M-8.2:3-4)

In other words, we know that what we desire is unreal, but we desire it so much that we make an illusory image of it to convince ourselves that it *is* real.

It seems hard to believe that we actually do this, yet we can see examples of it in our daily lives. We are all familiar with the phenomenon of denial, where people can live a lie for years, convinced on the surface that their lives are totally authentic, yet never quite escaping that nagging feeling deep down that they are just fooling themselves. This dynamic also expresses itself in our love of fictional books and movies. Think about what happens when you go to a movie. You know going in that it is pure illusion, projected images of actors who are pretending to be other people, filmed on artificial sets, perhaps even with computer-generated special effects. Yet you want to believe it—you want to forget it is an illusion—because you desire the experience the movie promises. In essence, you want to be convinced that the characters and events in the movie are real.

That's the whole point of going to movies, is it not? A good movie is one that delivers a convincing experience, one that feels real; a bad movie is one that is unconvincing, one that feels contrived and fake. Purveyors of fiction even have a term for the audience's process of forgetting that a fictional work is an illusion, a process they want to facilitate: "willing suspension of disbelief." The Course is saying that our entire world is rooted in a willing suspension of disbelief: our desire to make illusory images of things we want, and then forget we made them in order to convince ourselves that they are real.

But of course, different people like different movies. As we've seen, our illusory world is a world of differences, in which each "mind is separate, different from other minds, with different interests of its own" (M-8.2:8). All of us prefer illusions to the truth, but each of us prefers *different* illusions. And thus, the Course says, each of us has developed our own individual "hierarchy of illusions" (T-23.II.2:3), a kind of ranking system in which the more preferable an illusion is to us, the more "true" it is. (Remember, our whole purpose for making illusions is to convince ourselves that the things we desire are real, or true.) This hierarchy of illusions is maintained and reinforced by an ingenious process of selective perception described in M-8.4, a process on which "the judgment of all differences rests, because it is on this [process] that judgments of the world depend" (M-8.4:7). This process of selective perception can by summed up broadly in four steps:

1. Each mind creates a variety of mental categories, based on its own personal hierarchy of illusions.

2. The mind then directs the physical senses to go out into the world and find things that fit these mental categories. (The mind "forgets" that it has done this, so now we are not consciously aware of this selection process.)

3. The senses do as the mind directs, overlooking things that don't fit the categories and finding things that do.

4. The selective evidence brought back by the senses "proves" to the mind that its categories must be true.

We can certainly see this process at work in the example of racial prejudice. Let's say that a person starts with a mental category called "Jews," a category which, in this prejudiced person's mind, contains the subcategory "Jews are stingy." This person then directs her senses to look for stingy Jews and—surprise, surprise—that's exactly what her senses find. She doesn't spot the Jews who are giving millions to charity or generously helping their neighbors in need. But any Jew who also happens to be a stingy person is spotted immediately, and into the database he goes. Our person then examines the results of this selective survey and—guess what?—she concludes, "Yes indeed, those Jews sure are stingy. Look at all the stingy Jews I found!"

This same process is at work when we judge people on the basis of their behavior. Most of us have mental categories called "People who do *x* are evil sinners." (We may not express it that way, but that's basically how we feel inside.) So let's say that a person is a vegetarian, and has a mental category called "People who eat meat are evil sinners." He sends his senses out to look for evil meat eaters. The first thing those senses will probably do is find particular meat eaters who are disagreeable people in other respects. He will tend to overlook kind, good-hearted people who also happen to eat meat. (He probably won't notice a picture of Jesus eating a fish.)

Once he selects out his group of particularly nasty meat eaters, his senses will then make even further selections. He will overlook the acts of kindness and love done by these people, and focus on their faults. And of course, he will completely overlook the evidence that the vision of Christ *beyond* his senses would reveal to him, evidence which shows that these evil meat eaters are really holy Sons of God. As a result of all this selective perception, our vegetarian concludes, "Those meat eaters really *are* evil sinners, and I've got the evidence to prove it!"

Thus is our particular hierarchy of illusions "proven" true. And thus do we convince ourselves that the entire illusion of differences is real and true. The shocking punchline is this: It is only our *preference* for illusions that makes them "real" to us. We want illusions instead of truth, and so illusions are what we see. "What is seen as 'reality' is simply what the mind prefers" (M-8.3:6).

Some illusions (such as particular judgments) seem more difficult to give up than others only because we prefer those particular illusions—they rank higher in our personal hierarchy of illusions.

This follows logically from the idea that only our preference for illusions makes them "real" to us. The higher a particular illusion (such as a particular judgment) ranks on our hierarchy, the more "true" it is to us, and thus the less willing we are to give it up. It is only our lack of willingness to accept truth that makes a particular illusion seem more difficult to let go. The Course says as much in this passage:

> It is impossible that one illusion be less amenable to truth than are the rest. But it is possible that some are given greater value, and less willingly offered to truth for healing and for help. (T-26.VII.6:1-2)

Or, as another line puts it, when we believe that some illusions are more difficult to give up than others, "all [we] mean is that there are some things [we] would withhold from truth" (T-17.I.3:1).

Certainly it doesn't appear to us that our preference for certain illusions is the only reason they seem more difficult to let go. Indeed, as Course students, on a conscious level we may desperately want to let them go. It appears to us that the reason for our difficulty is that "harder" illusions are truly different than "easier" illusions—bigger, more deeply rooted, more heavily reinforced—and further, that those differences are quite external to our minds. But that perception is simply the result of the whole game of making illusions "true" that we just saw above. It is our minds, not the external world, that produce the illusion of differences, including the illusion that some illusions are harder to give up than others. And it is in our minds that this illusion must be overcome.

The solution to this problem is first to open our minds to the idea that all illusions are equally unreal and equally undesirable, and then to ask for a miracle to heal them. The miracle undoes all illusions regardless of seeming difficulty because "there is no order of difficulty in miracles."

It sounds insane to say that the illusions we prefer are truer than the illusions we don't prefer. And it is indeed insane:

> It appears some [illusions] are more true than others, although this clearly makes no sense at all. All that a hierarchy of illusions can show is preference, not reality. What relevance has preference to the truth? Illusions are illusions and are false. (T-26.VII.6:4-7)

Being willing to see this simple and obvious fact—that truth is truth, illusion is illusion, and never the twain shall meet—is the first step in overcoming the belief that some illusions are more difficult to give up than others. It doesn't matter whether the illusion is of Mount Everest or a jungle gym, of Tiger Woods or our Uncle Louie, of cancer or a cold, of advanced calculus or elementary arithmetic, of Osama bin Laden or a cell phone user, of judgments based on behavior or judgments based on skin color. Whatever the form of the illusion, it is *nothing*. It is totally unreal, and precisely because it is unreal, it is totally undesirable: "How can illusions satisfy God's Son?" (W-pII.272.Heading). How can illusions possibly be preferable to the truth that we are radiant Sons of a loving Father, basking in a Heavenly realm of pure, limitless joy?

Once we open our minds to the idea that illusions are equally unreal and equally undesirable, we will be more willing to ask for the Holy Spirit's means of dispelling them: the *miracle*. Whatever the seeming magnitude of the particular illusion we are dealing with, the miracle can undo it. Why? Because, as every Course student knows, the very first principle of *A Course in Miracles* is that "there is no order of difficulty in miracles" (T-1.I.1:1). Miracles can heal everything regardless of seeming difficulty, and so they are the answer to any seeming problem that could possibly confront us. This principle is vital to the Course, "a real foundation stone" (T-6.V(A).4:5) of its spiritual program. As such, it is an idea that the author of the Course really wants us to take to heart.

Why is there no order of difficulty in miracles? We've already seen the answer: because there is no order of magnitude in illusions. The entire belief in order of difficulty *is* an illusion, an illusion which is powerless before the truth. The miracle, being the expression of the all-encompassing truth and boundless love of God, has all the power of God behind it. In short, the miracle demonstrates that *illusion is nothing, and truth is everything.* If this is so, then how could one illusion possibly be more difficult to overcome than another? "Not one [illusion] is true in any way, and all must yield with equal ease to what God gave as answer to them all" (T-26.VII.6:9).

Overcoming the belief in order of difficulty: a practice

As discussed above, the belief in order of difficulty is central to the way we see the world. If we were able to totally overcome this belief, the miracle would heal all of our problems instantly and our journey through time and space would be over. Unfortunately, we are unlikely to overcome this belief overnight, but we can chip away at it with practice. The following practice is one I've devised to help us do just that:

Bring to mind a specific problem in your life that seems particularly resistant to solution. It could be anything from a distressing external situation to a judgment that you are finding difficult to let go. Anything that is disturbing your peace of mind is a suitable subject. Once you have your specific problem in mind, take it through the following process (feel free to use whatever words appeal to you and elaborate as much as you like; you might even use some of the Course lines I quoted above, or other personal favorites that are relevant):

1. Gently tell yourself that whatever the seeming magnitude of the problem, it is totally an illusion, no more substantial than any other illusion, and therefore no problem at all. Illusions are *nothing*, and so they cannot be difficult to overcome.

2. Gently tell yourself that because it is an illusion, you don't really want it, however much you may seem to. No illusion can ever make you happy; only the truth that you are God's holy Son, basking in His eternal Love, can make you happy.

3. Now, ask the Holy Spirit for a miracle that will dispel this illusion, reminding yourself that "there is no order of difficulty in miracles." There is literally nothing a miracle cannot overcome, because illusions *are* nothing, and miracles have all the power of God behind them.

How did that work for you? It's a very simple practice, but I find it very effective when I apply it to a problem I'm facing. One caution about evaluating the results of this practice: Don't consider yourself a failure if your problem doesn't immediately vanish. Especially if it is a particularly "big" problem as the world judges these things, it will probably take a lot more than one brief practice to overcome it (though it doesn't have to). Even if all you feel is just a little more peace around the problem, consider your practice a success. You've chipped away at the belief in order of difficulty, even if only a little.

Conclusion

I find the Course's teaching that all problems are totally illusory and thus easily undone by the miracle very reassuring. It comforts me to know that I don't really have a vast collection of problems of all shapes, sizes, and levels of difficulty, however much I may seem to. And it is a great relief to realize that in spite of all the apparent differences that seem to make life so difficult, the fact remains that all illusions are the same, and all of them will vanish in the light of the simple truth:

> Just as reality is wholly real, apart from size and shape and time and place—for differences cannot exist within it—so too are illusions without distinctions....The one answer to all illusions is truth. (M-8.6:7,9)

11

I find that when I get closer to God, my ego fights back, bringing painful experiences into my life. My fear of this has slowed my progress to God. How would the Course have us deal with this problem?

Short Answer

The ego does fight back when we get closer to God. However, we needn't be afraid of it, because it is powerless; only our decision to listen to it gives it any power over us. Therefore, when the ego fights back:

1. Don't be afraid of it, because it has no real power.

2. See ego lapses as no big deal, just an inevitable, normal part of the journey.

3. Refuse to learn the lesson the ego is attempting to teach you, and choose instead to learn the Holy Spirit's lesson of forgiveness.

4. Remind yourself that Jesus' strength can help you transcend the ego.

☺☺☺

Note: I find this question about what to do when the ego interferes with progress to God to be very similar to Q & A #12, entitled "What can I do when strong negative emotions seem to hinder my Course practice?" Much of my answer to that question applies to this one as well. Therefore, I recommend reading the answer to that question, in addition to what I've written below.

The ego does fight back when we get closer to God.

It seems to be a common experience among Course students that periods of progress toward greater peace and a deeper awareness of God are often followed by painful ego relapses. It's as if the ego senses that its walls are beginning to crumble, and so it strikes back with a vengeance, desperately trying to shore up its fortress against the onslaught of God. The Course tells us that the ego definitely does fight back as we approach God:

> Even the faintest hint of your reality literally drives the ego from your mind, because you will give up all investment in it....The ego will make every effort to recover and mobilize its energies against your release. It will tell you that you are insane, and argue that grandeur cannot be a real part of you because of the littleness in which it believes.
>
> (T-9.VIII.4:2,5-6; see also T-9.VII.4:4-5)

This passage tells us, in essence, that whenever we catch a glimpse of the majesty of our true Identity, the ego responds by fiercely reminding us of the "fact" that we are small, painfully limited creatures, and any belief that we might be more than that is just an insane pipe dream.

The ego tries to convince us of this bitter "fact" in a myriad of ways. It makes us sick. It bombards us with painful life events. It tells us to blame other people for our suffering, which only reinforces our own guilt. It tells us to scuttle our holy relationships, and lures us into special relationships in which its agenda can be served. It tempts us with worldly goodies and delusions of grandiosity. It tells us that God doesn't even exist, or if He does, that He is a vengeful, punishing Deity Whom we should do everything we can to keep at arm's length. But whatever method the ego chooses, it has one goal: to make us forget that tantalizing glimpse of our true Identity, so that we will once again accept *it* as our identity, assuring its own survival.

Since the ego does fight back when we come closer to God, the obvious question becomes: What do we *do* when the ego fights back? The following four points, rooted in the Course's teaching that the ego is truly powerless, are my answer to that question.

1. When the ego fights back, don't be afraid of it, because it has no real power.

The ego's retaliation against us for turning to God can feel very frightening. But the Course tells us quite plainly and emphatically, "*Do not be afraid of the ego*" (T-7.VIII.5:1). Why needn't we fear? Because, as the very next sentence says, "It [the ego] depends on your mind, and as you made it by believing in it, so you can dispel it by withdrawing belief from it" (T-7.VIII.5:2).

We're afraid of the ego because we see it as some sort of powerful demonic force outside of our own mind, poised to strike the instant we let our guard down. The Course's own language can sometimes give us this impression. But it just isn't so. We *made* the ego, and thus we have absolute power over it. Only our decision to listen to it gives it any power over us. Our job, then, is to refuse to give the ego any power by refusing to listen to it. Our job is to recognize that we made it, and so we don't have to listen to it. If we truly recognized the utter powerlessness of the ego, how could it frighten us?

2. When the ego fights back, see it as no big deal, just an inevitable, normal part of the journey.

This point, I think, is a crucial one. It follows directly from the idea that we needn't fear the ego because it doesn't have any real power over us. My impression is that many Course students do fear the ego and its seeming power, and so they feel weak and powerless when they experience an ego lapse. Others, perhaps repressing and denying this fear, underestimate their investment in the ego, and react with shock and surprise when they experience an ego lapse. All of these reactions end up having a devastating effect on the mind: They make the ego lapse into a major event, a setback of cosmic proportions. The end result is a state of hopelessness and despair at the prospect of ever overcoming the ego and returning home to God.

This phenomenon is particularly evident when Course students get sick. I've seen it happen again and again. A Course student gets sick—

anything from a minor touch of the flu to a serious, life-threatening illness—and immediately the questioning and self-recrimination starts. "What did I do to create this? Does this mean I'm a bad Course student? I thought I was so close to enlightenment, and now this! I'll never make it!" On top of the pain of illness, all too many Course students add guilt, fear, and despair.

Ironically, this is exactly what the ego *wants* us to learn from sickness and other painful life events. It uses sickness and pain to convince us that we are guilty, that we really are painfully limited creatures, and that we don't have a prayer of ever reaching God. The unfortunate upshot of this is that when we react to such events with guilt and despair, we are actually learning the ego's lesson! Therefore, the crucial question to ask whenever we experience an ego lapse of any kind is not "Why did this happen?" or "Does this make me a bad Course student?" Rather, the question is "Do I want to learn the ego's lesson?"

And one powerful way of refusing to learn the ego's lesson is simply to not see ego lapses as a big deal. If we respond to them with guilt, fear, and despair, we *are* making them a big deal. We are seeing them as real, rather than as the illusory and temporary setbacks that they are. Workbook Lesson 181 tells us that our concerns about ever learning the Course and about the ego fighting back after we have had a breakthrough "are but defenses against present change of focus in perception. Nothing more" (W-pI.181.5:3-4; see entire discussion in paragraphs 3-5). In other words, worrying about whether we will ever give up the ego, or worrying that the ego will fight back later even if we do give it up for a moment, is simply a way of avoiding a shift in perception *now*. Making a big deal out of ego lapses is simply a way of perpetuating them.

Therefore, don't waste time worrying about the ego's inevitable attempts to fight back. This is just something that is going to happen on the journey to God, and we might as well accept it as a given. It's not something to be disappointed about or surprised about. What else would we expect the ego to do? Ego lapses aren't a big deal, *unless we make them a big deal by allowing them to teach us the ego's lesson*. Responding to ego lapses without guilt, fear, or despair—all expressions of the ego's lesson—robs the ego of its seeming power over us. By denying that the ego's activities are anything to worry about, we are asserting that the ego is not real. And this is exactly what the Course wants us to learn.

3. When the ego fights back, refuse to learn the lesson the ego is attempting to teach you, and choose instead to learn the Holy Spirit's lesson of forgiveness.

Not worrying about the ego, however, doesn't mean that we take an attitude of utter passivity toward it. Although it is an illusion with no real effects, we do believe in the ego's reality, and so when it fights back, we do need to take active steps to dispel it. We need to watch our minds for ego thoughts and actively dismiss them when they arise—the Course's practice of mental vigilance. Above all, we need to refuse to learn the ego's lesson, and choose instead the Holy Spirit's lesson.

What is the Holy Spirit's lesson? His lesson is spelled out directly in Workbook Lesson 193, "All things are lessons God would have me learn." This Workbook lesson tells us that, in all the ego-based pain and suffering that we experience, no matter what its form, the Holy Spirit has embedded one simple lesson: *"Forgive, and you will see this differently"* (W-pI.193.3:7).

Expanding upon this basic idea that everything is a lesson in forgiveness, Lesson 193 goes on to say, "This is the lesson God would have you learn: There is a way to look on everything that lets it be to you another step to Him, and to salvation of the world" (W-pI.193.13:1). This way *is* forgiveness. This is the way, then, that we are to look upon the situation when the ego fights back.

Renouncing the ego's lesson and choosing the Holy Spirit's lesson: a practice

Based on the above idea, I have developed a practice to use whenever it seems that the ego is having its way with me. It is a variation on a practice I learned at a Circle of Atonement workshop on sickness and healing. The practice goes like this:

Bring to mind a painful situation in your life, one in which it feels as if the ego is fighting hard and you're losing the battle. Then, search your mind for the ego lessons you are learning through this situation. Basically, this means looking for all the negative thoughts you have about it, things like "I'm worthless," or "I'll never make it," or "It's all so-and-so's fault," or "I'm guilty." As you consider each thought one at a time, say slowly in response to that thought, trying as best you can to really mean it:

I have no use for this lesson. I will forgive, and I will see this differently.
(Based on M-5.II.2:12; W-pI.193.3:7; and W-pI.193.13:3)

"This lesson," of course, means the lesson the ego is trying to teach you through this situation, and "I will forgive…" is the lesson the Holy Spirit is teaching you through the exact same situation. I find this to be an extremely powerful practice. It takes the very situations the ego uses to keep me *away* from God, and uses them to rocket me more quickly *toward* God. As Lesson 193 says, it transforms these situations into "another step to Him." Once these situations are thus transformed for me, I find that it often doesn't even matter so much if the situations change externally or not. If I'm using a situation to learn the Holy Spirit's lesson, I find it much easier to be at peace with it.

4. When the ego fights back, remind yourself that Jesus' strength can help you transcend it.

Finally, I find it extremely helpful to remind myself that Jesus is with me as I walk the path to God. The ego will inevitably fight every step of the way as we make this journey, but Jesus reminds us that "you are invulnerable to its retaliation because I am with you" (T-8.V.5:7). As we are faced with the ego's attempts to thwart our journey to God, we would do well to accept Jesus' invitation to walk with him:

Reach, therefore, for my hand because you want to transcend the ego. My strength will never be wanting, and if you choose to share it you will do so. I give it willingly and gladly, because I need you as much as you need me.
(T-8.V.6:8-10)

12

What can I do when strong negative emotions seem to hinder my Course practice?

Short Answer

Based on the Course's instructions and my own personal experience, I recommend the following as ways to help deal with negative emotions that seem to hinder Course practice:

1. Build a foundation of Course study.

2. Build a foundation of Course practice.

3. Do what you need to do behaviorally to set up a situation that is conducive to practice.

4. Remember that your thoughts cause your emotions.

5. Develop a problem-solving repertoire of Course practices.

6. Remind yourself how important your practice is to you.

7. Practice with gentle firmness.

8. Get support.

☞☞☞

The Course claims to be a complete spiritual program "in which nothing is lacking that is needed, and nothing is included that is contradictory or irrelevant" (W-pI.42.7:2). It tells us that it is "a course in mind training" (T-1.VII.4:1) which can heal our minds completely if we do what it says. If this is so, then its program should certainly be effective in dealing with emotional upsets like fear, anger, or grief. Yet many if not most of us have experienced emotional upsets of such intensity that they seem to make impossible the very practice that is meant to help overcome them. What can we do in those moments when the disease is so strong that it seems to block the very thing that would cure it?

First off, I think we should remind ourselves that dealing with negative emotions is exactly what Course practice is for. Therefore, emotional upsets aren't *hindrances* to practice; effectively dealing with them is the *purpose* of practice. Keeping this in mind, here are some tips for how to make Course practice more effective when we are confronted with strong emotional upsets. Some are drawn from the Course itself, while others are more from my own personal experience. Applying these ideas in my own life has definitely helped me to deal with strong negative emotions more effectively, and I hope these ideas will be equally helpful for you.

1. Build a foundation of Course study.

Study of the Course's thought system is the foundation of effective Course practice, as the Introduction to the Workbook tells us:

> A theoretical foundation such as the text provides is necessary as a framework to make the exercises in this workbook meaningful....It is the purpose of this workbook to train your mind to think along the lines the text sets forth. (W-In.1:1,4)

Course practice consists mainly of frequently repeating ideas which are part of the Course's thought system, so that those ideas will sink more deeply into our minds. But for this to be effective, we must first *understand* those ideas, at least to a certain extent. If we are to train our minds to "think along the lines the text sets forth," we need to have some understanding of what the text sets forth. To get that understanding, we must study it.

The value of study has proven itself time and time again in my experience. I have found that the more I understand an idea from the Course, the more potent my practice of that idea becomes. Course practices that used to be total duds for me have become "mighty forces" (T-16.II.9:5) in my life as I've come to understand the theory behind them. And the more powerful my practice has become, the more effective it has been in helping me deal with strong emotional upsets.

2. Build a foundation of Course practice.

As important as study is, it is not enough in itself. In order for our study of the Course's ideas to really change our lives, we need to *practice* those ideas:

> Yet it is doing the exercises that will make the goal of the course possible. An untrained mind can accomplish nothing.   (W-In.1:2-3)

If we want to awaken to God, we must focus our minds on the ideas that God has given us through the Course, and this requires the mental discipline acquired through regular practice. How much practice are we to do? This depends on how far we've progressed through the Workbook, but the further we go, the more practice we are asked to do. Moreover, practice does not end with the Workbook; Section 16 of the Manual outlines the daily practice of the beginning teacher of God, a person who has completed the Workbook (see M-16.3:7) and has joined with at least one other person in a truly common goal (see M-1.1:1-2). Clearly we are to develop a firm foundation of daily practice.

My own practice currently consists of at least 30 minutes of quiet time with God morning and evening, along with a regular regimen of various Workbook-style practices throughout the day. (I'm doing what we at the Circle like to call "post-Workbook practice"; for more information about this, see my article "My Journey with Post-Workbook Practice," in Issue #35 of the Circle of Atonement's newsletter, *A Better Way*.) Though I have certainly not perfected this, and there are many days when my practice is not as strong and consistent as it could be, I try my best to build my day around regular Course practice, as the Course itself advises us to do.

I have found this foundation of practice to be an absolute lifeline for me when faced with intense emotional situations. Many of us, myself included, have a tendency to put off practice until we are confronted with a major crisis, which I have found to be a recipe for disaster. Asking an untrained mind to deal with a major crisis is like asking a couch potato to run a marathon. I find that my practice is cumulative. If I do a lot of it during the day, it grows in strength and power, as if I were constantly adding fuel to my spiritual gas tank. If I'm properly "fueled up" with Course practice when an emotionally distressing event comes my way, I'm much better able to handle it. But if I'm not properly fueled up, then I'm stuck; my gas tank is empty and I don't stand a chance. I think that developing a rock solid foundation of Course practice is an absolute must if we are to deal effectively with the more stressful situations that we're confronted with in our lives.

3. Do what you need to do behaviorally to set up a situation that is conducive to practice.

While the Course is adamant that healing comes from changing our minds rather than our behavior, taking behavioral action to make our situation more conducive to practice is simply practical. Done in the right spirit, such behavioral action is simply a temporary measure that we can use to keep our situation relatively calm as we work on healing our minds. I can think of at least three things we can do behaviorally to help us clear the way to better Course practice:

First, we can physically remove ourselves (temporarily) from whatever is triggering our negative emotions. This is such a simple thing to do, yet it can really make a difference. It's just so hard to deal with strong emotions when we're right in the middle of a stressful situation. Taking time out and stepping away can give us the space we need to calm our minds and do our practice.

Second, we can express our emotions in an appropriate, non-harming way: We can have a good cry, or pound a pillow to vent our anger. Now, I don't want to emphasize this idea too much, since the Course does not consider physical expression of emotions to be healing in and of itself. In fact, research has shown that venting anger through pounding pillows and using punching bags actually increases angry and violent tendencies. Rather than physical expression, the Course consistently counsels us to *immediately* counter negative emotions with a Course practice as soon as we're aware of them, as in this typical practice instruction: "The idea for today should...be applied immediately to any situation that may distress you" (W-pI.32.6:1). This is what we should try to do, if we are up to it.

However, that being said, certainly there are times when the emotion is simply too intense for us to practice with it right away, and at those times we needn't feel guilty if we decide simply to let it all out. The Course seems to suggest that there are times when this will happen as we progress along the path: "You will weep each time an idol falls" (T-29.VII.1:2). Taking the edge off our intense emotions through non-harming expression is only a temporary expedient, but it can be a useful one at times. It can get some of the raw emotional energy out of our system so that we can focus our minds on the Course practice that will truly heal negative emotions.

Third, we can set up our daily life situation to make it more conducive to practice. This can be done in a number of ways. For starters, I think that simply taking care of ourselves physically can make a big difference. It's very difficult to practice when you are hungry, sleepy, or in physical distress. I myself have found that something as simple as the amount of sleep I get can make or break my practice. If I don't sleep enough, I nod off during my meditations, which is hardly conducive to spiritual awakening!

In addition to taking care of ourselves physically, we can also make our practice easier by setting up regular times and a quiet place for daily practice. The Course recommends that we do this, at least at the beginning stage of our journey:

> Try, if possible, to undertake the daily extended practice periods at approximately the same time each day. Try, also, to determine this time in advance, and then adhere to it as closely as possible.   (W-pI.65.4:1-2)

> The exercises should be done with your eyes closed and when you are alone in a quiet place, if possible.

> This is emphasized for practice periods at your stage of learning.   (W-pI.rI.In.3:3-4:1)

Like all of the behavioral suggestions I've discussed, setting aside the time and space to practice is only a temporary measure. Ultimately we will need to get to the point where we "require no special settings"

(W-pI.rI.In.4:2) for our practice. Indeed, we are told that "you will need your learning most in situations that appear to be upsetting, rather than in those that already seem to be calm and quiet" (W-pI.rI.In.4:3). But until we have become so advanced that we can practice anytime and anywhere, I think we would be wise to set up our lives in such a way that regular practice is a scheduled priority. Doing this will greatly increase the odds that our practice will be effective in those unpredictable situations when strong negative emotions arise.

4. Remember that your thoughts cause your emotions.

Emotions seem so powerful; they seem to have a life of their own. Most of us, I think, truly believe that "emotions alternate because of causes you cannot control, you did not make, and you can never change" (W-pI.167.4:2). Compared with the tempestuous drama of our emotions, our *thoughts* can seem rather weak, pallid, and unimportant. Given these beliefs, addressing emotional upsets with the mental repetition of ideas from the Course can seem like facing a dragon with a rubber sword.

But the Course sees things differently: It tells us that thoughts *cause* emotions: "It is always an interpretation [i.e., a thought] that gives rise to negative emotions" (M-17.4:2). For this reason, "correction belongs at the thought level" (T-2.V.1:7). Repeating thoughts as the Course directs, then, is not weak and ineffectual; rather, it is the most powerful practice imaginable because it *changes our minds,* and "by changing his mind, [the Son of God] has changed the most powerful device that was ever given him for change" (T-7.V.7:6). I find that simply reminding myself of this both encourages me to practice more and makes my practice more impactful. As I face the dragon of my emotional upset, I try to remember that this is no rubber sword I have in my hand—this is Excalibur.

5. Develop a problem-solving repertoire of Course practices.

In Lesson 194 of the Workbook, we are encouraged to add the idea for the day to our "problem-solving repertoire" (W-pI.194.6:2). The implication of this is that in the course of doing the Workbook, we have developed a repertoire of various Course practices that we can use whenever we encounter difficult situations. Adding to this the Workbook's injunction to practice with "great specificity" (W-In.6:1), I believe that Jesus is encouraging us to learn through experience which specific practices are most effective for us in specific situations. Learning this will give us some powerful personalized tools to use when faced with these situations.

I've developed my own problem-solving repertoire over time, and I've found it to be indispensable. I have indeed found that certain practices are especially potent for me in particular situations. For instance, in fearful situations, I have found the simple repetition of "There is nothing to fear" (W-pI.48.Heading) to be effective. For pain of various kinds, I often use "Whatever suffers is not part of me" (W-pII.248.Heading). In situations where I must forgive a brother, mentally saying to him, "Give me your blessing, holy Son of God" (W-pI.161.Heading) seems to do the trick. Each of us, I'm sure, will find different practices that are effective for us. The key is to find what works for you and *use it*. Having such a repertoire is really helpful when confronted with negative emotions; if your past experience has already shown you what practices are especially effective for you in dealing with a particular emotion, your practice is much more likely to really work.

6. Remind yourself how important your practice is to you.

Simply holding an attitude in your mind which says, "Course practice is important to me" can really strengthen that practice. The Course encourages this attitude in its practice instructions:

> What is needful is a sense of the importance of what you are doing; its inestimable value to you, and an awareness that you are attempting something very holy.
> (W-pI.44.8:1)

For me, keeping this in mind helps to counteract my tendency to believe that other things in my life are more important than practice. So often, I tend to let practice slide because "it interferes with goals [I] hold more dear" (W-pI.rIII.In.4:2). I think most of us are probably prone to this. It especially happens when we are faced with emotional upset—in upsetting situations, we often spend a lot more time trying to fix the external situation or get back at the person who "hurt" us than we do practicing. Reminding ourselves of the importance of our practice can help make our practice a priority; reminding ourselves that we are "attempting something very holy" can make that practice much stronger.

7. Practice with gentle firmness.

Practicing with an attitude of gentle firmness has, perhaps more than anything else, made my own practice come alive. What is "gentle firmness"? The phrase itself occurs in Workbook Lesson 73, where we are told to repeat the idea for the day with "gentle firmness and quiet certainty" (W-73.pI.10:1). To me, this phrase conveys an entire attitude toward Course practice, an attitude I believe the Course wants us to adopt.

This attitude is rooted in the recognition that, all appearances to the contrary, our true will is one with God's: "There is no will but God's. I cannot be in conflict" (W-pI.74.3:2-3). It certainly seems as if we have *two* wills—God's and the ego's—that constantly battle for control of our minds, but only the will we share with God is real, while the other "will" is literally nothing. There is, therefore, no real battle (which means one shouldn't take my sword and dragon analogy above too literally). Based on this understanding, practicing with firmness means *firmly committing* our minds to the will we share with God by affirming that God's Will is the only will, the only thing we really want. Practicing with gentleness means *gently letting go* of our false "will" (the ego) rather than fighting it, by reminding ourselves that the ego is nothing, and therefore *not* something we really want. Putting firmness and gentleness together, practicing with gentle firmness means practicing in a way that firmly reinforces our true will *and* gently lets go of our false "will."

I think that an attitude of gentle firmness is absolutely vital in applying our practice to negative emotions. If we see practice as a battle between opposing wills, we will have the tendency to use Course practice to hammer our emotions into submission. This is not the kind of firmness the Course is advocating. Using practice to crush emotions we don't like will just drive them into hiding, where they will continue to run our lives.

Instead, we are to be gentle in dealing with such emotions. We are not to strain or try to fight them off. The kind of firmness we are to apply to them is not an iron fist, but rather a gentle but firm *recognition* that however powerful they may seem to be, negative emotions are nothing, and the will we share with God is everything. We don't really want painful emotions, and we have both the desire and the power to let go of the thoughts that cause them. Practicing with gentle firmness does not attack and destroy our negative emotions—it simply shines them away. This shining away is hard to describe in words, but when you experience it, you know what it feels like. Course practice done with the right attitude doesn't just repress negative emotions—it truly releases them.

(For more about the idea of practicing with gentle firmness, see my article "Gentle Firmness: A Powerful Antidote to Our Resistance to Practice," in Issue #26 of the Circle of Atonement's newsletter, *A Better Way*.)

8. Get support.

"Salvation is a collaborative venture" (T-4.VI.8:2). I don't think that any of us can deal with intense emotions like fear, anger, or grief without help from another person. The Course's program is a challenging one, and we need each other's support for it to be successful. We can get help from Course teachers, our fellow Course students, and, if needed, from healing professionals. The last one, in particular, is one I don't think we should overlook. If we are wrestling with very intense emotional trauma, the help of a trained psychotherapist may simply be required. We should take every opportunity to accept the help that is available to us. And, of course, one of the most powerful ways to facilitate our own healing is to *give* help to others, both in our minds and behaviorally when asked.

Conclusion

To conclude, I would simply reiterate that dealing with negative emotions is exactly what Course practice is for. If we practice the Course with understanding, consistency, diligence, commitment, and support, I truly believe that there are no limits to the healing it can offer us. As the Course says, "Your practicing can offer everything to you" (W-pI.rIII.In.4:5). Course practice can undo the core beliefs from which all of our distress arises, and thus it offers much more than a quick fix or temporary alleviation of emotional pain. Since it undoes the root cause of negative emotions, Course practice will ultimately undo them for all time.

13

What is the role of silence (stilling the mind) in the practice of *A Course in Miracles*?

Short Answer

Silence, the practice of stilling the mind and experiencing the quiet peace of God, plays a prominent role in *A Course in Miracles*. There are three broad aspects to this practice:

1. We still the mind by withdrawing our attention from the chaos and conflict of the external world, and the ego thoughts that normally occupy the mind.

2. God enters our still, open mind and gives us His gift of peace.

3. We return to the world, bringing the peace of God with us as we act in the world, extending that peace to everyone.

ᗢᗢᗢ

Note: Two of the most time-honored ways of stilling the mind and allowing the peace of God to enter are meditation and prayer, both of which are featured prominently in the Course. For an in-depth presentation of the theory and practice of Course-based meditation and prayer, I recommend reading Robert Perry's excellent article entitled "Meditation and Prayer," on the Circle of Atonement's website, as well as his article "Meditation in *A Course in Miracles*," in Issue #29 of the Circle's newsletter, *A Better Way*.

The cultivation of silence—primarily inner silence, though outer silence can certainly help facilitate inner silence—is indeed a vital part of the practice of *A Course in Miracles*. In fact, it could be said that the Course's path as a whole is essentially one of silencing the clamorous voice of the ego, allowing the quiet, peaceful message of God's Voice to replace it, and extending that peace to the world. Let's now take a closer look at the three aspects of this practice:

1. We still the mind by withdrawing our attention from the chaos and conflict of the external world, and the ego thoughts that normally occupy the mind.

From the Course's standpoint, our "normal" state of mind is not a pretty picture. The picture of our ego mind that the Course presents is similar to what the Buddhists call "monkey mind": a mind that is constantly leaping from one thing to another, endlessly chattering, never still. The thoughts which normally occupy this mind are described in the Course as "raucous screams and senseless ravings" (T-21.V.1:6). This mind is constantly occupied with "the frantic, riotous thoughts and sights and sounds of this insane world" (W-pI.49.4:4). In a nutshell, this mind is in a state of *conflict*. It is constantly at war, both with the external world and within itself.

This picture of our normal state of mind may sound extreme. It can be hard to believe that the everyday content of our mind is comparable to the bedlam of an insane asylum. Yet if we pause and examine our ongoing stream of thoughts, we can see that this is so. We are focused almost exclusively on the task of surviving and hopefully triumphing in a chaotic external world. Our days are spent devising battle plans to successfully combat the myriad external forces that threaten us at every turn: hunger, thirst, germs, injury, traffic, obnoxious co-workers, you name it. It seems as if the whole world is against us.

Yet even when we look within, we don't see a united front: our *own thoughts* are in conflict. Part of us wants to do this, part of us wants to do that. Our ego thoughts conflict both with our spirit-based thoughts, and with each other. In the midst of such conflict, peace of mind seems like an airy-fairy pipe dream, a delusion of naive people who hide their heads in the sand and refuse to acknowledge the senseless chaos of the real world.

But according to the Course, this conflict—both in the external world and within the mind—is entirely unreal. The conflict of the external world is an illusion, a projection of the conflicting thoughts in the mind, thoughts which are themselves illusions. Both the world we see and the conflicted thoughts that produce and maintain it are completely divorced from reality (see W-pI.45.1).

Therefore, if we want to end the conflict and find peace, the first step is simply to turn our attention away from both the cacophony of the outside world and the constant stream of warring thoughts in our mind. This is what the Course wants us to do when it asks us to still the mind: to empty the mind of its usual conflicted content, so that it is open to receive new content. The Course frequently invites us to take a moment and let go of everything that normally occupies our mind, as in the following passage:

> Let us be still an instant, and forget all things we ever learned, all thoughts we had, and every preconception that we hold of what things mean and what their purpose is. Let us remember not our own ideas of what the world is for. We do not know.
> (T-31.I.12:1-3; see also T-31.II.8 and W-pI.189.7)

I think it is vitally important to see passages like the one above not just as pretty, poetic words, but as an invitation to do a real spiritual practice. The author of the Course really wants us to take some time to still our minds here. Given how often he instructs us to do this (the phrase "be still" occurs 36 times in the Course), it is clear that this is important to him. The Text encourages us to still our minds frequently. The Workbook introduces meditation practice (though it doesn't use the word "meditation" to describe it) starting with Lesson 41; as we advance through the Workbook, regular extended periods of quiet time with God become a staple of our practice, until they become the main practice of every lesson in Part II. This quiet time is a major part of post-Workbook practice as well (see M-16).

Given the chaotic nature of our normal state of mind, it is not hard to see why this practice is important. As anyone who has tried to still her mind can tell you, monkey minds need a lot of training to set aside their incessant chattering and be still. And it is this stillness, this openness, this willingness to set aside what we think we know, that paves the way for something new to enter.

2. God enters our still, open mind and gives us His gift of peace.

Once we have stilled the mind and emptied it of its old content, God (through the Holy Spirit) fills it with His new content. God Himself takes the place of the conflicting illusions that battled in the mind before, bringing His truth with Him:

> An empty space that is not seen as filled...[becomes] a silent invitation to the truth to enter, and to make itself at home....For what you leave as vacant God will fill, and where He is there must the truth abide. (T-27.III.4:1,3)

God lays His gifts into the mind that is open to receive them. The Course tells us of a number of gifts that we receive when we still the mind: the miracle, the holy instant, forgiveness, healing, God's Word, the Holy Spirit's guidance, our function, etc. But the greatest gift of all, the gift that all the other gifts bring with them, is the gift of *peace*. The conflict that raged in the mind before is gently replaced by "the stillness of the peace of God" (W-pII.273.Heading). This peace is above all what the Course is speaking of when it uses the word "silence" and its many synonyms, such as quiet, stillness, calmness, and tranquility. This peace is the deep, abiding peace that dawns on the mind when the truth beyond the mad illusions of the world stands revealed. This peace is the Course's goal.

How does God's gift of peace come to us? In some Course passages, the implication is that God's gifts come to us automatically once we open our mind to them, while in other passages we are invited to actively ask for those gifts. An example of God's gifts coming to us automatically is the above quote from T-27.III, in which the very openness of our mind invites God to replace our illusions with the truth. This makes a lot of sense, since the truth was always there to begin with, awaiting only our recognition of it; stilling our mind automatically puts us in touch with a part of our mind that is always at peace.

An example of actively asking for God's gifts is the following prayer, which is typical of the prayers in Part II of the Workbook. We ask God to speak to us and give us His gift of peace, and then wait in silence to receive it:

Greg Mackie

Father, I come to You today to seek the peace that You alone can give. I come in silence. In the quiet of my heart, the deep recesses of my mind, I wait and listen for Your Voice. My Father, speak to me today. I come to hear Your Voice in silence and in certainty and love, sure You will hear my call and answer me. (W-pII.221.1:1-5)

But whether the gifts are given automatically or we actively ask for them, the key is that *we* must extend the invitation to God by stilling the mind and clearing a space for Him. Actively turning away from our conflicted ways of thinking and seeing is the gateway to the peace of God. It is *our* stillness that opens our mind to *His* stillness. In "this empty space...is Heaven free to be remembered" (T-27.I.10:1).

3. We return to the world, bringing the peace of God with us as we act in the world, extending that peace to everyone.

All of this withdrawing attention from the world, stilling the mind, taking quiet time, and inviting the peace of God to enter may sound very self-absorbed and impractical. After all, most of us are not solitary Himalayan masters who can spend all day in meditation; we have to actually relate with other people and live in the rough and tumble of everyday life. How can ordinary people actually *live* this teaching?

The Course's answer is that we are not to turn away from the world for good. Once we have received God's gift of peace (in our practice, our quiet time of stilling the mind and inviting Him to enter), we are to *come back* to the world, bringing this peace with us and extending it to others. Extending our peace to others reinforces our peace, for it is in giving that we receive. All of our gifts are thus gifts to the Self we all share, and so the Course encourages us to return from our quiet time to the world and be thankful for the opportunity to give our gifts to others: "Be grateful to return, as you were glad to go an instant, and accept the gifts that grace provided you. You carry them back to yourself" (W-pI.169.14:1-2).

The extension of peace to others can happen in two ways. The first way actually takes place before we return from our quiet time to the world: Just as God's gifts are extended to us automatically once we still our mind, so those gifts are extended automatically from our mind to other minds once we receive the gifts.

One Workbook lesson which speaks of this is Lesson 106. The lesson instructs us to frequently take time out for quiet listening to the Voice for God, but also reminds us that our periods of quiet time are not for ourselves alone. On the contrary, "For each five minutes spent in listening, a thousand minds are opened to the truth and they will hear the holy Word you hear" (W-pI.106.9:2). Simply by taking the time to quiet our mind and allow truth to enter, we automatically extend truth (and the peace that comes with it) to other minds as well. This first way, then, is essentially extending peace passively.

The second way is extending this peace actively. This may take the form of a purely mental practice, as when the Course instructs us to mentally say to specific people, "Let peace extend from my mind to yours, [name]" (W-pI.82.2:2). But while all extension is ultimately mind-to-mind, the Course definitely sees us communicating our peace behaviorally as well. The Course would have us literally go out into the world and perform miracles, and by so doing extend God's peace to those whose minds are still torn by the conflict and chaos of the world.

The following prayer from Part II of the Workbook is a beautiful evocation of this extension. This prayer is both an expression of the uplifting truth that our peace blesses all who come into contact with us, and an invitation to God to bring to us those who particularly need our help:

> *Your peace surrounds me, Father. Where I go, Your peace goes there with me. It sheds its light on everyone I meet. I bring it to the desolate and lonely and afraid. I give Your peace to those who suffer pain, or grieve for loss, or think they are bereft of hope and happiness. Send them to me, my Father. Let me bring Your peace with me.*
> (W-pII.245.1:1-7)

The form this communication takes is to be guided by the Holy Spirit, and could be anything that gets the message of peace across to the one in need of peace. It could be an act of kindness, a word of reassurance, a gesture of forgiveness, or simply our peaceful presence. Many of us have had the experience of a stressful situation being instantly defused simply by the entry of a calm, peaceful person. If you are such a person, just being there may be enough to extend stillness and peace of mind to others: "You bring [God's] happiness to all you look upon; His peace to everyone who looks on you and sees His message in your happy face" (W-pI.100.6:5).

One section of the Course which describes all three aspects we are discussing—stilling the mind, allowing God's peace to enter, and bringing His peace back with us to the world—is the well-known section of the Text entitled "I Need Do Nothing" (T-18.VII). This section was originally addressed specifically to Helen, who was facing a distressing life situation of both outer and inner conflict, and wondering what to do about it. This section's advice, which applies to us today every bit as much as it did to Helen, is as follows:

1. When we are in a conflicted situation, we should remind ourselves that we need do nothing (T-18.VII.5:5-6). In other words, we should take time out and still the mind by withdrawing our attention from the external situation and letting go of our worries about what to do.

2. This creates an opening in our mind, an empty space free of the mind's usual focus on externals (T-18.VII.7:7). God then places His gift of peace into this empty space, through His Voice, the Holy Spirit (T-18.VII.7:8). We now have an abode of peace within us, a "quiet center" (T-18.VII.8:2).

3. Once we have found this place of peace, we don't just sit there in solitary bliss, permanently oblivious to the external world. Eventually, we return and bring this peace with us as we go about our business in the world, allowing the Holy Spirit to guide us to where we can best bestow the gift of peace we have received: "This quiet center, in which you do nothing, will remain with you, giving you rest in the midst of every busy doing on which you are sent" (T-18.VII.8:3).

Thus even in the external situation we were originally worrying about, we won't necessarily do nothing externally. We may be guided to do something about it, or we may not. But whatever we do externally, we will in essence be doing nothing, because all of our actions will be coming from a place of deep stillness within us. Even as we go about our work in this tumultuous, chaotic world, we "will be more aware of this quiet center of the storm than all its raging activity" (T-18.VII.8:2). Before, our mind was buffeted about by the storm, thrown here and there by its fierce winds, seemingly at its mercy. But now, we are in the eye of the storm, so to speak; even in the midst of the often frenetic activity of everyday life, we will be still, basking in the peace of God. And this peace is a gift to everyone we meet. By stilling our mind we allowed God's stillness to enter, and now we extend that stillness to the world. We have become the living embodiment of peace.

Stilling the mind, receiving the peace of God, and extending it to the world: a practice

Here's a brief practice which incorporates all three elements of stilling the mind, receiving the peace of God, and bringing His peace back with us to the world. It uses the prayers from Lessons 221 and 245, reproduced above. I would suggest reading through all of the instructions first, and then giving the practice a try.

1. As a prelude to entering into a period of silent listening, close your eyes and slowly say the prayer from Lesson 221 to God. Don't just read the words, but offer them as a personal invitation to your Father, an invitation for Him to speak to you and give you His peace. Bring as much sincerity as you can to the words you say. Use the prayer to still your mind, to turn your attention away from the thoughts of the world and toward God. Use it to enter the quiet center of your mind, where God your Father abides.

2. When you have concluded the prayer, sink into the silence at the center of your mind and listen for God. Patiently await the gift of peace that He has promised you, confident that you will receive it. When your mind wanders and thoughts of the world enter (as will almost certainly happen), quietly reaffirm your commitment to be silent and listen for God. You might repeat a short line from the prayer, such as "I come in silence" or "I seek the peace that You alone can give," to refocus your mind each time it wanders from its intent. Or you might use a variation on a technique given in the Introduction to Review VI of the Workbook: When you have a distracting thought, say, "This thought I do not want. I choose instead the peace of God" (based on W-pI.rVI.In.6:2). Spend as much time in this silence as you like; you might want to set a specific time, perhaps 15 minutes.

3. When you are ready to leave your quiet time and return to the world, open your eyes and say the prayer from Lesson 245 to God. Again, don't just mouth the words, but make it a sincere prayer of the heart, addressed personally to your Father. Use this prayer to affirm your commitment to bringing God's peace with you as you return to the world. Really see yourself bringing peace to all the people God sends to you today. If particular people come to mind who are in need of the gift of peace, mentally extend peace to them now, and also see yourself extending that gift behaviorally to them. When you have concluded the prayer, return to the world, committed to bringing the peace you have found in the stillness of your mind to everyone you meet.

Obviously, we won't have a deep experience of peace every time we do this practice. Our monkey minds can be pretty stubborn, and so we should be patient with ourselves. Most of us are pretty inexperienced at stilling the mind, and so it will take time to learn. But that is exactly why it is called *practice*. We need practice, and the more we practice, the more skilled we will become. And along the way, we should take heart in whatever small gains we make. If we do nothing more than strengthen our desire to find the peace of God, we will have accomplished something worthwhile. For if the desire is there, it is only a matter of time before we find the stillness and peace we seek.

In fact, the Course traces our entire journey to peace from beginning to end in Review I of the Workbook (see W-pI.rI.In.3:3-5:2). This journey consists of four basic phases of learning:

1. At first, we will need externally quiet situations in order to find peace. In other words, we will need to get away from the hustle and bustle of our everyday lives and create "special settings" for quiet time with God. I suspect that most of us are still at this step much of the time.

2. Then, we will learn how to bring peace with us into our everyday lives, and use it to deal with whatever difficult situations we are confronted with.

3. In time, we will learn that peace is part of us, and so it is always with us, wherever we are.

4. Finally, we will learn that our true Self is everywhere, and so peace is everywhere.

All we are asked to do is begin this journey. If we take the first step, the others will follow. The peace of God will be ours.

Conclusion

In conclusion, I encourage you to really *do* the practice of stilling the mind and inviting the peace of God to enter. Make it a habit. In addition to the short practice I put together above, the Course itself contains a treasure trove of other practices and prayers to choose from.

Ultimately, the practice of silence in *A Course in Miracles* can be boiled down to an exceedingly simple formula: *Withdraw your attention from the world, and place your attention on God.* By silencing the voice of the ego and its world, we open to the deep, eternal silence of God's peace. And it is here we will find our Father, and remember our true Identity as His Son:

> There is a resting place so still no sound except a hymn to Heaven rises up to gladden God the Father and the Son. Where Both abide are They remembered, Both. And where They are is Heaven and is peace.   (T-29.V.1:3-5)

14

How can we distinguish between the ego and the Holy Spirit?

by Allen Watson

Question

How do we know that it is actually the voice of the Holy Spirit and not the voice of the ego that we are listening to?

Answer

Another way of phrasing the question might be, "How can we distinguish between illusions and the truth?" The actual answer is, "Do the Course." But that seems to beg the question. My point, though, is that learning to tell the difference between illusion and truth, or learning to hear only the Voice for God and not the voice of our egos, is really what the Course is meant to train us in doing. The only way, really, to learn how to distinguish between the ego and the Holy Spirit, or between illusion and truth, is to completely devote oneself to the Course's training program.

Recognizing the Holy Spirit's Voice May Take Time

Learning to recognize the Holy Spirit's Voice is, for most people, a lifelong process. The Course tells us: "Only very few can hear God's Voice at all, and even they cannot communicate His messages directly through the Spirit which gave them" (M-12.3:3). So hearing the Holy Spirit is not something we hear about and do, without any effort or training, the next day. A lot of people think they hear God's Voice, but that doesn't necessarily mean that they actually *do* hear it.

Indeed, Jesus tells us that even for him, hearing the Holy Spirit's Voice was no easy matter. He says:

> It is possible even in this world to hear only [the Holy Spirit's] Voice and no other. It takes effort and great willingness to learn. It is the final lesson that I learned, and God's Sons are as equal as learners as they are as sons.
>
> (T-5.II.3:9-11)

These lines are simultaneously discouraging and encouraging. They are discouraging in that they let us know that pure, unadulterated reception of the Holy Spirit's guidance is not an easy goal to attain. Learning to hear only that Voice "takes effort and great willingness to learn." Not only that, but it was also Jesus' *final* lesson, so it isn't something elementary, something we can learn quickly. It takes a while! However, on the encouraging side, Jesus points out that we are his equals as learners; therefore, if he learned it, so can we.

Clues in Discerning between Ego and Holy Spirit

There are some practical tips on recognizing the Spirit's voice. There are several signs that are pretty clear indicators that the voice we are hearing is the ego. There are also a few signs that indicate what we are hearing is the Spirit's Voice. And, since the ego attempts to counterfeit these positive signs, there are also warnings about false signs.

Signs that say "ego"

The Holy Spirit is often referred to as a "still" voice, or a quiet voice. We are told that "the Holy Spirit never commands" (T-6.IV.11:1). So if the voice you hear is commanding you, it isn't Him.

We are also told, "The Holy Spirit never itemizes errors" (T-6.V.4:1). So if the voice you are hearing is fault finding, it isn't Him. By extension, if the voice you hear is making you guilty, it isn't Him.

The Holy Spirit is very clear that you are the innocent, holy Son of God. The Course says: "The Holy Spirit never varies on this point, and so the one mood He engenders is joy" (T-6.V(C).1:10). If the voice you are hearing is engendering something besides joy, it isn't Him.

"The Holy Spirit never asks for sacrifice, but the ego always does" (T-7.X.5:5). So if the voice you are hearing is calling for sacrifice, it's the ego.

The Holy Spirit's answer always benefits everyone equally: "Be certain any answer to a problem the Holy Spirit solves will always be one in which no one loses" (T-25.IX.3:1). Therefore, guidance from the Holy Spirit will always arrange things in such a way that everyone is blessed, and no one is hurt in any way. He probably won't guide you to steal your brother's car, for instance.

Qualifications of the above rules

Despite these seemingly simple rules, we need to watch out here. Sometimes we can be hearing the Holy Spirit, but then *reacting* with our egos. The ego will always react negatively to the Holy Spirit, and will try to confuse us, to cause us to react to love as if it were fearful, and to fear as if it were lovely.

Negative reactions to God's Voice

Sometimes we have what seem to be negative reactions to the Voice for God. This occurs when we are genuinely hearing guidance from the Holy Spirit, but we are allowing our egos to hear and respond to it. Although the Holy Spirit never commands, if we are hearing Him with our egos, it will seem to us that we are being asked to do something against our will. Prayerful self-examination at such times will usually reveal that we *really do want* what the Holy Spirit is asking us to do; only our ego or our independent self, which insanely wants autonomy at all costs, feels imposed upon.

The Course also speaks of a kind of false guilt that can arise in us as we listen to God's Voice. This is to be expected in a mind that has not wholly lost its fear of God. For instance, when we begin to realize that our projection of guilt upon the world is a mistake, and that the guilt we are seeing is in fact our own, "the beginning phases of this reversal are often quite painful, for as blame is withdrawn from without, there is a strong tendency to harbor it within" (T-11.IV.4:5).

Some people have even stopped reading the Course (few students would question that the Course itself is an expression of the Holy Spirit) on the grounds that "It makes me feel guilty." The Course's own answer to this kind of false guilt is quite simple:

> Only the ego blames at all. Self-blame is therefore ego identification, and as much an ego defense as blaming others. (T-11.IV.5:4-5)

In other words, give up the guilt. Guilt is *always* an indication of the ego. You may be thinking that you are feeling guilty because you are listening to the Holy Spirit, but if you are feeling guilty, *you are listening to the ego*. It isn't what the Holy Spirit is saying that gives rise to guilt; it is your own ego's interpretation of it. The Holy Spirit may be saying, "Your loss of peace is not your brother's fault; you, yourself have chosen to give up peace." If that seems to make you feel guilty, however, it is only because your ego is telling you so; the Holy Spirit *never* blames, and never condemns.

Similarly, what the Holy Spirit has to say never makes our *egos* feel joyful; on the contrary, the ego is fearful and depressed when the Voice for God is heard. So the mere absence of a joyful feeling does not mean that the voice you are hearing is not the Holy Spirit. If some inner guidance seems to be from God, and yet does not give rise to joy, look carefully at the reasons behind the lack of joy. If the guidance is truly of God, you will find that the lack of joy is being caused by some belief in fear or sacrifice, or some false perception of loss of specialness.

Likewise, many times our ego will perceive sacrifice where there is none, and sometimes, therefore, what the Holy Spirit asks of us seems, at first, to be sacrifice. We think nothing is something; if the Holy Spirit asks us to give it up, we think "sacrifice," but really we are sacrificing nothing. If you feel the Holy Spirit is asking a sacrifice of you, ask yourself what you are sacrificing, and if that something is truly something of God. Possibly, the only way to resolve the doubt is simply to *let go* of whatever it is, and so discover that losing it was not really a sacrifice after all (see M-4.I(A).5:5-8).

Positive reactions to the ego's voice

On the other hand, there are times when we are hearing the ego's voice, and the ego attempts to simulate the positive reactions of joy and peace.

We can often mistake a feeling of *triumph* for a feeling of joy. True joy is always a shared feeling. It never arises from besting someone else. Beating out the competition for that new job may seem to feel good, but it is a simulated joy that arises from specialness and competition. The Holy Spirit, being an equal-opportunity Helper, will never lead you to gain at the expense of someone else's loss.

There is also a kind of false peace that the ego can give us. As an obvious example, think of the "peace of mind" that effective denial can bring. If we take some problem or negative emotion and bury it deeply enough, cover it over with layers of darkness, we seem to achieve a certain kind of "peace." But such denial is only a temporary palliative. It is only masking the problem rather than healing it. Ask yourself, "Is my peace coming from resolving the problem, or from avoiding it?" Another kind of false peace is referred to in the Workbook discussions of meditation as "withdrawal." One discussion of this is W-pI.74.5:1-4, which I invite you to read now before continuing.

The clear instruction in this passage tells us that true peace brings with it "a deep sense of joy and an increased alertness," as opposed to the "drowsiness and enervation" (a loss of energy) that will come from false peace. God's peace is awake and energetic, confident that all problems can and will be resolved, rather than retreating into withdrawal and avoidance.

Signs that say "Holy Spirit"

The section of the Text that speaks to this question most directly is Chapter 14, Section XI. The fifth and sixth paragraphs are key. As with the passage from the Workbook discussed above, I invite you to read those paragraphs now before continuing.

The fifth paragraph says the ultimate test that can tell us we have heard God's Voice is that we are wholly free of fear of any kind, and that everyone who meets or even *thinks* of us shares that same peace. Now, honestly, that lofty criterion seems to put the whole thing completely out of my reach! Don't you agree? And it *is* the only final test, the one sure test. No wonder Jesus tells us that learning to hear God's Voice is difficult, and was so even for him. But it is *not* out of our reach; it is attainable, as we saw earlier. If Jesus, who is no different from any of us, could do it, that means we can also.

Realizing I don't know

Yet, until we have achieved that extremely high standard, the passage continues, it means that we all have "dark lessons" in our minds that hurt and hinder us and those around us. Despite that, Jesus assures us that all is not lost, because we are not expected to overcome these dark lessons on our own (see T-14.XI.6:1-4). Help is available to us, if only we will do the little he asks of us:

> Your part is very simple. You need only recognize that everything you learned you do not want. (T-14.XI.6:3-4)

To me, what this is in essence saying is that all we really need to "do" is to recognize our dark lessons—the ego's voice—and when we realize we are hearing the ego's voice, to be willing to see how undesirable its lessons are and to let them go. Adopt the attitude at all times of "I do not know what this means." Sentence 6:10 makes it clear for me: "By this refusal to attempt to teach yourself" means refusing to try to figure things out, to determine what things mean or, in a word, a refusal to judge. That is all we need to do. If we do just that, the Holy Spirit will speak to us. If we get out of the way, and don't interfere, He will guide us. And when He does, we will have that perfect peace spoken of.

So, how we learn to hear His Voice isn't the real question. Since all I need to do is stop listening to the ego, the real question is, how do I recognize the ego's voice? If I learn that, I do not need to concern myself about how I will learn to hear the lesson of the Holy Spirit. He'll take care of that.

My own opinion is that we learn this very gradually. We can start with the basic assumption that virtually everything we hear is at least tainted by the ego, and therefore assume the attitude of "I don't know." As the Course says, "I don't know" is our "firm beginning" in learning (see T-11.VIII.3:1-4).

Don't be stopped by the ego

At first, I think most of the "guidance" we get will be a mixed bag at best. "Not one thought you hold is wholly true" (T-11.VIII.3:2), the Course tells us. The ego will wriggle in almost every time. We can't let that stop us, though. I've come to look on life as a process of learning to hear one Voice: "Learning is living here" (T-14.III.3:2). I once wrote an article titled "Don't Let the Ego Stop You!" My idea was that as we begin, the ego will always manage to work its way into our choices, and we can't avoid that. It will be by making choices and experiencing the results of the ego's directions—usually pain of some sort—that we learn to disregard them. We will "fall down" a lot while learning to "walk" in the Spirit. But that's how we learn.

Summary

In summary, my advice in answer to this question is:

1. Recognize you don't know anything.

2. Be willing to let go of all your preconceptions.

3. Ask the Holy Spirit for help.

4. Evaluate what you hear: Commanding, demanding, sacrificing, specialness-supporting, guilt-inducing, or non-joyous guidance is almost always from the ego.

5. When you think you hear His guidance, act on it as purely as you can.

6. Evaluate the results, and look to see where the ego crept in. Be willing to adjust and change your mind.

Over time, with willingness and practice, we will learn to hear only the One Voice. Be patient with yourself; be willing to learn; be a happy learner.

15

I have a Course friend who frequently points it out when he thinks I am coming from my ego. Is this something the Course recommends? What would the Course have us do when it appears to us that someone else is coming from the ego?

Short Answer

This is definitely *not* something the Course recommends. What the Course would have us do is this: When it appears to us that our brothers are coming from the ego, we should not judge our brothers and attempt to "correct" their ego errors on the basis of our judgment. Instead, we should accept the Holy Spirit's judgment of our brothers, and let Him guide our behavioral response to their ego errors.

�☺☺☺

I think this question is a crucially important one to address, because it is my experience that we Course students have a great propensity for pointing out each other's egos. I have seen countless exchanges between Course students degenerate into this kind of *ad hominem* attack. It seems to me that "You're coming from your ego!" (or variations on the same basic theme, such as "You're projecting!") has become the ultimate Course put-down, the Course student's equivalent of one born-again Christian saying to another, "The devil made you do it!"

I think it's no real surprise that we engage in this, given the Course's contention that all of us have such a strong investment in attack. Yet while it is not surprising, I think it is still very unfortunate. It *is* an attack, a weapon that is brandished whenever someone feels threatened by something another person is saying or doing. I think that dropping the "You're coming from your ego!" bomb has torn asunder many potentially fulfilling relationships and scuttled many potentially fruitful dialogues among Course students. Thus, I think that finding an alternative to this approach has the potential to bring great benefit to all of us.

Fortunately, the Course itself speaks directly to this issue, and provides the alternative we need. It is my hope that we as Course students will learn to choose this alternative more frequently, and thus come to treat one another with greater love, kindness, courtesy, and respect. Now, let's take a closer look at what the Course would have us do when faced with our brothers' egos.

We should not judge our brothers and attempt to "correct" their ego errors on the basis of our judgment. Instead, we should accept the Holy Spirit's judgment of our brothers, and let Him guide our behavioral response to their ego errors.

This, in a nutshell, is the counsel of four Course sections (T-9.III; T-12.I; M-17; and M-18) that speak directly to the topic of how to respond to other people's seeming ego errors. But before we look at those sections, let's consider for a moment our typical response when someone else makes what we consider to be an ego error. Since all of us have egos ourselves, most of the time we immediately go into attack mode. First comes our mental response: We judge the error, get angry about it, and mentally condemn the other person for making it. This is often followed by a behavioral response: We attempt to correct the other's error by letting her know about it and trying to convince her that she's wrong. Though all of this is really an attack, we who identify with the ego think we are actually doing this person a big favor by showing her the error of her ways: "To the ego it is kind and right and good to point out errors and 'correct' them" (T-9.III.2:1).

To put it bluntly, the Course considers this to be a profoundly wrong-minded approach to ego errors. This point is made loud and

Greg Mackie

clear in the four Course sections I mentioned above. All of them tell us clearly both what we should *not* do and what we *should* do in response to our brothers' errors. The following is my summary of the counsel offered by these sections (I recommend reading all of them in their entirety):

T-9.III, "The Correction of Error," addresses the question of what we should do when it seems to us that a brother is making an ego-based error. What we should not do is focus on the error and attempt to set our brother straight: "The alertness of the ego to the errors of other egos is not the kind of vigilance the Holy Spirit would have you maintain" (T-9.III.1:1). We shouldn't do this because rather than truly correcting our brother, this will actually magnify and reinforce the seeming reality of both his errors and our own: "To perceive errors in anyone, and to react to them as if they were real, is to make them real to you" (T-9.III.6:7; see also T-9.III.5:2). What we should do is give all of our brother's errors to the Holy Spirit for correction (T-9.III.5:3). We should look past his errors to the truth of who he really is: "When a brother behaves insanely, you can heal him only by perceiving the sanity in him" (T-9.III.5:1). This perception, the Holy Spirit's perception, truly corrects both our brother's errors and our own (T-9.III.7:4).

T-12.I, "The Judgment of the Holy Spirit," addresses the question of what we should do when it seems to us that a brother's actions are motivated by the ego. What we should not do is decide for ourselves what our brother's motivation is: "Analyzing the motives of others is hazardous to you" (T-12.I.1:6). Nor should we try to "help" him in our own way (T-12.I.6:10). We shouldn't do this because this will actually reinforce the seeming reality of his errors (T-12.I.1:7-8). What we should do is accept the Holy Spirit's interpretation of our brother's motivation, an interpretation that sees everything he thinks, says, or does as either an expression of love or a call for help (T-12.I.3:1-4). We should respond to our brother's call for help by *offering* true, Holy Spirit-inspired help (T-12.I.3:5-6). By offering help to our brother, we ourselves receive what we have offered: "Only by answering [your brother's] appeal *can* you be helped" (T-12.I.5:6).

M-17 and M-18, "How Do God's Teachers Deal with Magic Thoughts?" and "How Is Correction Made?" are companion sections that together address the question of what we, as teachers of God, should do when one of our pupils presents us with magic thoughts (ego thoughts that assert that a power other than God can save us). What we should not do is respond to magic thoughts with anger (M-18.2:1). Nor should we try to forcibly correct them (M-18.1:2). We shouldn't do these things because they will actually reinforce the seeming reality of both the pupil's errors and our own: "If [a teacher] argues with his pupil about a magic thought, attacks it, tries to establish its error or demonstrate its falsity, he is but witnessing to its reality" (M-18.1:2; see also M-17.1:6). What we should do is let go of our angry, ego-based judgment of our pupil's magic thoughts (M-18.4:2). Then we should "turn within to [our] eternal Guide, and let Him judge what the response should be" (M-18.4:3). We should allow the Holy Spirit to respond to the pupil's magic thoughts *through* us (M-18.2:3; M-18.4:3). We should see such thoughts as calls for help, and respond with true, Holy Spirit-inspired help (M-17.3:5-7). Doing this will bring healing to our pupil and ourselves: "So is [the teacher] healed, and in his healing is his pupil healed with him" (M-18.4:4).

These sections give us an extremely consistent teaching on the issue of what to do when it appears to us that someone else is coming from the ego. None of them suggests that "You're coming from your ego!" is a helpful response. On the contrary, all of them say the same basic thing in different ways: We should not judge a brother's ego error, get angry about it, and try to correct it—our typical response—because all this does is make the error real in our minds and cement the ego more firmly into place. Instead, we should allow the Holy Spirit to reinterpret the error as a call for help, and then we should offer true help based on His guidance. This help could take many forms, I'm sure, but the key is that the inspiration for it comes from the Holy Spirit, not from the ego. Only in this way will we see beyond our brothers' errors to the truth of who they really are. Only in this way will their errors *and* our own be truly corrected.

Is it ever okay to correct a brother's errors?

This is a question that inevitably arises, given the Course's radical teaching on this issue. My short answer to this question is yes, there are times when correction of a brother's errors is warranted. I know this answer may seem surprising, in light of the material we've just covered. Yet I do think that there are times and situations when this is appropriate, *if* we are truly motivated by love and guided by the Holy Spirit (and that's a big "if"). I say this because Jesus himself clearly approves of certain exceptions to the "no correcting" rule, either explicitly by stating them in the Course material, or implicitly by engaging in them himself in the course of his own teaching.

What are some situations in which correcting a brother's errors may be appropriate? First, while I think "You're coming from your ego!" is virtually never helpful, clearly there are many everyday situations in which correcting a brother's errors in a loving way is truly helpful, and even expected. For instance, it would certainly be loving to point out to a driver that she's driving the wrong way down a one-way street, so that she doesn't have a horrible accident. The Course itself gives us an example of loving correction when it speaks positively of correcting a child who mistakenly sees ordinary objects in his room at night as terrifying monsters (see T-11.VIII.13). In situations like these, correction is just common sense. I don't think Jesus expects us to take this idea of not correcting errors to the point of absurdity.

Second, I think it is certainly okay to correct a brother's errors when the correction is *asked for*. Even gently pointing out a person's ego thoughts can be appropriate when the other person welcomes it. Certainly Jesus did this all the time with Helen and Bill, and they did welcome it, even if it brought up resistance at times. To share a personal example of this, I have a standing agreement with my wife that she will remind me to do my Course practice whenever she notices that I'm angry. Because this is something I have asked for, I truly appreciate it when she does this (though I admit that resistance comes up at times!).

The "asked for" category can also include relationships in which one person is mentoring another, such as a teacher and her pupil or a psychotherapist and his patient. These are relationships in which one person has asked for another's expert help, and pointing out errors and ego patterns in a loving way is often a vital and welcome part of such relationships. It is worth noting that two sections after coming down so hard on pointing out errors in the "Correction of Error" section, Jesus acknowledges that in the context of a spiritual teaching or therapy relationship, "it may help someone to point out where he is heading" (T-9.V.7:2). Clearly, Jesus' caution against pointing out errors is not an absolute rule.

Finally, I think it can sometimes be quite proper to correct other people's errors in the context of taking a stand for what we believe to be the truth. (This Q & A is an example of such a stand.) Taking a stand of any kind automatically implies that we believe those who disagree with us are in error, even if we don't overtly point this out. Taking a stand simply *has* to be permissible, because we literally can't help but stand for *something*, whatever it may be. Even to say that we should never correct errors is a stance that attempts to correct a perceived error!

Jesus himself often corrects other people's errors—such as the errors of traditional Christianity and the errors of modern psychotherapy—as he presents his teaching in the Course. He has taken a firm stand for truth, and he calls on us to do the same in this world: "As you share my unwillingness to accept error in yourself and others, you must join the great crusade to correct it" (T-1.III.1:6). This passage refers to correcting error through extending miracles, but even this is a stand for truth which may well involve verbally pointing out errors at times.

While I do think that taking a stand for what we believe to be the truth is both desirable and inevitable, I would like to end this Q & A with a few suggestions for how to do this in a truly loving way. First, I think it is wise to remain open-minded even as we take our stand; we may well be wrong, so we should always be open to other ways of seeing things. Second, as a general rule, I think we should make sure that our views are asked for, and not attempt to force them on others; while there may be times when we are truly called to offer unsolicited advice, for the most part people do not like to be preached to. Third, I want to make a heartfelt plea that as we Course students take our stands and discuss our ideas with others, we resist the temptation to accuse those who disagree with us of coming from their egos. Let's be charitable with one another, and not let character assassination get in the way of our common goal of finding the truth.

Finally, since the desire to point out errors does so often come from the ego, I would suggest that we think twice when the urge to do so arises. I've said that pointing out errors must be permissible at times because Jesus himself does it, but it is also true that we don't have the wisdom and clear perception that he does. Yes, there are times when pointing out our brothers' errors is appropriate, but I think that we should always do our utmost to make sure that this is truly motivated by love and guided by the Holy Spirit.

Conclusion

Our tendency to accuse one another of coming from the ego is unfortunate, but it is not a sin. It is just a mistake that all of us who have egos tend to make, and as such, it is simply one more opportunity to practice forgiveness. Let us, then, choose to forgive instead of focusing on one another's egos. Let us choose to treat one another with love, kindness, courtesy, and respect instead of condemnation and attack. As we slowly but surely learn to do this, I think all of us will be much happier, our relationships will be much more fulfilling, and our dialogue with one another will be much more fruitful. In the spirit of true brotherhood, let us replace the curse of "You're coming from your ego!" with the blessing of "I see you as God's Son and my brother" (T-9.II.12:6).

Forgiveness and Relationships

16

The Course tells us frequently that much of the "joining" we do is not really joining. But it also tells us that truly joining with our brothers is essential to salvation. What, then, is the difference between false joining and true joining?

Short Answer

False joining is the "joining" of egos (and bodies) in the pursuit of separate ego goals; this kind of joining actually reinforces and maintains the separation. True joining is the joining of minds in the pursuit of a truly common goal; this kind of joining is what heals the separation.

☫☫☫

False joining is the "joining" of egos (and bodies) in the pursuit of separate ego goals; this kind of joining actually reinforces and maintains the separation.

Joining with other people for the sake of mutual gain is something that we are seemingly engaged in all the time. We make friendships with others who share our personality traits. We come together to promote the causes we believe in, and to oppose our common enemies.

We unite in relationships of mutual give and take, in which we share resources both tangible (material things) and intangible (emotional support, encouragement, validation, etc.). We unite with one another in the thrill and intimacy of romantic love relationships. Joining seems to be simply part of the fabric of everyday human life.

But is all of this really joining? According to the Course, most of the time, the answer is no. Why? Because most of the time our "joining" is simply a joining of *egos*, and egos are only in it for themselves, not for truly mutual gain. As the Course puts it, "Egos do join together in temporary allegiance, but always for what each one can get *separately*" (T-6.V(A).5:9). Thus, what looks like joining is often the very antithesis of joining. True joining affirms a common interest and a common goal, but the ego's "joining" is all about *separate* interests and *separate* goals. It is thus pseudo-joining, a false joining.

One example of this kind of false joining is the typical scenario of two people joining in a business venture. I think if we're honest with ourselves, we have to admit that as a general rule, we enter into such ventures in order to serve our own ego goals: to make money for ourselves, acquire material possessions, give ourselves the means to live a life of luxury, gain prestige, etc. Our business partners, in our eyes, are simply useful means to accomplish these personal goals. We may deny this and claim that our partner's success is equally important to us. We may have the best of conscious intentions, and really be striving to see our business ventures as truly collaborative enterprises. But given our heavy investment in the ego, I think that in most cases the bottom line is still "What's in it for me?" This is made evident by the fact that we are very quick to jettison our business partners when they don't hold up their end of the bargain. Our primary motivation is to accomplish our separate, personal ego goals, not to truly join with the other person.

Another example of false joining is one I mentioned above, a kind of "joining" that is near and dear to all of our hearts: the romantic love relationship. At least if our popular music, literature, TV shows, and movies are any indication, the romantic love relationship is easily the most sought after prize on earth. In our eyes, finding that special someone to join "body and soul" in wedded (or at least cohabitating) bliss is the deepest, truest kind of joining imaginable.

But again, I think we have to admit that as a general rule, we enter into such relationships to serve our own ego goals. We see our romantic partners as the perfect fulfillment of our personal ego fantasies, and "love" them as long as their bodies satisfy us sexually, say the right things to us, and do the things we want them to do. Our romantic relationships are thus pretty much the same as our business relationships: However much we may say that we care about our partner's welfare, the bottom line is what's in it for us. And just as with our business partners, the tenuous, illusory nature of romantic "love" is revealed by just how quick we are to dump our romantic partners when they no longer satisfy. Once they stop fulfilling our ego fantasies, we no longer want anything to do with them, and may even come to hate them. (Our penchant for bitter divorces is certainly a testament to this.) As with our business ventures, our primary motivation here is to accomplish our separate, personal ego goals, not to truly join with the other person.

In the Course's view, this is a basic law of the world the ego made: Things "join" only to serve their separate interests. And the Course has a name for this false joining, which it identifies as the crown jewel of the ego's thought system: the *special relationship*. The special relationship, according to Robert Perry's succinct definition in his *Course Glossary*, is a relationship in which we "try to a) have a special or exclusive interaction with b) a special person so that c) we can feel more special."

On the surface, special relationships are our "good" relationships, such as friendships and the business and romantic relationships discussed above—in other words, relationships in which we seem to join with one another. But as we can see from Robert's definition, the ego's underlying goal for the special relationship is not really to join, but to acquire the ego's ultimate prize: *specialness*, the heady feeling of being separate from and superior to others. The "joining" that seems to take place in the special relationship is merely a facade that hides each participant's real goal. That goal is to serve his own ego by wresting specialness from the other:

> [The participants in the special relationship] come together, each to complete himself and rob the other. They stay until they think that there is nothing left to steal, and then move on. (T-22.In.2:6-7)

In short, the special relationship is a "joining" of egos, each in pursuit of specialness at the expense of the other. Moreover, since the body is the ego's dwelling place, the special relationship is a "joining" of *bodies*. (This is especially evident in the romantic love relationship.) This is not a joining that includes everyone, but one that *excludes* everyone except the chosen partner; the essence of the special relationship is "separate bodies, seeking to join each other in separate unions" (T-16.VI.5:2). Thus, as I said above, this relationship is about separate interests and separate goals, not true joining.

Indeed, the ego's ultimate goal for the false joining of the special relationship is the *prevention* of true joining. True joining ends separation, and so the ego—which depends on separation—must avoid true joining at all costs. It therefore offers us an illusion of joining as a substitute for true joining. It offers the "joining" of illusory egos as a replacement for the joining of our real minds. It offers "the union of bodies" as a means to "keep minds apart" (T-15.VII.11:5). The special relationship is thus "a kind of union from which union is excluded" (T-16.V.6:4), a way of separating that only *seems* to be joining. And it is precisely because it seems to be joining that the special relationship is "the ego's most boasted gift" (T-16.V.3:1). Through the special relationship, the ego entices us to take the bait of false joining by making it into a shiny lure that looks like true joining. In this way, the ego ensures that the separation is reinforced and maintained.

Before I move on, I want to add an important qualifier to all that has been said here: Although I do think that the vast majority of our relationships are rooted in false joining, the *forms* these relationships take are quite neutral in themselves. There is nothing inherently wrong with joining with another person in a business venture, a romantic love relationship, or any of the many other forms relationships take in this world. The problem is not the forms in themselves, but the separate, ego-based goals that usually motivate us to pursue these forms. Many of these same forms can also be used by the Holy Spirit as vehicles for true joining, which I will discuss below.

True joining is the joining of minds in the pursuit of a truly common goal; this kind of joining is what heals the separation.

As we've seen, what usually passes for joining in this world is the "joining" of egos and bodies. Now, egos can "join" in the very limited sense of "temporary allegiance" noted above. The Course speaks of egos joining together to reinforce ego ideas like sickness, suffering, fear, and body identification; in fact, the Course says that the entire illusory world we live in arose as the result of our sharing ego thoughts with one another (see W-pI.54.3:3). And just as egos can join in this limited sense, bodies can "join" in the limited sense of coming together to serve ego goals, as we saw in the discussion of special relationships.

However, none of this is real joining. According to the Course, the truth of the matter is that neither the ego nor the body can truly join with anything, because both are illusions, and "illusions cannot join" (T-23.I.3:6). Indeed, the sentence immediately following the statement that the world we live in arose as the result of sharing ego thoughts reveals the illusory nature of that sharing: "Yet that sharing was a sharing of nothing" (W-pI.54.3:4). All of the seeming joining our egos and bodies do is the joining of illusions, and thus false joining.

If our egos and our bodies cannot join, then what can? The Course's answer is clear: Only *minds* can truly join—not our false ego minds, but our real minds, the Mind of God and the minds of His Sons as He created them. Only minds can join because, as the Course repeats again and again, "minds *are* joined" (T-15.XI.7:1 and nine other references; emphasis mine). Because egos are inherently separate, they are capable only of false joining; but because minds are inherently joined, they are capable of true joining.

True joining is a joining that affirms the inherent unity of minds by recognizing our common interests. "Common interests," as I'm using the term here, does not refer to the idea of being interested in the same things (like sharing a hobby or similar political views), but to the idea of mutual benefit: Because our minds are one, we gain or lose together.

In the Course's view, this recognition of common interests is the most crucial turning point in our entire spiritual journey, the key insight that tilts our minds away from the ego and toward God. If one person recognizes common interests with another (which can be done even if the other person doesn't consciously see common interests himself), then that one person becomes a teacher of God (see M-1.1:2). And if *two* people see common interests with *each other* and join in a unified goal, then they enter into what the Course calls a *holy relationship*, a relationship which "represents the reversal of the unholy [special] relationship" (T-17.V.2:4). For while the special relationship is a false joining of egos in the service of separate ego goals, the holy relationship is a true joining of minds in the service of a truly common goal (or "common purpose," which in the Course means the same thing), a goal established by the Holy Spirit.

This leads to a big question: What constitutes a truly common goal? What makes the common goal of the holy relationship different from the ego goals that masquerade as "common goals" in the special relationship? In a nutshell, the Course says that a common goal is *anything that can be truly shared*. The *Psychotherapy* supplement, in a discussion of how the joining of two people in a common purpose invites God into their relationship, says that "it does not matter what their purpose is, but they must share it wholly to succeed" (P-2.II.6:6). So now the question becomes: What kind of purpose or goal is wholly shareable?

Based on my understanding of the Course, I would say that in order for a goal to be wholly shareable, there are two properties it must have. First, it must be an *idea*. The goal of acquiring material things cannot be truly shared, because material things themselves cannot be truly shared; even if we jointly own something, in truth we "divide its ownership" (T-5.I.1:10). A goal rooted in an idea, however, is a completely different story, because as the Course tells us many times, ideas *can* be truly shared:

> If you share an idea...you do not lessen it. All of it is still
> yours although all of it has been given away.
>   (T-5.I.1:11-12)

Second, and more specifically, it must be an idea that *reflects the goal of universal salvation*. That is, the goal must involve the realization of a saving idea, the facilitation of someone's internal healing or awakening. It must be focused on the healing of one or both participants in the relationship, or the healing of someone outside of the relationship—healing that, wherever it is specifically focused, will ultimately include everyone and benefit the entire world.

Thus, we cannot truly join in the "common goal" of hateful ideas like white supremacy, getting revenge, or forcibly establishing our religion as the one true faith, because these ideas are obviously ideas of separation, not ideas that reflect the goal of universal salvation. We cannot truly join in any ego idea, because the ego is the very antithesis of salvation—in fact, the ego is the very thing we are saved from. This means that we certainly cannot join in the goal of acquiring specialness—the goal of the special relationship—because specialness by definition is an attempt to "save" the special one at everyone else's expense. Only an idea that leads to the salvation of all can serve as the common goal of a holy relationship.

To get a sense of what such a holy relationship might look like, it may be helpful to look at some of the examples that the Course material offers us. A prime example is the act of joining that led to the genesis of the Course itself: Helen and Bill joining in the goal of finding "another way" to deal with their interpersonal conflicts. In the Course material, we have the example of a teacher and pupil joining in the goal of walking a particular path of awakening together (see M-2.5:7), and the example of a psychotherapist and his or her patient joining in the goal of bringing healing to the patient's mind (see the *Psychotherapy* supplement). The Course also speaks of joining in goals like truth, peace, holiness, and love. Notice how all of the goals in these examples fit the two criteria given above for a wholly shareable goal: The goals are ideas, and they are ideas that reflect the goal of universal salvation.

I think there are certainly other things that could qualify as truly common goals under these criteria. And the Course is clear that even if a particular relationship began as a false joining based on ego goals, a shared goal can emerge within that relationship at any time and transform it into a true joining. Jesus makes it a point to say that our special relationships need not *remain* special relationships: "I have said repeatedly that the Holy Spirit would not deprive you of your special relationships, but would transform them" (T-17.IV.2:3). Within every special relationship is a holy relationship waiting to be born. And while that newly born holy relationship will most likely still have elements of specialness in it that must be weeded out over time, it is truly a new creature, because it has a new goal blessed by the Holy Spirit. So the good news, as I said above, is that the forms we have used for false joining (including the body) can also be used by the Holy Spirit as vehicles for true joining. The key is allowing the Holy Spirit to replace our goals for our relationships with His.

Where does true joining ultimately lead us? To the very goal that

I've already mentioned: universal salvation. Just as the ego uses false joining to reinforce and maintain the separation, the Holy Spirit uses true joining to heal the separation. "Healing is the effect of minds that join" (T-28.III.2:6).

How does the joining of minds in a common goal bring about the healing of the separation? By affirming the inherent unity of minds, as I alluded to earlier. The Course tells us that "what shares a common purpose is the same" (T-27.VI.1:5); therefore, when we join our minds in a common purpose, we come to recognize that our *minds* are the same. We learn that "those who share a purpose have a mind as one" (T-23.IV.7:4). What the following Course passage says about the joining of teachers and pupils applies equally to us all. Whenever true joining occurs, those who join are blessed with a living experience of their oneness:

> The demarcations they have drawn between their roles, their minds, their bodies, their needs, their interests, and all the differences they thought separated them from one another, fade and grow dim and disappear.　(M-2.5:6)

The ultimate result of true joining, then, is the recognition that we have always *been* joined with each other and with God. We are restored to awareness of "the joint will of the Sonship" (T-5.IV.7:4), the will we share with God. Through this restoration, we come to realize that we have never been separate; we are forever one with each other and with our Creator. We are forever joined in the embrace of God's Love.

17

The Course urges us to heal our relationships, but how can I heal my relationship with someone when the other person apparently has no desire for the relationship to be healed?

Short Answer

I believe that in this situation, the Course would have us do the following:

1. Do everything in our power to allow our own perception of the other person to be healed.

2. Let the Holy Spirit guide the form the relationship takes, including the form in which we extend our healed perception to the other person.

3. Trust that the other person will accept the healing we have extended when he or she is ready, and that the ultimate healing of the relationship is inevitable.

☯☯☯

We've all experienced this situation: We dearly want a strained or ruptured relationship to be healed (or at least we think we do), but the other person wants no part of it. Perhaps it is a close relationship in which we see a rift that needs to be repaired, but the other person doesn't acknowledge the rift or want to address it. Perhaps it is a formerly close relationship that has been shattered, but which we would like to put back together. Perhaps it is a relationship of longstanding enmity, in which we are now holding out an olive branch. Whatever the specific situation, it can feel frustrating when our attempts to bring healing to the relationship seem to have no positive effect. It can be distressing when we want to bring peace, but the other person seems bent on continuing the war.

As Course students who want to heal all of our relationships, what can we do about this? I've given my short answer to this question above. Now let's look at the three points of that short answer in more detail:

1. Do everything in our power to allow our own perception of the other person to be healed.

This, of course, is our primary responsibility. We cannot sit around and wait for the other person to wake up one day and say to us, "Hey, let's heal our relationship today." Our job is to *do our part* to facilitate that healing, and our primary part in the Course's view is to allow our own perception to be healed. It starts with us.

I think that often the first step in allowing our perception to be healed is to get in touch with our *unhealed* perception of the other person. A number of the Course's forgiveness exercises include this as a preliminary step. So, we may want to begin by asking ourselves questions like: What are my grievances against this person? What has she done to arouse my anger? What do I blame and condemn her for? Personally, I find it very helpful to get a clear and specific picture of my resentments toward the person I'm trying to perceive truly. Only when we bring our resentments out of the darkness can the light of healing shine them away.

There is one form of resentment I think we should especially be on the lookout for here: We are often angry at the other person precisely *because* she doesn't seem to share our desire to heal the relationship. We think that this relationship could be healed, if only this pig-headed relationship partner of ours would hold up her end of the bargain. The Course warns against this tendency in its discussion of holy relationships: "Perhaps you are now entering upon a campaign to blame [your relationship partner] for the discomfort of the situation in which you find yourself" (T-17.V.11:9). Needless to say, this is not a very healing attitude to adopt, and one I think we would do very well to confront in ourselves.

As part of this process of uncovering our unhealed perception, I think it is also a good idea to question our very perception that the other person has no desire for the relationship to be healed. Now, clearly there are cases where the other person is truly resistant to healing, at least outwardly. However, I think that all too often, our belief that the other person doesn't want healing is simply a projection of our own resistance to healing. It is an expression of our unforgiveness, a declaration that this person's heart is just too black with sin to respond to healing. It can become a convenient excuse for us to withhold healing from the other person, and thus stave it off ourselves.

So, to expose this unforgiving perception, we might ask ourselves questions like: Is it really true that this person doesn't have any desire to heal the relationship? Is it possible that what I'm seeing is only my own resistance to healing? Even if this person really is outwardly resisting healing, isn't there something deep inside her that dearly wants this relationship to be healed? And wouldn't I rather see that something, the innocent Son of God in her who yearns to join with me in peace, instead of seeing her as an evil sinner who is beyond hope of healing? Questions like these can help us get in touch with our unhealed perception, and open our minds to the truth in the other person—an opening that is vital to the process of healing.

Once we get in touch with our unhealed perception of the other person, how do we allow it to be healed? The Course offers us a veritable treasure chest of tools that can help bring this healing about, if we use them. We can ask the Holy Spirit or Jesus for a new perception of the other person. If we are going through the Workbook, we can apply the idea for the day to this relationship. We can do a favorite practice from the Text or Workbook. Personally, I find it useful to counter my specific resentments with Course practices that directly address those particular resentments. (That is one reason why I like to get in touch with my specific resentments.) For example, if I'm angry at someone because he has seemingly betrayed my trust, I might counter that anger with Lesson 181, "I trust my brothers, who are one with me."

The key thing, as I said above, is to do our part. This is what we should be concentrating on instead of waiting for the other person to be struck with the desire for healing, or blaming the other person for not getting with the program. The Course, in fact, tells us that attending to our own responsibility is all we need do to ensure that the other person *will* get with the program: "Be certain, if you do your part, he will do his, for he will join you where you stand" (T-28.IV.5:1). And while sometimes the other person might not join us outwardly right away, I think that if we look honestly at our relationships, we will find that when we truly do our part and experience a genuine shift in our perception, our relationship partner often will join us outwardly right away. A real healing on our part is simply bound to have some sort of positive effect on the relationship. By healing our own perception, we pave the way for the healing of our relationship partner's perception as well.

2. Let the Holy Spirit guide the form the relationship takes, including the form in which we extend our healed perception to the other person.

So often, we equate the healing of a relationship with certain external events. In our eyes, a healed relationship means that our friend forgives us for that rotten thing we did, our ex-lover returns to us after years of estrangement, or our enemy has a change of heart and persecutes us no more. We think that there must be some form of external resolution.

But while these kinds of external resolution can and do happen, things don't always work out the way we want. As everyone knows, we don't always get the Hollywood ending. Why don't we always get the resolution we want, even when we've worked very hard on healing a relationship? I can think of at least three reasons. First, our own perception of the other person may not be as healed as we think it is, and our still-buried resentments may contribute to the lack of resolution. Second, however much our perception of the other person may be healed, he has free choice and therefore might not consciously *accept* the healing himself, which can also block outward resolution. (I'll discuss this idea in more detail below.) Third, even in a situation in which both people consciously accept the healing of their relationship, the Holy Spirit is in charge of how it unfolds in form, and He is not beholden to Hollywood.

In this third case, I think the relationship probably will be healed outwardly in some form that can be recognized. As I said above, a real healing on our part is simply bound to have some sort of positive effect on the relationship, and this positive effect will be especially evident when both people are open to healing. However, the Holy Spirit chooses whatever outward form of healing will best serve His plan of salvation, and this form may not be the particular resolution we expect or hope for.

So, for any of these reasons (or perhaps a combination of them), sometimes our friend isn't going to outwardly forgive us, the flame of a former love isn't going to be rekindled, and our enemy isn't going to have an immediate change of heart. We may not see an outward resolution today, next week, next year, or even in this lifetime. And sometimes, relationships are simply meant to end for the time being. The Course, in its discussion of teacher-pupil relationships, tells us that this can be the case even with relationships in which a lot of healing has taken place; such relationships can end simply because "each person involved [has learned] the most that he can from the other person at that time" (M-3.4:1).

Given all of this, I think that it is important to make our peace with the fact that sometimes things just don't change on the outside, however much we may want an outer healing. We need to realize that a lack of change in an external situation doesn't necessarily mean that no healing has taken place. Healing often does lead to miraculous changes in external situations, but the Course also reminds us that miracles "may not always have observable effects" (T-1.I.35:1). External situations are in the Holy Spirit's hands, and I think we would be wise to allow Him to guide the forms that our relationships take.

This same principle of allowing the Holy Spirit to guide us applies to the question of how to extend our healed perception to our relationship partner. Such extension is vitally important in the Course's view, because it communicates our healed perception to the other person, and thus reinforces the healing that took place in our own mind. It is definitely something the Course wants us to do. But how do we do it? In what form should we communicate our healing, especially when the other person doesn't even want to talk to us? The Course's answer is clear and simple: What we must do is ask for Help. *The Song of Prayer* stresses this point when it says, "And let it not be you who sets the form in which forgiveness comes to save God's Son" (S-2.III.5:3). Instead, we are to turn to our inner Guide, Who "will say exactly what to do, in words that [we] can understand and...can also use" (S-2.III.5:7).

The guidance we receive could vary a great deal, depending upon the situation. In some cases, we may be guided to do nothing but extend a silent blessing to the other person's mind. In others, we may be guided to say or do some kind thing that communicates the love we feel without bringing up the particulars of the relationship problem at all. In still others, we may be guided to address the relationship problem directly in some way. Every situation is different. The important thing is that we do the inner work needed to bring about a real healing in our mind, and that we follow our Guide in how to communicate that healing in a way that will be understood by the other person as a communication of love.

3. Trust that the other person will accept the healing we have extended when he or she is ready, and that the ultimate healing of the relationship is inevitable.

In the last point, I stressed the importance of making peace with the fact that sometimes things just don't change on the outside, in spite of our best efforts to bring about healing. This peace can be difficult to find, however, because in situations where the other person doesn't seem to share our desire for healing and there is no external resolution, it can be easy to conclude that all of our healing work has been for naught. Perhaps it has made *us* feel better, but the relationship seems to be no better off than it was before. How can we make peace with that?

We can do so by reminding ourselves that, appearances to the contrary, the relationship is actually much better off than it was before. We may think that our healing work has been for naught, but the Course assures us that this is not really the case. In its view, our healing has not been for us alone: It *has* extended to our relationship partner, and thus extended to the relationship as a whole. The Course gives us the exceedingly good news that "whenever a teacher of God has tried to be a channel for healing he has succeeded" (M-7.2:1). What is true for teachers of God is, in this case, true for all of us: Simply by attempting to extend healing, we have healed ourselves, our relationship partner, and the relationship itself on a deep level.

But if healing on a deep level always happens, why isn't the relationship always healed on the surface? I discussed three possible reasons above, but I want to focus on the second one here: According to the Course, outward healing may not occur because even when a genuine deep-level healing happens, the healed person may not be ready to consciously *accept* that healing. If he still has a heavy investment in his ego, he may be afraid of healing, and if this is so, external "healing must wait, for his protection" (M-6.1:9). So, when our relationships show no signs of outward healing in spite of all our healing work, the reason may simply be that one or both of the relationship partners is not yet ready to fully accept the healing that has been offered. When this is the case, our job is to trust that healing has been given and received on a deep level of the mind, and it is being held in trust by the Holy Spirit until the day when it can be fully embraced on a conscious level without fear. The healing will be accepted and experienced by all parties when they are ready.

If every attempt to heal leads to healing on a deep level, then this phenomenon of deep healing followed by delayed conscious acceptance of that healing must happen all the time. I had something happen in my own life recently which may be an example of it. My wife and I have a dear friend who is a recovering drug addict, and doing very well in his recovery. But that wasn't the case several years ago; at that time, he was very much in the throes of his addiction. We knew he was in trouble and attempted to help him, but he would have none of it. He isolated himself from us and totally disappeared from our lives. Our relationship with him had seemingly come to an end.

But just a month ago, he reestablished contact with us by writing a letter. As I read the letter, one of the things he said had a powerful impact on me: He said that he remembered how much we had tried to help him when he was hitting bottom, and although he rejected our help at the time, in hindsight he recognized what a gift that attempted help was. He came to realize how much we really loved him. Moreover, he said that the memory of this love sustained him over the last few years as he began to walk the road to recovery.

This strikes me as an excellent example of what the Course is saying here about delayed acceptance of healing. When my wife and I attempted to help our friend (however clumsy our attempt may have been), we did give him healing on a deep level. But since he had a heavy investment in his addiction at the time, he wasn't ready for the healing and didn't consciously accept it. The relationship came to an end. But in time, as he began to free himself from the grips of addiction with God's help (as he told us), this deep-level healing began to rise to the surface. He was ready to accept it, and as he did, he began to consciously recognize the love we had given him years ago. As a result, he contacted us again, and our relationship was blessed with a wonderful outward healing. What was planted as a healing seed deep in the mind sprouted and bore fruit when the time was ripe. When all of us were ready, the outward healing appeared.

This readiness will come to everyone sooner or later, for the Course tells us time and time again that healing on all levels is inevitable. We cannot hold it off forever; however long it takes, it will happen. Even those who apparently have no outward desire for a healed relationship have a deep inner desire for healing, and it is only a matter of time before this desire is acknowledged and fulfilled. If we remember this, we can be patient and trust that the healing we give will manifest in form when the minds that receive it are open to fully accept it.

Conclusion

If you have an unhealed relationship in which the other person seems to have no desire for the relationship to be healed (and who doesn't have such a relationship?), I recommend going through the steps I just outlined above with that relationship in mind:

1. Attend to the healing of your own mind by getting in touch with your misperceptions of the other person, and allowing those misperceptions to be healed through Course practice. (For this purpose, I recommend the six Workbook lessons that focus on forgiving particular individuals: Lessons 46, 68, 78, 121, 134, and 161.)

2. Ask the Holy Spirit for help in how to appropriately extend your love, and let Him determine the form the relationship is meant to take.

3. Remind yourself that even if your relationship doesn't look healed on the outside, it *is* healed on the inside, and trust that the healing will manifest in time.

I think it is also good to keep in mind that this healing may take quite a bit of time. We need to be patient with the process, and go through the above steps over and over again. There are relationships in my life that I've been working on for years. None of them are perfectly healed yet, but I have experienced increased peace and some genuine breakthroughs in those relationships through using the tools the Course offers me. I know I am peeling the layers of darkness off one by one, and I am heartened by the Course's assurance that I'm bringing the day of perfect healing nearer each time that I do this.

It can certainly feel frustrating when our desire to heal our relationships seems to meet with indifference or even hostility on the part of those with whom we are in relationship. It can be especially difficult when relationships seem to come to an end. But the Course tells us that even when we must part ways with one another in the world of form, "what appears to be the end of the relationship [is not] a real end" (M-3.4:4). Jesus promises us that "all who meet will someday meet again, for it is the destiny of all relationships to become holy" (M-3.4:6). As we work to bring healing to our unhealed relationships, it is in this promise that we can rest secure.

18

If the sins we see in our brothers are really *our own* sins, then is forgiveness based on recognizing that the particular "sinful" character trait that I'm seeing in my brother is really my projection of a character trait that I'm seeing and not acknowledging in myself?

Short Answer

No, this is not the basis of forgiveness in the Course. When the Course says that we see our own sins in our brothers, it means that we project our own *sense of sinfulness* onto our brothers, and thus interpret their particular character traits and behaviors as sinful. Forgiveness is based on recognizing that this *interpretation* is our own projection, a recognition that enables us to reinterpret our brothers' character traits and behaviors as expressions of love or calls for love, rather than sins.

☉☉☉

When the Course says that we see our own sins in our brothers, it means that we project our own *sense of sinfulness* onto our brothers, and thus interpret their particular character traits and behaviors as sinful.

This is my interpretation of the following passage, which clearly states what is really going on when we condemn our brothers:

> You never hate your brother for his sins, but only for your own. Whatever form his sins appear to take, it but obscures the fact that you believe them to be yours.
>
> (T-31.III.1:5-6)

Another possible interpretation of this passage, of course, is that the *specific* sins that we see in our brothers are always projections of specific sins we see but don't acknowledge in ourselves. To illustrate this idea with an example, if I hate Bill Clinton because I see him as a philanderer, it must be because I secretly see myself as a philanderer (or at least a potential philanderer), and I'm projecting that character trait, along with the self-hatred that goes with it, onto him.

Certainly, this kind of thing does happen. We've all heard of cases where the anti-homosexual activist turns out to be gay, the anti-porn crusader is caught with a prostitute, and the anti-Semite is found to have Jewish ancestry. However, I think this is too narrow an interpretation for the above passage. While it is undoubtedly true that we often hate our brothers because we're projecting our own unwanted character traits onto them, this particular dynamic isn't *always* the cause of our hatred. Thus, the hated "sins" referred to in this passage must be something broader than the particular character traits that we dislike and disown in ourselves.

Why do I say that seeing our own unwanted character traits in our brothers isn't always the cause of our hatred? Because there are some situations in which this simply cannot be the case. For instance, it is clear that in the case of a white supremacist who hates black people, it isn't because he is a closet black person who has projected his unacknowledged black identity onto black people. Obviously, the hatred is based on a physical trait that the white supremacist doesn't have. Even with nonphysical traits, there are many cases where one person hates another for a character trait that the hateful person clearly

Greg Mackie

doesn't have. For instance, if a highly educated person condemns illiterate people, it is not because she is projecting her unacknowledged illiteracy onto these people.

In the above examples, the white supremacist's and educated person's hatred is based not on seeing their own traits in the people they hate, but on seeing *different* traits in those people. The Course, in fact, describes this very dynamic in its discussion of the first law of chaos (T-23.II.2). There, we are told that each of us develops our own "hierarchy of illusions" (T-23.II.2:3): our own personal ranking system in which we rate the world's illusions on the basis of which ones we prefer. It says further that we defend our own hierarchies and establish their "truth" by attacking other people's hierarchies.

To illustrate this with one of our examples, when the educated person condemns an illiterate person, she does so to defend the "truth" of her own hierarchy (on which the trait of literacy ranks very high) against the "threat" of the illiterate person's hierarchy (on which the trait of literacy seemingly ranks very low). Everyone in this world is playing this game of dueling hierarchies, in which competing value systems battle for supremacy. The result is a world in which people hate and attack each other because their "values differ, and those who hold them seem to be unlike, and therefore enemies" (T-23.II.2:5). In short, people hate and attack each other because of their differences, not their similarities.

I'm sure there are situations in which one person hates another because of a combination of the two dynamics described above. For instance, a homophobic person might condemn homosexuals both because he overtly rejects their values *and* because he covertly shares their homosexual orientation, and is projecting his self-hatred for his own "sin" onto them. But my point is that since both of these dynamics can be a source of hatred, the idea that we always hate our brothers for our own sins can't refer only to the dynamic of hating our brothers for our own "sinful" character traits that we have projected onto them. At the very least, it has to refer to something that encompasses both dynamics. As I said above, the "sins" referred to in this passage must be something broader.

That "something broader" is the general *sense of sinfulness* that I referred to in my interpretation above. To restate that interpretation: The idea that we see our own sins in our brothers means that we project our own sense of sinfulness onto our brothers, and thus interpret their particular character traits and behaviors as sinful. How we see ourselves determines how we see the world. Because we believe we have separated from God, we see ourselves as guilty sinners, and "who looks upon himself as guilty and sees a sinless world?" (T-21.VI.2:4). Seeing ourselves as sinners leads inevitably to the perception of a sinful world.

The bottom line is that the particular form this takes doesn't matter. In a situation in which I condemn a brother for his "sins," he may actually have the particular character trait that I hate, or he may not. I may actually have the particular character trait that I hate in him, or I may not. He may have actually done the thing I hate, or he may not have. All of this is beside the point. The point is that whenever I condemn a brother's character traits or behaviors, it is always because I am projecting my own belief that I am a sinner onto him, and thus seeing him as a sinner too. I see my own sinful nature in him, and so I interpret his character traits and actions as sins. This is true "whatever form his sins appear to take" (T-31.III.1:6). Undoing this interpretation and allowing a new interpretation to replace it is the true basis of forgiveness, which brings me to my next point.

Forgiveness is based on recognizing that this *interpretation* is our own projection, a recognition that enables us to reinterpret our brothers' character traits and behaviors as expressions of love or calls for love, rather than sins.

This is how forgiveness is accomplished. The problem isn't that we're seeing the *form* of our own sins in our brothers, but that we're seeing the *content* of our own perceived sinfulness in them. The first step in forgiveness, then, is simply the recognition that the sinful content we're currently seeing in our brothers' character traits and behaviors comes from our own mind, and nowhere else. Our first task is to remind ourselves that "I have given what I see all the meaning it has for me" (W-pI.51.2:1). By recognizing that our current view of our brothers is our interpretation rather than a fact, we open the door to a new interpretation that is not the projection of our own sense of sinfulness.

Once the door is open to a new interpretation, how do we invite this new interpretation in? The Course provides a number of practices to help us do this, such as the following practice from Lesson 21 of the Workbook. This lesson says that when we are angry with a brother because of a particular attribute of his, we should apply the idea for the day to that situation by saying the following: "I am determined to see ___ [specify the attribute] in ___ [name of person] differently" (W-pI.21.5:4). Notice that this does not say that we should see the anger-inducing attribute as the projection of an attribute that we're not acknowledging in ourselves. Rather, it is simply a declaration of our willingness to see a different mental content in the empty form of that attribute, something other than the sinful content that seems to justify our anger. It is an invitation to a new interpretation of our brother's attribute.

What is this new interpretation? It is the Holy Spirit's interpretation. And, as virtually every Course student knows, everything in His eyes is either an expression of love or a call for love. This is the new interpretation we can give to all of our brothers' character traits and behaviors, with the Holy Spirit's help. As we learn to see through His eyes, we begin to withdraw our projection of sin from our brothers. When this is fully accomplished (a process that will take a lot of time and practice for most of us), we will no longer see our brothers as sinners, and therefore will not interpret their traits and behaviors as sins. Instead, our brothers' authentic expressions of love will be seen as such, and we will gratefully extend a loving response. Our brothers' attacks will be seen as innocent mistakes that also call for a loving response. Thus, regardless of what form our brothers' traits and behaviors take, our minds will see only the content of love in all of them. This is the vision that forgiveness through the Holy Spirit reveals. And through this forgiveness of our brothers, we will come to forgive ourselves as well.

Conclusion

Forgiveness is not based on recognizing that the *form* of our brothers' sins is a projection of the form of our own sins. Rather, it is based on recognizing that the *content* of sinfulness that we see in our brothers is a projection of the content of sinfulness we see in ourselves.

Personally, I find this to be a much more solid basis for forgiveness. Why? Because the idea of tying forgiveness to the particular form of sin we see in a brother, besides being unsupported in the Course, has a fatal flaw: It subtly implies that if the form we see is not our projection—if that brother really has that particular character trait, or really did that particular thing—then it is not forgivable. But if forgiveness has nothing to do with forms and everything to do with healing our interpretation of forms, then *everything* is forgivable. Through forgiveness, we learn that our interpretation of our brothers as sinners is always false, no matter what form their seeming sins take. This ultimately teaches us that our brothers' sins are totally unreal, and it is on this foundation that forgiveness—both for our brothers and for ourselves—ultimately rests. Forgiveness "sees there was no sin. And in that view are all your sins forgiven" (W-pII.1.1:3-4).

19

What is the difference between false forgiveness and true forgiveness?

Short Answer

According to the Course, the basic difference between the two is that false forgiveness sees sin as *real*, while true forgiveness sees sin as *unreal*. False forgiveness assumes that sin is real and then attempts to overlook it; this doesn't work, because it only ends up reinforcing the "reality" of the sin. True forgiveness recognizes that sin is unreal, and thus *truly* overlooks it; this works, because it reawakens us to the truth that God's Son is sinless. We can exchange false forgiveness for true forgiveness by allowing the Holy Spirit to teach us how to forgive.

ಠಠಠ

False forgiveness assumes that sin is real and then attempts to overlook it; this doesn't work, because it only ends up reinforcing the "reality" of the sin.

Forgiveness, whether false or true, is a response to situations in which we perceive that another person has wronged us and caused us pain. The key feature of false forgiveness is that this perception is assumed to be the truth. False forgiveness says, in essence:

> You have caused me real harm, and therefore, you are a sinner. Your sin against me gives me the right to resent you and punish you, because this is what you deserve. However, because I want to be loving, I will overlook your sin against me. I will sacrifice my right to resent you and punish you, and I will get no benefit from this except

the solace of knowing that I made a sacrifice for the sake of love. In the name of love, I will release you from the punishment you truly deserve. I will forgive your sin against me, and thereby show how good and innocent I am by overlooking your guilt.

This kind of forgiveness basically asserts that the sin against us was undeniably real, but we can somehow drop the emotional and behavioral responses—resentment and punishment—that are the natural consequences of sin. This "forgiveness" may seem to be a loving act, and indeed, this is what generally passes for true forgiveness in the world. However, the Course material dismisses it in no uncertain terms. T-30.VI calls it "false forgiveness" (T-30.VI.4:1), a kind of forgiveness that "pardons 'sinners' sometimes, but remains aware that they have sinned" (T-30.VI.3:7). Earlier in the Text, it is called "the ego's plan for forgiveness" (T-9.V.1:1), a plan in which we are to "see error [sin] clearly first, and then overlook it" (T-9.IV.4:4).

But perhaps the most striking name the Course material gives this kind of forgiveness is one that unveils the true motive behind this seemingly loving act: "forgiveness-to-destroy" (S-2.I.2:1). (This is from Chapter 2 of *The Song of Prayer*, a chapter entitled "Forgiveness"; I recommend reading this chapter in its entirety, because it has a great discussion of false versus true forgiveness.) Forgiveness, of course, was given to us by the Holy Spirit as a means of healing, not of destruction. But distorted by the ego's appetite for death and destruction, forgiveness as typically practiced in the world has become "a scourge; a curse where it was meant to bless, a cruel mockery of grace, a parody upon the holy peace of God" (S-2.I.1:2).

The Song of Prayer goes on to describe some of the specific forms that forgiveness-to-destroy takes, forms that I'm sure are familiar to most of us. One form is forgiveness based on moral superiority, in which a more "righteous" person affirms that a "baser" person has indeed sinned, but condescends to let this hopeless sinner off the hook (S-2.II.2). Another form is forgiveness based on false empathy, in which the forgiver basically says, "I'm just as rotten a sinner as the person I'm angry with, so who am I to hold his sin against him?" (S-2.II.3). Still another form, like the first rooted in the idea of moral superiority, is forgiveness as martyrdom, in which a person "forgives" another by meekly and patiently enduring the sufferings that the

Greg Mackie

other's "sins" have inflicted upon him (S-2.II.4-5). Finally, there is the form of conditional forgiveness, which says, "You sinned against me, but I will forgive you *if* you repent, show remorse, change your ways, apologize, recompense me for my injury, give me a backrub, etc." (S-2.II.6).

Most all of us use these various forms of forgiveness-to-destroy, but they never really give us the peace and sense of release from the ravages of sin that we seek. Why? The following passage tells us plainly why the ego's plan of seeing a brother's error clearly and then trying to overlook it—the core idea behind all forms of forgiveness-to-destroy—simply cannot work:

> How can you overlook what you have made real? By seeing it clearly, you have made it real and *cannot* overlook it. (T-9.IV.4:5-6)

Forgiveness-to-destroy cannot really free us from sin, because it actually affirms and reinforces the reality of sin. As I said above, false forgiveness asserts that sin is real, but we can somehow let go of sin's natural consequences. However, the Course is clear that as long as we believe in the reality of sin, its consequences will inevitably follow in our experience. There is no way around this, because the consequences simply come with the territory. If sin is real, the Course says, then eternal guilt (see W-pI.134.5:4) and punishment (see W-pI.101.2:1) are our inescapable lot. Real sin "must forever be beyond the hope of healing" (T-19.III.8:1). It is a declaration that we truly succeeded in attacking God and separating ourselves from Him.

This, in fact, is the ego's very goal for false forgiveness: to make sin real, so that the separation from God and our brothers can never be healed. Now we can see why it is called "forgiveness-to-destroy." False forgiveness, while it masquerades as a means to heal us, is really the ego's means to *destroy* us. In place of the eternal life that only our true relationship with God and our brothers offers us, false forgiveness offers us permanent separation from eternal life. False forgiveness proclaims sin forever real, and "if sin is real, its offering is death" (W-pI.101.4:4). In the ego's hands, God's healing gift of forgiveness "has become a twisted knife that would destroy the holy Son He loves" (S-2.I.2:6).

True forgiveness recognizes that sin is unreal, and thus *truly* overlooks it; this works, because it reawakens us to the truth that God's Son is sinless.

True forgiveness is the exact opposite of false forgiveness. As I said above, the key feature of false forgiveness is that the perception that another person has wronged us and caused us pain is assumed to be the truth. True forgiveness, on the other hand, declares that this perception is false. Sin is unreal, because our true Self cannot really be harmed. True forgiveness says, in essence:

> You didn't cause me harm; only my false *perception* of what you did caused me apparent harm. Therefore, you are not a sinner. You have not sinned against me, and so I have no "right" to resent you and punish you, because this is not what you deserve. Because I want to be loving, I will *truly* overlook your seeming sin against me. When I choose to see you as you really are—a holy Son of God, who deserves only love—my resentment and desire to punish you will disappear automatically. This will not feel like a sacrifice, because I will benefit from this as much as you. In the name of love, I will release you *and myself* by giving you the love you truly deserve. I will forgive your seeming sin against me, and thus see both your innocence and my own.

True forgiveness really does give us the peace and release from the ravages of sin that we seek, because it undoes the problem at its source: our *perception* that our brother really sinned. False forgiveness has the same outward goal as true forgiveness: the relinquishment of our resentment and our desire to punish a person who has seemingly wronged us. But as we've seen, it doesn't work because it upholds our perception of our brother as a sinner, a perception which is an attack. This attack is the underlying goal of false forgiveness, whatever its outward goal may be. True forgiveness withdraws this attack, and only in this way can our resentment and desire to punish be truly relinquished.

This, then, is the difference between false and true forgiveness: False forgiveness tries to keep our perception of sin intact, but somehow magically remove its consequences; true forgiveness replaces our perception of sin with the recognition that "there is no sin; it has no consequence" (W-pI.101.6:7). False forgiveness attempts to forgive our brother for what he did; true forgiveness forgives him "for what he did not do" (T-17.III.1:5). False forgiveness doesn't work because it simply reinforces the "reality" of sin; true forgiveness works because it reasserts the reality that all of God's Sons are forever sinless: "God's Son is guiltless, and sin does not exist" (M-10.2:9).

We can exchange false forgiveness for true forgiveness by allowing the Holy Spirit to teach us how to forgive.

False forgiveness doesn't work because it doesn't really alter our fundamental perception of the world. To use a biblical analogy, it is basically an attempt to take the new wine of forgiveness and pour it into the old wineskin of our ego-based worldview. As *The Song of Prayer* puts it, we take God's gift of forgiveness and try to "set it in an earthly frame" (S-2.III.7:3). Since the whole point of true forgiveness is to help us *transcend* our earthly frame, this move on our part effectively robs forgiveness of its power to heal.

What, then, can we do if we want to escape the trap of false forgiveness and learn how to truly forgive? The Course is full of instructions on how to forgive and gives us many practices for that purpose, but here I want to focus on a basic principle underlying all of them: Of ourselves, we can do nothing, because of ourselves we cannot really see beyond our ego-based frame of reference. Therefore, in order to learn how to truly forgive, we need a Teacher from outside our frame of reference. We need the Holy Spirit (or Christ, for Whom the Holy Spirit speaks). That is why *The Song of Prayer* gives us this succinct advice for how to transform forgiveness-to-destroy into forgiveness-for-salvation: "Let Him take charge of how you would forgive, and each occasion then will be to you another step to Heaven and to peace" (S-2.III.3:4).

Letting Him take charge of how you would forgive: a practice

Let's take this advice right now and apply it to a real-life situation. Bring to mind a person against whom you have a grievance, a person whom you need to forgive. Visualize the person's appearance—see him or her in your mind's eye—and briefly review the "sins" you believe this person has committed against you.

Now that you have the situation clearly in mind, think of some of the ways in which you have tried to forgive this person in the past, or ways that you are considering now. Do you have a sense of moral superiority when you think of forgiving this person? Do you empathize with the person's faults, and feel like letting him or her off the hook because you've done some pretty bad things yourself? Are you attracted to the idea of silently enduring this person's abuses and showing him or her how "spiritual" you are? Do you find yourself going through a list in your mind of the things this person needs to do in order to "earn" your forgiveness?

Recognize that these are all forms of false forgiveness. Keeping the situation in mind, let go of your own ideas of how to forgive this person by saying the following:

> *I do not know what anything, including this, means. And so I do not know how to respond to it. And I will not use my own past learning as the light to guide me now.*
> (T-14.XI.6:7-9)

Now, with your mind clear and open to receiving a new way of seeing the situation, ask for the Holy Spirit's help in forgiving this person by saying the following:

> *Holy Spirit, please take charge of how I would forgive this person. Guide my mind, and let this situation help me learn what forgiveness means.*
> (based on S-2.III.3:4 and W-pI.81.4:2)

Now, simply be still, and open your mind to receive His guidance. Perhaps you will be given words to mentally say to this person. Perhaps you will receive a visual image, such as an image of loving light extending from you to him or her. Perhaps you will receive guidance on how to outwardly communicate forgiveness to this person the next time you meet. Or your guidance may be something totally unexpected. Whatever you receive, accept it with gratitude. You have taken another step to Heaven and to peace.

Some personal reflections on false versus true forgiveness

Personally, I find the Course's sharp distinction between false and true forgiveness to be truly mind-bending. The shocking but unavoidable implication of this teaching is that the vast majority of what passes for forgiveness in this world is in fact false forgiveness. I've seen a lot of different rationales for forgiveness in various spiritual paths and psychotherapeutic systems, and in my opinion, the bulk of them fall squarely within the parameters of false forgiveness as described above. I say this not to disparage other paths, but simply to point out that the contrast is there, and we would do well to look at it honestly.

As I've looked at this contrast, one of the questions that I've pondered for years is the following: If most of what the world presents as forgiveness is really false forgiveness, has anyone in this world (besides Jesus) truly forgiven? This question is particularly challenging when applied to people like Mother Teresa and Martin Luther King, Jr., two people who developed great reputations for forgiveness, but who also unquestionably (based on their public statements) believed that sin is real, an idea that makes true forgiveness impossible.

The answer that I've personally come up with is this: Yes, there have been (and are) people in this world who have truly forgiven, though most likely not perfectly. (The impression I get from the Course is that very few people have ever forgiven perfectly.) I believe that it is possible to extend true forgiveness even if one's professed doctrine is false forgiveness. True forgiveness is a shift in perception that happens deep in our minds; our surface beliefs can help or hinder this process, but the shift can happen regardless of what we outwardly profess. Therefore, I believe that the great spiritual masters in the history of our world—including Mother Teresa and Martin Luther King, Jr., two of my personal heroes—did indeed extend true forgiveness. Whatever their outer doctrines may have been, the loving fruit they produced in the world bore witness to what was really in their minds: Deep down, they truly recognized the sinlessness of their brothers. By their fruits, we have come to know them as bearers of true, forgiving love.

I think that many of us who are less well known than Mother Teresa and Martin Luther King, Jr. have been bearers of true, forgiving love as well. As clouded as our minds are by the ego, true forgiveness does shine through at times. While I'm certainly no spiritual giant, I'm convinced that I have given true forgiveness, however imperfectly, at various times in my life. I'm equally convinced that I've received it at times, both from those who are Course students and those who are not. And I think that deep down, all of us know when we've experienced true forgiveness. Giving and receiving false forgiveness simply doesn't feel good; there's just something grimy, hollow, and unsatisfying about it. But giving and receiving true forgiveness *does* feel good; it brings a sense of sweet release that is unlike anything else I have experienced. This is the fruit that tells us we have given and received the blessing of true forgiveness.

Conclusion

False forgiveness damns, while true forgiveness blesses. False forgiveness is a bitter curse disguised as a gift, while true forgiveness is the greatest gift we can give and receive in this world. We have seen how cruel forgiveness can become in the hands of the ego, and how beneficent it is in the hands of the Holy Spirit. The obvious question then becomes: In whose hands will we place it? The equally obvious answer, if we want the blessing of true forgiveness, is to place it in the hands of the Teacher God has given us. He alone knows how to use it wisely; He alone can use it to open the door to the redeeming vision of our true Self, revealed in our holy brothers. With this vision, we come to recognize what all of the great teachers of forgiveness in human history have seen, the joyous truth that lies at the heart of every path of awakening: "God's Son is guiltless, and in his innocence is his salvation" (M-1.3:5).

20

How can we forgive murderers? How can we forgive people like rapists and child molesters? How can we accept these people as loving children of God who perpetrate "bad" behaviors without judging the behavior?

Short Answer

We forgive people who perpetrate such acts by recognizing the Christ in them. From this perspective, we realize that no matter how "bad" their behavior seems to be, it is only a mistake, *not* a sin. Through seeing this, we forgive our own "sins" as well as theirs. This is the Holy Spirit's judgment of their behavior, and we are to allow His judgment to replace ours. We forgive by using the practices the Course itself offers us for this purpose. Through forgiving the "unforgivable," we follow Jesus' own example, and learn the lesson that is at the very heart of his teaching.

☡☡☡

We forgive people who perpetrate such acts by recognizing the Christ in them.

Forgiveness is a decision to look past what we *think* people are, and invite the Holy Spirit's vision of what they *really* are into our minds. What they really are is the Christ, the Son of God. The following quote, which describes how the teacher of God heals his patients, captures the essence of seeing the Christ in our brothers:

> He [the teacher of God] overlooks the mind *and* body, seeing only the face of Christ shining in front of him, correcting all mistakes and healing all perception.
>
> (M-22.4:5)

Recognizing the Christ in a brother who has committed grievous acts like rape and murder is no different than recognizing the Christ in anyone, although it certainly seems more difficult. To see the Christ, we must look past our brother's acts, since the acts were done by the body, and the Christ in him is not a body. We must also look past the faulty decisions and beliefs of his mind that led to such acts, because the Christ in him is beyond those faulty decisions and beliefs. The vision we will experience when we look past these things is a vision of our brother's reality: the face of Christ, his true Identity, which sweeps away the mistakes his body and his mind seemed to make.

Certainly, this is a lofty vision of people whom society generally regards as the scum of the earth. Yet this is the vision the Course is calling us to offer all of our brothers without exception—even those who commit what we consider to be horrible crimes. "When a brother acts insanely, he is offering you an opportunity to bless him" (T-7.VII.2:1). We bless him by forgiving him, by seeing him with the vision of Christ. How can we actually do this? More on that below.

From this perspective, we realize that no matter how "bad" their behavior seems to be, it is only a mistake, *not* a sin. Through seeing this, we forgive our own "sins" as well as theirs.

When we see the Christ in our brothers, we see all the horrendous things we thought they did as simple mistakes, rather than sins. What is the difference between a sin and a mistake? In a nutshell, a sin is a real violation of God's laws which inflicts real harm on God and His creation: "To sin would be to violate reality, *and to succeed*" (T-19.II.2:2, emphasis mine). A sin, because it did real harm, would merit punishment. A mistake (or error), on the other hand, is simply our mind's foolish *attempt* to violate God's laws, an attempt that is completely illusory and thus has no real effects. God's laws cannot really be violated. Therefore, since it did no real harm, a mistake calls for simple correction, not punishment.

Applying this to people like murderers, rapists, and child molesters, what this means is that these people did not truly injure their "victims." There is no denying that they did so on the level of form, but in truth, the eternal reality of their "victims'" true Identity is completely untouched. "Injury is impossible" (W-pI.198.1:1), and so all of the heinous crimes that we think we and our brothers have committed are merely mistakes rather than sins. They are illusion, not reality. And this recognition is the basis of forgiveness:

> Forgiveness recognizes what you thought your brother did to you has not occurred. It does not pardon sins and make them real. It sees there was no sin. And in that view are all your sins forgiven. (W-pII.1.1:1-4)

The last line of the above quote clues us in to a very important benefit of forgiveness: *Forgiving others is how our own "sins" are forgiven.* As the Course tells us, "You never hate your brother for his sins, but only for your own" (T-31.III.1:5). Now, this doesn't mean that if you condemn a rapist, you secretly believe that *you* are a rapist (or at least a potential rapist); hating your brother for your own sins has nothing to do with the particular form that your brother's "sin" takes. What it does mean is that your *interpretation* of the rapist's act as sinful is a projection of your belief that *you* are sinful, though your "sin" may well take different forms. The crucial point is that withdrawing our belief that our brothers have sinned is what allows us to recognize that we ourselves have not sinned. Thus forgiveness is not an act of sacrifice on our part in which we let a criminal off the hook at the cost of our sacred "right" to punish him. Instead, it is the way we claim our sacred right to forgiveness ourselves: "[Forgiveness] *keeps* your rights from being sacrificed" (T-30.VI.2:9).

Being willing to see our brothers' seeming sins as mere mistakes is thus the key to seeing the Christ in them, and in ourselves. The world that the belief in sin shows us "stands like a block before Christ's face" (C-4.4:1); but "mistakes are tiny shadows, quickly gone, that for an instant only seem to hide the face of Christ, which still remains unchanged behind them all" (S-2.I.6:5).

For an excellent discussion of the distinction between sin and error, I recommend reading the Text section entitled "Sin versus Error" (T-19.II).

Our job is to let the Holy Spirit's judgment of behavior replace ours.

The vision described above is how the Holy Spirit sees everyone. He sees the Christ in everyone, and sees all "bad" behavior as a mistake, not a sin. Our job, then, is to let go of our own judgment of what other people's behavior means, and allow it to be replaced by the judgment of the Holy Spirit. As Section 10 of the Manual says, when a person gives up his own judgment, it puts him "in a position where judgment *through* him rather than *by* him can occur" (M-10.2:7). When we give up our own way of seeing things, which is rooted in the ego's belief in sin, we become conduits through which the Holy Spirit can extend his forgiving judgment.

I think it's very important to realize that when the Course tells us not to judge, it is not telling us that we cannot have an opinion about something, or that we are not to see genuine mistakes *as* mistakes. It is literally impossible not to have an opinion or viewpoint about a situation; even to say "We shouldn't have an opinion" is an opinion!

Instead of refraining from opinions, not judging simply means letting go of our own viewpoint and, as the above passage says, letting the Holy Spirit's viewpoint be expressed *through* us. And since "in time, the Holy Spirit clearly sees the Son of God can make mistakes" (T-19.III.5:1), it follows that when we are using the Holy Spirit's judgment, we can see mistakes as well, both other people's and our own. Jesus himself frequently discusses our mistakes in the Course, and stresses the importance of "the recognition of a mistake as a mistake" (M-7.5:8). Of course, when we think someone made a mistake, we would do well to question this judgment; it may be coming from the ego. But it is also possible that this judgment is not coming from the ego. Because of this, I don't think that it is necessarily a violation of the Course's injunction against judgment to see the acts of people like Hitler and Charles Manson as mistakes that had tragic, painful consequences in time. People do make mistakes, and we certainly shouldn't pretend otherwise.

In addition, giving up judgment doesn't necessarily mean that we shouldn't do anything behaviorally to deal with people who commit crimes. According to the Course, the same judgment that is to guide our *perception*—the Holy Spirit's judgment—is to guide our *behavior* as well. The question, then, is: What would the Holy Spirit have us do behaviorally to deal with crime? I don't know the answer, and certainly this issue is a controversial one. But I suspect that at the very least, the Holy Spirit would have us do things to physically protect law-abiding citizens from those who commit criminal acts. He may well guide us to sequester people who commit particularly violent or abusive acts, so that they will not be able to harm others or themselves. This is certainly not the change of mind that alone can really solve the problem of criminal behavior, but it may be the best our society as a whole can do at its present level of development.

Whatever we do behaviorally, the crucial thing from the Course's standpoint is that we heal our perception. We must do the mental work so that we can see criminal acts as merely mistakes rather than sins, and see the perpetrators as innocent Sons of God, regardless of their acts. This is the Holy Spirit's judgment.

We forgive by using the practices the Course itself offers us for this purpose.

To say that we should forgive criminals is all well and good, but this brings up the obvious question: Just how do we actually do it? The question of how we actually forgive is one that many Course students ask. Fortunately, we need look no further than the Course itself to find all the instructions we need for how to forgive.

These instructions are sprinkled throughout the Course; indeed, one could say that the entire Course is a course in how to forgive. But in particular, there are six lessons in the Workbook that give us specific practices for forgiving particular people: Lessons 46, 68, 78, 121, 134, and 161. These lessons offer forgiveness exercises that all follow the same basic pattern:

1. You choose a person to forgive.

2. You get in touch with your current perception of him as a sinner.

3. You invite a new perception of him as the Christ, your savior.

(Robert Perry has written an excellent article on this topic, from which I have drawn some of this material. The article contains a composite forgiveness exercise based on these six lessons. It is entitled "How Do We Forgive?" and appears in Issue #24 of the Circle of Atonement's newsletter, *A Better Way*. I highly recommend it.)

How to forgive: a practice

One lesson that is particularly powerful for me is Lesson 161, "Give me your blessing, holy Son of God." Of course, I recommend reading the lesson in its entirety, but just to offer a brief example of forgiveness in action, here is a short version of the Lesson 161 practice. You might want to give it a try.

First, bring to mind the specific person you want to forgive. It could be anyone, of course (though I would recommend picking a person other than yourself). But in keeping with the topic of this Q & A, perhaps you might want to choose a notorious "bad guy" from the past or present, someone whom society vilifies for his atrocious acts, someone who elicits a particularly strong response of anger and hatred in you. Once you have this person vividly in mind, warts and all, invite a new perception of him into your mind, using the words of Lesson 161:

> What you are seeing now [your current picture of this person] conceals from you the sight of one who can forgive you all your sins; whose sacred hands can take away the nails which pierce your own, and lift the crown of thorns which you have placed upon your bleeding head. Ask this of him, that he may set you free:
>
> *Give me your blessing, holy Son of God. I would behold you with the eyes of Christ, and see my perfect sinlessness in you.* (W-pI.161.11:5-8)

How did that exercise go for you? Did you feel a shift in your attitude toward this particular person? I really find this practice powerful. To me, it is the flip side of the idea presented above that we are to respond to our brother's insanity with a blessing. When we bless him, we see him as a Son of God rather than a sinful criminal; then, in return, this Son of God turns around and blesses *us*. Through seeing him with Christ's vision, we behold his sinlessness; then, the Christ in him shows us that we too are sinless. Through forgiving the sins of our

Greg Mackie

brother, we too are forgiven, for as we saw above, it is our sins we see in him.

Through forgiving the "unforgivable," we follow Jesus' own example, and learn the lesson that is at the very heart of his teaching.

We may well wonder if the kind of radical forgiveness advocated by the Course is truly possible. Can we really forgive *everything*, even criminal acts like murder, rape, and child molestation? Jesus' answer is an unequivocal "Yes," but he doesn't just ask us to take his word for it. In the Course, he reminds us that he also offered us his own "extreme example" (T-6.I.2:1) of it: his loving, forgiving response to his own crucifixion.

Jesus discusses this example at length in the Text section entitled "The Message of the Crucifixion" (T-6.I; the Introduction to Chapter 6 is also relevant to this discussion). His response to his crucifixion is the perfect answer to the question that we are discussing in this Q & A: How do we forgive people who commit horrible crimes? His short answer: Recognize that because the "crime" is only an illusion that causes no real injury and has no effect on reality at all, it doesn't really matter:

> I elected, for your sake and mine, to demonstrate that the most outrageous assault, as judged by the ego, does not matter. As the world judges these things, but not as God knows them, I was betrayed, abandoned, beaten, torn, and finally killed. (T-6.I.9:1-2)

I included the second line of this passage because it tells us just how horrific the assault on Jesus was in worldly terms—his example was extreme indeed. Robert Perry wrote a commentary on this line that, to me, perfectly captures the vicious nature of the attack on Jesus and the radical nature of his response:

> When you think about the intensity of the attack (as we would judge it), this [the fact that the attack didn't matter to Jesus] is virtually beyond belief. It wasn't just a physical attack. He was betrayed by a close friend. He was abandoned by his closest followers. He was rejected

by the people he came to save. He was publicly judged to be a criminal, worthy of the most humiliating form of death available. He was subjected to all the hatred of an angry mob. It looked like his mission had failed, his purpose had come to naught. It looked like God had abandoned him. Even by conventional standards, the whole episode was totally unjust, since he had harmed no one and helped many. On top of all that, he was subjected to an excruciating and torturous death that we simply cannot imagine.

This is what, in his eyes, did not matter.

The Course doesn't deny that Jesus was attacked, in worldly terms. It acknowledges that he was viciously assaulted by brothers who were deeply and profoundly mistaken in their perception of him. But he didn't see their mistakes as sins, because he recognized that their attack wasn't real. He allowed the Holy Spirit's judgment to come through him, looking past the acts of his brothers' bodies to the Christ in them, Who is forever unaffected by their mistakes. Later in the section, we are told that the message of the crucifixion is "Teach only love, for that is what you are" (T-6.I.13:2). In the context of this section, that well-known line means: "No matter how horrible and unjustified other people's attacks on you seem to be, respond with love rather than counterattack, because that is the way you ultimately learn that you *are* love."

Responding like this when we are brutally attacked may sound like too tall an order for us, and indeed it probably *is* too tall an order at our present level of development. Fortunately, Jesus tells us that we aren't expected to be able to do this right away in the kind of extreme circumstances that he faced. All we are asked to do is "to follow my example in the face of much less extreme temptations to misperceive" (T-6.I.6:7). We can start small, with the things that are right in front of us. We probably won't be ready to forgive the person who is coming at us with a knife. But perhaps we *can* forgive the next-door neighbor who's blasting his AC/DC tapes at midnight again. Perhaps we *can* forgive the girlfriend who just broke up with us because she fell in love with our best friend. Perhaps we *can* forgive the boss who fired us for no apparent reason. And perhaps we *can* forgive the mass murderer we read about in the paper, who's now on death row at the State Pen.

And who knows? Perhaps we may surprise ourselves. We might find that with time and practice, we are able to forgive far more than we ever imagined. It is said that Gandhi had a prayer on his lips for his attacker when he was shot. I have seen well-documented accounts of ordinary people who in time have been able to forgive the murderers of their children. I have read of Jews who were able to forgive Hitler for the Holocaust. Such extraordinary forgiveness is relatively uncommon, but it happens frequently enough to give us real hope that we truly can follow Jesus' example.

Personally, I think that forgiving seemingly "unforgivable" acts is at the heart of Jesus' teaching, both in his earthly life and in the Course. In the Gospels, he spoke of loving our enemies and blessing those that persecute us; in the Course, he tells us that we *have* no enemies and we cannot really *be* persecuted in truth. Central to his teaching is the radical idea that when someone attacks you, not only do you not attack him back, you respond by giving him a gift—a gift of love, which demonstrates that *attack is nothing and love is everything*. Forgiving our seeming "attackers" is, in Jesus' view, the central way in which this saving message is taught and learned.

Such profound forgiveness may sound difficult, but learning how to forgive the seemingly "unforgivable" is exactly what the Course's program is for. It will take time and practice. It will likely take most of us a long time to reach the level of forgiveness exemplified by Jesus' response to the crucifixion. But all we have to do is start moving in the right direction. Let's simply roll up our sleeves and get to work on the program, trusting that if we will do the work, we will make progress. If we do our part, then slowly but surely the day will come when we "will see the love beyond the hate, the constancy in change, the pure in sin, and only Heaven's blessing on the world" (W-pI.151.11:3).

Topical Issues

21

How does the Course regard the birth of a child into this world? Since birth into this world represents birth into a world of illusion and separation, the implication seems to be that we shouldn't have children. Is this what the Course is suggesting?

Short Answer

I don't think so. The Course never explicitly says that we shouldn't have children. Not having children would make sense if birth into this world represented a fall from perfect unity with God into the belief in illusion and separation. But the Course strongly implies that we believe in illusion and separation *before* we are born into this world, and so this birth is simply a transition from one form of illusion and separation to another. Therefore, being born into this world is basically neutral; but while we are here, we can choose to make the most of our experience by seeing the world as a teaching device for restoring our awareness of perfect unity with God.

☽☽☽

The Course never explicitly says that we shouldn't have children.

If the Course really considered having children to be a bad idea, one would think that it would tell us this directly. But it never does. In fact, it contains very few references of any kind to people having children (though it does contain a number of references to children themselves, often using childhood as a metaphor for our current level of spiritual maturity). On the rare occasion that the Course does refer to people having children (for instance, T-7.I.1:7-8), it says nothing about whether having children is a good or a bad thing. In my mind, this fact alone is strong evidence that the Course is not against having children.

Not having children would make sense if birth into this world represented a fall from perfect unity with God into the belief in illusion and separation.

In some philosophies and spiritual systems, it is believed that before a child is born, he or she exists in a blissful state of primordial unity with the Source. According to this view, the unborn entity basks in an oceanic, totally egoless Oneness, absolutely free from the illusion of separation. In this scenario, when this entity is born into the world, he or she "falls" from this state of primordial unity into the illusion of separation. The state of egoless Oneness is replaced by the experience of a separate, ego-bound existence. There are even some philosophies that suggest that the birth of a child into the world should be mourned rather than celebrated, because birth represents a fall from blissful unity into painful separation.

If this scenario or something like it is really true, then one could certainly see in it a good rationale for not bringing children into the world. If it is true that we exist in a state of perfect unity with God before birth, and only experience the belief in illusion and separation (the ego) after we are born into this world, then it would make sense not to have children. Why deprive the children of God of their blissful unity and subject them to the pain of separation by dragging them into this world? However, I think the Course sees the situation quite differently, which leads me to my next point.

But the Course strongly implies that we believe in illusion and separation *before* we are born into this world, and so this birth is simply a transition from one form of illusion and separation to another.

There are several passages in the Course that carry this implication. Here are two of them:

No one who comes here but must still have hope, some lingering illusion, or some dream that there is something outside of himself that will bring happiness and peace to him.   (T-29.VII.2:1)

The world believes in idols. No one comes unless he worshipped them, and still attempts to seek for one that yet might offer him a gift reality does not contain.
                                                (T-29.VIII.8:4-5)

According to the Course, seeking outside ourselves for happiness and seeking after "idols" (which amounts to the same thing) are expressions of the belief in illusion and separation. These things are ego goals. Therefore, both of these passages strongly imply that we already believed in illusion and separation—in other words, we already had an ego—*before* we were born into this world. Our purpose for coming here was to continue a search for illusions and idols that began some time before our birth. If this is so, then birth into this world isn't a fall from primordial unity into a belief in illusion and separation; rather, it is a transition from one form of illusion and separation (the state we were in before our birth) to another (our present life in this world).

If our pre-birth state was, like our present life, characterized by the egoic belief in illusion and separation, what did this pre-birth state look like? The Course doesn't really say anything about this, and I don't think it's really all that important to know. Personally, I suspect that we must have had a "body" of some sort, since the belief in separation is a thought that seems to require some kind of separate form in which to live, and the Course tells us that "all thinking produces form at some level" (T-2.VI.9:14). One possibility, if one believes in reincarnation, is that the pre-birth state was a series of previous earthly bodies. Another possibility is that we had some sort of ethereal body that existed in another illusory realm. Who knows? Various religions and spiritual systems have offered many different theories about the nature of the pre-birth state, and I really have no idea which of them, if any, is true. The point I want to make here is simply that in the Course's view, there is at least a strong implication that we believed in illusion and separation before we were born into our current earthly life. We had an ego before we came here.

As an aside, I want to mention that I think the same situation exists on the other side of the human life cycle: death. I think that just as we had an ego and some sort of "body" before birth, so we continue to have an ego and some sort of "body" after death—unless, of course, we fully awaken to God in this lifetime. For more on this topic see Q & A #5, entitled "What happens to the ego after the death of the body? Does the ego have less 'reality' after bodily death?"

Therefore, being born into this world is basically neutral; but while we are here, we can choose to make the most of our experience by seeing the world as a teaching device for restoring our awareness of perfect unity with God.

I don't think that the Course sees having children as bad *or* good, because birth into this world, in and of itself, doesn't really have an effect on our belief in illusion and separation one way or the other. What does have an effect on that belief, however, is how we choose to see the world while we're here. We can choose to see this world as a means of reinforcing our belief in illusion and separation, or we can choose to see it as the Holy Spirit does, "as a teaching device for bringing [us] home" (T-5.III.11:1). We can choose to continue the futile search for illusions and idols that brought us to this world, or we can choose to search for something much more satisfying. Though we came to search for hell, our real heart's desire is for Heaven. And if we choose to spend our time on earth in search of *this*, we cannot fail:

> Be glad that search you must. Be glad as well to learn you
> search for Heaven, and must find the goal you really want.
> No one can fail to want this goal and reach it in the end.
> (W-pI.131.4:1-3)

In the end, we will not only find Heaven, but we will also realize that we never really left Heaven. We never really fell from our perfect unity with God. It is this awareness of eternal, blissful Oneness with our Source that following the path of the Course will ultimately restore to us.

22

T-13.VII.2:1 says, "The world you see must be denied, for sight of it is costing you a different kind of vision." Does this mean that we should totally deny that there is pain and suffering in this world? How can we deny that people are in pain and need help?

Short Answer

There are two very different kinds of denial—which I will call *false denial* and *true denial*—and here as elsewhere, the Course is advocating true denial. One form of false denial is denying that we have made mistaken, ego-based choices which have led to pain within the illusion, and thus call for help. True denial is denying the ultimate reality of those mistaken choices and the pain that comes from them, affirming that our true Self is totally unharmed by those choices. The goal of the Course's program is to get us out of falsely denying the painful effects of the ego *so that* we can practice true denial, the Course's means of healing pain and suffering in ourselves and others. This process enables us all to stop denying the truth about ourselves, restoring our awareness that we are the beloved creations of a loving Father, forever free of pain and suffering.

ʊʊʊ

One form of false denial is denying that we have made mistaken, ego-based choices which have led to pain within the illusion, and thus call for help.

What is false denial? To deny something is to declare that thing untrue; false denial, then, is to declare something untrue that really *is* true, at least on some level. False denial is refusing to look at the truth because we think the truth threatens us in some way. It is the lie we tell ourselves to avoid the truth that we think will destroy us.

The primary form of false denial that the Course talks about is the ego's denial of our true Identity and everything that goes with It. Because the ego is "made out of the denial of the Father" (T-4.III.4:3), it must blot out of our awareness everything that reminds us of our Father, because if we remember the truth about ourselves, the ego will be "destroyed." It must deny the truth, and get us to deny the truth, in order to survive.

The ego blots out the truth about us by convincing us that we are limited, separate beings, vulnerable to pain and suffering inflicted upon us by an external world. And one form of false denial the ego uses to keep us from recognizing what it is doing is the form that is the main focus of this Q & A: The ego gets us to deny (or at least minimize) the painful effects that choosing to listen to it has brought us. These effects are not ultimately true, of course, but they are "real enough in time" (T-3.VII.3:2), and the ego encourages us to deny this fact so that we won't see just how undesirable the ego is.

This refusal to look at the problems brought on by the ego is the kind of denial that is usually meant when people say, "You're in denial." It is sticking our head in the sand, pretending that we don't have a problem and don't need any help, despite all evidence to the contrary. Like an alcoholic who denies he has a drinking problem even as he loses his job, his wife and friends abandon him, and he lies face down in the gutter, this form of false denial is a misguided attempt to shield our awareness from the devastating effects of the ego even as it makes a train wreck of our lives. It is a defense mechanism which is used not to heal the problem, but to conceal it.

Just as we can use false denial to sweep our own problems under the rug, so we can use it to deny the pain and suffering in the outer world. We can turn away from the suffering people all around us and lose ourselves in trivial pursuits. We can find all sorts of rationalizations to convince ourselves that things aren't really as bad as they seem. We can even, as Course students, blithely dismiss the world's pain by saying, "It's all an illusion, so it doesn't matter anyway."

But this kind of denial—either of our own ego-based suffering or that of others—is definitely not what the Course is advocating. The Course tells us that while delaying our awakening by listening to the ego will not cause us any *real* harm, such delay "is tragic in time" (T-5.VI.1:3). It tells us that whenever our brothers are not expressing love they are calling for help, and urges us to respond to their call by *giving* help. It even implores us to take an unflinchingly honest look at the world around us and ask ourselves if we are moved to do our part to heal the pain and despair surrounding us:

> Look about the world, and see the suffering there. Is not your heart willing to bring your weary brothers rest?
> (W-pI.191.10:7-8)

Thus when the Course tells us to deny the world, it is not asking us to callously pretend that the suffering brought on by mistaken ego-based choices isn't happening *within the illusion*. That is false denial, which does nothing but hide the suffering, thereby ensuring that it will continue. The Course is talking about a very different kind of denial, which I will discuss below.

True denial is denying the ultimate reality of those mistaken choices and the pain that comes from them, affirming that our true Self is totally unharmed by those choices.

If false denial is to declare something untrue that really *is* true (at least on some level), then true denial is to declare something untrue that really is *untrue*. False denial refuses to look at the truth, denying that it is true; true denial looks straight at untruth, affirming that it is untrue. This is the kind of denial that the Course is advocating. One of the best discussions of true vs. false denial in the Course occurs in the first two paragraphs of T-2.II, which I recommend reading. The following lines from the second paragraph are a good description of true denial:

> True denial is a powerful protective device. You can
> and should deny any belief that error can hurt you. This
> kind of denial is not a concealment but a correction.
>
> (T-2.II.2:1-3)

Notice the implied distinction between false and true denial here. What I am calling "false denial" is *concealment*, one form of which is the denial of the ego's painful effects that I discussed above. True denial, on the other hand, is a *correction* of the mistaken belief that our true Self can really be altered by our mistaken choices; it "denies the ability of anything not of God to affect you" (T-2.II.1:11). As we saw above, this doesn't mean denying the fact that error can be very painful within the illusion; instead, it means denying that what happens within the illusion has any effect on our reality. No matter what the appearance, our true Self is as pure, holy, complete, and perfect as the moment God created It.

Therefore, when T-13.VII.2:1 tells us that we must deny the world we see, it doesn't mean that we should literally not use our physical eyes (which would certainly make driving a car difficult), nor does it mean that we should pretend that the things our physical eyes behold aren't happening within the physical world. Rather, it means that we should deny the reality of those things. Believing in the reality of the things our physical eyes show us blocks the experience of true vision: the vision of Christ, a kind of seeing that "does not depend on the body's eyes at all" (W-pI.30.5:1). This is the vision that reveals to us the real world beyond the world of form. T-13.VII.2:1 is saying, in essence, "Don't depend on the body's eyes to tell you what is real. They see only form, and so they can't see reality. If you want to see what is real, turn to true vision, for only true vision can show you reality."

Indeed, the Course tells us that even after we attain true vision, our physical eyes will continue to see the same things everyone else sees, as long as we remain in a physical body. The difference lies in how we interpret those things:

> The body's eyes will continue to see differences....But
> the healed mind will put them all in one category; they
> are unreal. (M-8.6:1,4)

Even when our minds are healed, then, we will not deny that the choice to listen to the ego has produced a world of different forms which can be perceived by physical senses, a world which brings pain and suffering as long as we believe those differences are real. Jesus himself does not deny this, since he speaks of it so often in the Course. What we will deny, however, is the reality of this world of differences. We will see it, but we will also see beyond it to the truth beyond appearances, to our true Identity which remains forever untouched by those appearances. We will look straight at what is untrue, and affirm that it is untrue. This is true denial.

The goal of the Course's program is to get us out of falsely denying the painful effects of the ego *so that* we can practice true denial, the Course's means of healing pain and suffering in ourselves and others.

Turning away from our false denial of the ego's darkness and practicing true denial is the very essence of the Course's healing program, a program of "bring[ing] the darkness to the light" (T-18.IX.1:1) and allowing that light to "shine it away" (T-8.IV.2:10). In short, the Course's process of healing consists of two basic steps:

1. Getting out of false denial by bringing our illusions into the light of truth.

2. Undoing those illusions with true denial, allowing the light of truth to dispel them.

In other words, we must first look squarely at our illusions, and then deny the reality of those illusions with the help of the Holy Spirit or Jesus. Both steps are necessary. We must first look squarely at our illusions because we can't truly deny the reality of something that we're not even aware of: "No one can escape from illusions unless he looks at them, for not looking is the way they are protected" (T-11.V.1:1). The ego uses false denial to protect itself and its illusions from the light of truth, and so we must actively decide to bring our illusions out of hiding if we want to be healed.

But once we do so, we must then move to the second step, because it is only by denying our illusions' reality that we *are* healed. Once the illusions caused by our mistaken choices are brought out of hiding, we must refuse to hold onto our mistakes, and allow them to be undone by the Holy Spirit:

Having accepted the errors as yours, do not keep them. Give them over quickly to the Holy Spirit to be undone completely, so that all their effects will vanish from your mind and from the Sonship as a whole.   (T-7.VIII.5:5-6)

Both steps, then, are equally important, for the first one sets up the second. Bringing our illusions into the light of truth allows that light to dispel them. The following passage is perhaps the Course's clearest statement of the necessity of looking directly at our illusions (referred to here as *conflict*), and allowing them to be undone by the truth:

Conflict must be resolved. It cannot be evaded, set aside, denied, disguised, seen somewhere else, called by another name, or hidden by deceit of any kind, if it would be escaped. It must be seen exactly as it is, where it is thought to be, in the reality which has been given it, and with the purpose that the mind accorded it. For only then are its defenses lifted, and the truth can shine upon it as it disappears.   (W-pII.333.1:1-4)

Getting out of false denial and practicing true denial is therefore the way to our own healing. But it is also more than that: It is the way we heal others. We have already seen above (especially in W-pI.191.10:7-8) that the Course wants us to look with unflinching honesty at the suffering in the world around us and be willing to help our brothers in need. And once we get out of false denial concerning the suffering of the world, the Course would have us heal that suffering by practicing true denial: denying the ultimate reality of that suffering, and affirming that the true Self of everyone is totally untouched by that suffering.

This is the idea behind the Course's statement that "the task of the miracle worker [is] *to deny the denial of truth*" (T-12.II.1:5). In the context of the paragraph from which this line is taken, this statement means that a miracle worker—a person who extends miracles of healing to others—has the function of denying *the miracle receiver's* denial of the truth (though of course the miracle worker must do this for herself before she can do it for someone else). This is how the miracle worker heals sick and suffering people. The person in need of healing is suffering because he has denied the fact that his true Self is whole and complete, forever beyond suffering of any kind. (Notice that this denial is the primary form of false denial mentioned above: the ego's denial of our true Identity.) The miracle worker undoes this denial by looking beyond this person's suffering to his true nature, and in so doing denying his denial of the truth about himself. This is true denial, the vision that shines the light of truth into his mind, healing him of his suffering.

What does this look like on a form level? Does this mean that the miracle worker goes around telling suffering people, "Your suffering is only an illusion"? I don't think so. While there may be some instances where this is appropriate, I think such instances are probably extremely rare. Saying this to someone in pain would hardly be regarded by most people as loving, and the miracle worker is above all an extender of love. The miracle worker's job is to deny *in her mind* the reality of the other's suffering; the form through which this mental content is expressed should be left in the hands of the Holy Spirit or Jesus. They will guide the miracle worker to express the healed content of her mind in whatever way is most helpful to the miracle receiver.

Given most people's firm belief in the reality of their pain and suffering, I think that most of the time, the Holy Spirit will counsel miracle workers to help in a way that addresses and acknowledges that pain and suffering in a loving way. Denying the reality of what happens in the physical world doesn't mean that the miracle worker should do nothing physically to help suffering people. Such people usually need some sort of help on a form level, and giving that help when guided is simply the most loving thing to do. But whatever help the miracle worker gives on a form level, the key is that the inner content of her mind is healed perception, which acknowledges that painful mistakes have been made within the illusion, but also recognizes that it *is* an illusion. It is this recognition that truly heals.

This process enables us all to stop denying the truth about ourselves, restoring our awareness that we are the beloved creations of a loving Father, forever free of pain and suffering.

This is the ultimate payoff of turning away from our false denial of the ego's darkness and practicing true denial. For the denial at the root of all our suffering—the falsest denial of them all, the one that began and still maintains the separation—is the denial of the glorious truth that we are "God's Son, complete and healed and whole, shining in the reflection of His Love" (W-pII.14.1:1). The false denial of our true Identity led to the ego; the false denial of the pain the ego has caused keeps the ego in place. But by fearlessly bringing the ego and its illusions out of the fog of false denial and allowing the sunlight of true denial to shine them away, all of us will remember the truth that we denied, and be free of suffering forever.

This may seem difficult, but the good news is that it is inevitable. No matter how long we persist in hanging on to denial, the truth cannot be staved off forever. In the end, "The awareness of truth cannot be denied" (T-12.I.10:3).

23

What is the Course's stance toward money and material wealth? Since the Course asserts that we are all equal and encourages sharing, would it advocate equal distribution of wealth?

Short Answer

From the Course's standpoint, money is *nothing*—it is simply illusory form, with no meaning in itself. Any meaning or purpose money seems to have has been assigned to it by us. Therefore, the key question we should ask concerning money and material wealth is: "What is it *for*?" Used for the ego's purpose, it is an idol that reinforces separation; used for the Holy Spirit's purpose, it is a simple tool which can help us fulfill the function He has given us in His plan for salvation. When we accept the function the Holy Spirit has given us, He will give us everything we need, including money and material things, to fulfill that function. And as more and more people accept the function the Holy Spirit has given them, we will increasingly live in a world in which each brother gives freely of what he has to anyone who needs it.

☾☾☾

Money is *nothing*, with no meaning in itself. Any meaning or purpose money seems to have has been assigned to it by us.

I think the most succinct statement about money in the Course material is from the *Psychotherapy* supplement: "Money is not evil. It is nothing" (P-3.III.1:5-6). I would add that since money is nothing, it is not good either. It is simply empty form, "green paper strips and piles of metal discs" (W-pI.76.3:2), with no real meaning whatsoever. Our problem is that we attach meaning to money. Rather than seeing money as nothing, we see it as something vitally important, something which we must have to sustain us in this world. In truth, only God can sustain us, both in Heaven and on earth. But

> in this world, you believe you are sustained by everything but God. Your faith is placed in the most trivial and insane symbols...an endless list of forms of nothingness that you endow with magical powers. (W-pI.50.1:2-3)

One of those symbols, of course, is money. Money is one of the world's prime examples of what the Course calls *idols*: external things that we believe can give us the happiness and security that only God can truly provide—things that we use as substitutes for God. As substitutes for God, they are false gods whom we worship and "endow with magical powers," like the stone idols of ancient times.

I think it is clear that money is one of the most universally worshipped idols on earth. Virtually all of us see money as something very meaningful, something which has a powerful impact on our lives. All one has to do is throw a twenty dollar bill into a crowd to see what importance people attach to money. For some, this idol worship takes the form of *loving* money. They see acquiring money as the royal road to happiness. They glorify the rich, and promote political systems like free-market capitalism that support and encourage the accumulation of wealth. This even takes a "spiritualized" form in churches that emphasize material prosperity through positive thinking, a spiritual philosophy that proclaims our "divine right to be rich."

On the other end of the spectrum are those whose idol worship takes the form of *despising* money. They see money as "the root of all evil." They condemn the rich, and promote political systems like communism that aim to distribute wealth equally. This too has its "spiritualized" form in movements like liberation theology, and in ascetic religious orders that emphasize the virtue of poverty. (Of course, the *form* of either acquiring money or renouncing money is neutral in itself, and can be used just as easily by the Holy Spirit—it is the ego *content* of seeing money as an idol that I'm focusing on in this paragraph and the preceding one.)

Most of us undoubtedly fall somewhere in between these two extreme positions. But the irony, from the Course's point of view, is that these seemingly opposite poles—loving money and despising money—are actually different forms of the exact same thing. Both views assume that money is important in itself, that it is real and truly meaningful, rather than the nothingness it really is. Both views, then, are forms of idolatry, because both views grant meaning and power to money that in truth belongs to God alone.

Therefore, the key question to ask about money and material wealth is: "What is it *for*?" Used for the ego's purpose, it is an idol that reinforces separation; used for the Holy Spirit's purpose, it is a simple tool which can help us fulfill the function He has given us in His plan for salvation.

Since money is nothing in itself and *we* assign meaning and purpose to it, the most important question to ask ourselves about money and material wealth is the same question that the Course would have us ask about everything: "What is it *for*?" (T-24.VII.6:1). What purpose are we seeing in it? Of course, there are really only two choices in this matter, regardless of how many choices there seem to be: the ego's purpose, or the Holy Spirit's purpose.

The ego uses money, as it uses everything, to reinforce our belief in separation. More specifically, the ego uses money to reinforce body-identification, to "prove [the body] is autonomous and real" (T-27.VIII.2:1)—which is, of course, the ultimate proof of separation. Money is simply one of the myriad lures the ego dangles in front of us in an attempt to tie us to the body and blot out awareness of our true Self:

> Power, fame, money, physical pleasure; who is the "hero" to whom all these things belong? Could they mean anything except to a body?...By seeking after such things the mind associates itself with the body, obscuring its Identity and losing sight of what it really is.
>
> (M-13.2:6-7,9)

I think it's pretty obvious that the ego's ploy to tie us to the body through money and other worldly goodies has been extremely successful. We've taken the bait and swallowed it hook, line, and sinker. We really do think that we are bodies, and that money and the things it buys are absolutely necessary for our survival. This belief seems to be the epitome of common sense, but it is instructive that the Course considers this belief extremely bizarre. At one point, Jesus remarks in an incredulous tone, "You really think you would starve unless you have stacks of green paper strips and piles of metal discs" (W-pI.76.3:2). The fact that the Course dismisses this belief as preposterous is a good indicator of just how divorced from reality our current view of things is. Our belief in separation is very strong, which is exactly what the ego strives to accomplish through money and material things.

The Holy Spirit uses money, as He uses everything, to serve His plan for salvation. In a section of the *Psychotherapy* supplement which deals specifically with the issue of whether psychotherapists should accept money for their services, we are told that "it is...part of His plan that everything in this world be used by the Holy Spirit to help in carrying out the plan" (P-3.III.1:2)—including money. While the ego sees money as a powerful means of hooking us into separation, the Holy Spirit sees it as a simple, neutral tool which can be used to help free us from the belief in separation. We will explore how the Holy Spirit uses money to serve His plan below.

When we accept the function the Holy Spirit has given us, He will give us everything we need, including money and material things, to fulfill that function.

Even though money is nothing and, strictly speaking, we don't really need it to survive, the Course material does acknowledge that as long as we live in this world, we do have earthly needs. In a line which speaks of psychotherapists but certainly applies to us all, the *Psychotherapy* supplement says, "Even an advanced therapist has some earthly needs while he is here" (P-3.III.1:3). These needs are ultimately illusory, but as long as we *believe* in the illusion, these needs must be met.

How, then, do we meet our earthly needs? In a nutshell, the Course tells us that the Holy Spirit will give us whatever we need, including money and material things, to fulfill our function in His plan for salvation. The Text puts it this way:

> Once you accept His plan as the one function that you would fulfill, there will be nothing else the Holy Spirit

will not arrange for you without your effort....Nothing you need will be denied you....You need take thought for nothing, careless of everything except the only purpose that you would fulfill. (T-20.IV.8:4,6,8)

We can boil down the teaching in this passage to the following two points:

1. *If* you focus only on fulfilling your function in the Holy Spirit's plan for salvation, rather than on meeting your needs,

2. *then* the Holy Spirit will give you everything you need to fulfill your function.

The key, then, is to focus our minds on discovering and fulfilling the Holy Spirit's function for us: the function of forgiveness or healing, in whatever form He has specifically designed for us. Discovering and accepting His function for us is a long-term goal that will not be accomplished overnight, but to the degree we can do this, our earthly needs will be met. We tend to think that we must first meet our earthly needs before we can even think about serving a larger function, but in truth, accepting our function comes first. If we don't accept our function, the Holy Spirit can't give us what we need—not because He is withholding anything from us, but because we are refusing to ask Him for what we need. We've thrown in our lot with the ego, and are thus at the mercy of its laws of lack and deprivation.

Indeed, even the idea that the Holy Spirit will meet our earthly needs can be co-opted by the ego. Once we get ahold of this idea, it is easy to begin seeing Him as a kind of divine butler at our beck and call, who will bring us all the goodies our ego craves. But the Holy Spirit only gives us things to serve His agenda, not ours. In the Text (T-13.VII.10-13), Jesus says that if we strive for what the ego tells us we need, we will be hurt, because we will be reinforcing our belief in separation (as we saw above). Instead, we should ask the Holy Spirit for what we *really* need. If we do so, He will give us what we really need, *and nothing else*. He understands that our earthly needs are only temporary illusions, and so He will give us things in a way that does not reinforce our belief of separation. He will even make sure that we don't misuse the things He gives us. In a nutshell, He will give us only those things which help us make progress to salvation, and keep us away from things that hinder it.

The punch line in this Text passage is my favorite statement in the Course concerning our earthly needs and the attitude we should have toward them: "Leave, then, your needs to Him. He will supply them with no emphasis at all upon them" (T-13.VII.13:1-2). This tells us two very important things: First, it reassures us that the Holy Spirit will indeed supply our earthly needs. Second, it tells us that the Holy Spirit doesn't *emphasize* those needs, an attitude I think Jesus wants us to adopt as well. We should rest assured that the Holy Spirit will meet our needs as long as we do our part in His plan, and with that assurance, not spend a lot of time dwelling on them.

I don't think this means we should never think about our earthly needs or ask the Holy Spirit for specific things. I think that's a pretty unrealistic standard for most of us. In *The Song of Prayer*, we are told that a certain amount of "asking-out-of-need" (S-1.II.2:1) is inevitable at the beginning stages of our journey. We are also told that, while God's Love is our only real need, we certainly believe that we need earthly things, and we "cannot be asked to accept answers which are beyond the level of need that [we] can recognize" (S-1.I.2:5). Therefore, we shouldn't consider ourselves bad Course students if we occasionally ask the Holy Spirit for earthly things.

Yet this should never be our emphasis, for as we saw above, this kind of asking can very easily become an invitation to the ego. Instead, our emphasis should be on finding and fulfilling our function, and giving the Holy Spirit free rein to supply our earthly needs as *He* sees fit. To whatever degree we are able, we should turn our minds away from our earthly needs and toward the Love of God which alone can truly satisfy us. As much as possible, we should bring to our asking the attitude exemplified by this prayer from the Workbook:

> *We come with wholly open minds. We do not ask for anything that we may think we want. Give us what You would have received by us. You know all our desires and our wants. And You will give us everything we need in helping us to find the way to You.* (W-pII.242.2:2-6)

The Course material applies these ideas to a specific earthly situation in a section of the *Psychotherapy* supplement that I've quoted from already: "The Question of Payment" (P-3.III). This section presents some profound and radical teaching about the place of money in healing professions, and I recommend reading it in its entirety. For the sake of brevity, here is my summary of the section's basic teaching:

1. Healing is a free gift from God, so no therapist should attempt to give healing to a patient for the purpose of receiving money. To do so is not to heal the patient, but to demand a sacrifice of him.

2. However, if a therapist extends genuine healing to her patients, she will be given money in one way or another (including often receiving money from her patients) in order to get her earthly needs met so she can continue to fulfill her function as a healer.

Notice that these two points are essentially a specific application of the two points I mentioned above: 1) *If* you focus only on fulfilling your function rather than on your own needs, 2) *then* you will be given everything you need to fulfill your function.

The practical import of this teaching for psychotherapists is summed up in one succinct line, the only firm behavioral rule given in all of the Course material: "No one should be turned away because he cannot pay" (P-3.III.6:1). This rule makes perfect sense in light of the section's teaching: If you're turning away people who cannot pay, then you must be healing for the purpose of money, and anyone who does this "loses the name of healer" (P-3.III.2:9). Yet this rule is flexible enough to allow the therapist a variety of options for how she handles the question of money. She might accept only free-will offerings, she might offer a sliding scale starting at zero, or she might even charge a flat fee, with the understanding that those who can't pay it don't have to. As long as she doesn't turn away anyone, she can be a true healer to all whom the Holy Spirit has sent to her, even if she accepts money.

As more and more people accept the function the Holy Spirit has given them, we will increasingly live in a world in which each brother gives freely of what he has to anyone who needs it.

What would our world be like if a sizable number of people—both within healing professions and in society at large—really took the Course's radical teachings about money to heart? What would it be like if more people truly lived by the dictum "No one should be turned away because he cannot pay"? To say the least, we would live in a radically transformed world, a world in which the old Communist party slogan "From each according to his ability; to each according to his needs" would become more and more a living reality.

Yet the key to this transformation, as always with the Course, is in changing our entire *perception* of needs, not in what we do outwardly to meet people's material needs. In spite of the idealistic vision of that old Communist party slogan, large-scale communist systems like the former Soviet Union failed, because their ideology was rooted in the ego thought system. Orthodox Marxism rejected God entirely, and insisted that material needs were the only needs that really mattered (a perfect expression of the ego's teaching that we are bodies). Needless to say, communist regimes didn't ask the Holy Spirit for guidance, but tried instead to determine for themselves both what people's abilities were and what people needed.

The result was really no different in content than the capitalist systems these communist regimes aimed to replace: Anything rooted in the idea that only material needs are important will be a system of greed and exploitation, regardless of its form. Only a true change of mind—not a mere rearranging of form through revolution or governmental legislation—will give birth to a world in which people are truly helpful to one another, a world in which people meet each other's material needs simply as an outward expression of meeting their real need: the need for love, forgiveness, and healing.

All of this leads to the whole question of equal distribution of wealth. Personally, I doubt this will happen anytime soon if at all, but if we truly took to heart the Course's teachings about money, it wouldn't really matter. Certainly the Course says that we are equal, but this is a matter of *content*, not form. We are equal Sons of God, equally deserving of His and each other's everlasting Love, but on a form level, we *are* different. As I said above, the Holy Spirit will give each of us what we need to fulfill our function in His plan for salvation— no more, no less. And since each of us has a different special function in that plan, it stands to reason that each of us will have different material requirements to fulfill our special function.

Therefore, I'm convinced that there are some people whose role in the Holy Spirit's plan requires them to be rich, and others whose role

Greg Mackie

requires them to renounce riches. Some will give to the world as Princess Diana did; some will give to the world as Mother Teresa did. I don't think any of us is in a position to judge someone's acceptance of the Holy Spirit's function on the basis of her bank account.

Conclusion

The vision of money and material wealth I have presented here is an extraordinarily lofty vision to be sure. It is not something that is likely to be fully attained right away, either individually or collectively. On an individual level, it will take most of us some time to really accept the Holy Spirit's function for us as our *only* function, and until then we will undoubtedly use money to pursue ego goals much of the time. I'm sure it will be even longer before we will see real changes on a global scale concerning money and distribution of material goods. Yet even as we acknowledge this, we can aspire to the lofty goal the Course has given us, set our sights firmly on that goal, and resolutely move in that direction. As we do so, we bring the Course's vision of truly selfless giving and receiving that much closer to fruition:

> The right to live is something no one need fight for. It is promised him, and guaranteed by God. Therefore it is a right the therapist and patient [and all brothers] share alike. If their relationship is to be holy, whatever one needs is given by the other; whatever one lacks the other supplies. Herein is the relationship made holy, for herein both are healed. (P-3.III.4:1-5)

24

What is the Course's stance on physical violence? Does the Course advocate total nonviolence?

Short Answer

The Course does not advocate total nonviolence as a behavioral injunction. The Course advocates nonviolent *thought,* from which nonviolent behavior would naturally follow. While the Course clearly implies that a person with a totally healed mind would be extraordinarily nonviolent in behavior, it does not follow that the Course advocates total nonviolence as a behavioral injunction for those with unhealed minds. Our behavior should be guided by the Holy Spirit (or Jesus), Who will guide us to do the most loving thing we are realistically capable of doing, given our level of development. Because He adjusts His guidance to our level of development, what we are guided to do may well fall short of total nonviolence.

The Course advocates nonviolent *thought,* from which nonviolent behavior would naturally follow.

The Course states unequivocally that its program is aimed at changing our minds:

> You must change your mind, not your behavior....You do not need guidance except at the mind level. Correction belongs only at the level where change is possible. Change does not mean anything at the symptom level [behavior], where it cannot work. (T-2.VI.3:4-7)

Applying this to the question of nonviolence, it is clear that the Course's aim is nonviolent *thought.* Workbook Lesson 23 says that "I can escape from the world I see by giving up attack *thoughts*" (W-pI.23.Heading, my emphasis), and goes on to say that "nothing else will work" (W-pI.23.1:2). The mind is cause; behavior is effect. "You cannot behave appropriately unless you perceive correctly" (T-1.III.6:5). Turning this around, if you *do* perceive correctly, you *will* behave appropriately. Nonviolent behavior will naturally flow from nonviolent thought.

The Course clearly implies that a person with a totally healed mind will be extraordinarily nonviolent in behavior.

In keeping with the idea that nonviolent behavior will naturally flow from nonviolent thought, the advanced teacher of God, as described in Section 4 of the Manual, is an extraordinarily nonviolent person. Such a teacher is the epitome of harmlessness in thought, word, and deed:

> Harm is impossible for God's teachers. They can neither harm nor be harmed....No teacher of God but must learn,—and fairly early in his training,—that harmfulness completely obliterates his function from his awareness.
> (M-4.IV.1:1-2,8)

Jesus, of course, was himself the epitome of harmlessness. He tells us that in his earthly life he "had not harmed anyone and had healed many" (T-6.I.9:3). In that earthly life, he instructed his disciples to love their enemies, turn the other cheek, and face evil without resistance. He himself submitted without resistance to the crucifixion in order to demonstrate the total unreality of attack. And he invites us to take him as our role model for every aspect of our lives, which we can accomplish by joining him in following the Guide that God has given us:

> I have enjoined you to behave as I behaved, but we must respond to the same Mind to do this. This Mind is the Holy Spirit, Whose Will is for God always. He teaches you how to keep me as the model for your thought, and to behave like me as a result. (T-5.II.12:1-3)

But it does not follow that the Course advocates total nonviolence as a behavioral injunction for those with unhealed minds.

From the above depictions of the advanced teacher of God, one might conclude that the Course is advocating total nonviolence as a behavioral standard for everyone. But this, I think, is a mistaken conclusion based on a faulty logic that goes something like this: "A person with a totally healed mind is nonviolent behaviorally; therefore, if we want a totally healed mind, we must practice nonviolent behavior to get it." But this logic essentially puts the cart before the horse. Advanced teachers of God are nonviolent in behavior *as a result* of being nonviolent in thought; they did not become nonviolent in thought as a result of being nonviolent in behavior. Trying to attain nonviolent thought through practicing nonviolent behavior simply won't work: "You cannot change your mind by changing your behavior" (T-4.IV.2:1).

The characteristics presented in Section 4 of the Manual are not behavioral injunctions. Rather, as the introduction to that section tells us, they are "special gifts" (M-4.1:4) given by God to help the advanced teacher of God fulfill his function, gifts that come as a result of the mental healing that makes him an advanced teacher of God in the first place. And though Jesus does invite us to emulate his behavior, the passage above (T-5.II.12:1-3) tells us that this depends on us emulating his thought. As always in the Course, thought is cause; behavior is effect.

Thus, while nonviolent behavior can be a powerful teacher of love when it is the expression of a healed mind, nonviolence is not a behavioral injunction for those with unhealed minds. Simply trying to imitate the nonviolent behavior of an advanced teacher of God while leaving the mind unhealed will not be beneficial; in fact, it will teach the exact opposite of love, "for all behavior teaches the beliefs that motivate it" (T-6.I.16:6). A person whose mind is motivated by fear and anger (as some nonviolent protesters seem to be) will teach fear and anger, regardless of how "nonviolent" her acts may be on the surface. Nonviolent behavior will only teach love if it is the expression of a truly nonviolent mind.

I don't think this means that as long as our minds are unhealed, we should just go ahead and physically attack people. I think nonviolent behavior is a good idea for all sorts of reasons. Nonviolence is certainly more loving on the world's terms. It contains a glimmer of recognition that there is a better way than attack, and thus it may reinforce whatever healing our minds do have. It keeps situations relatively peaceful while we're in the process of letting our minds be healed. At the very least, it keeps us out of a lot of trouble! My point is simply that adopting nonviolence as a behavioral standard *without working on healing the mind* will not lead to real healing. Healing the mind is our primary responsibility; adopting a standard of nonviolent behavior is at best a temporary expedient that can keep our lives and our world running relatively smoothly as we work on the crucial business of healing our minds.

Our behavior should be guided by the Holy Spirit (or Jesus), Who will guide us to do the most loving thing we are realistically capable of doing, given our level of development.

If nonviolence is not a behavioral injunction, how then should we behave? The Course's answer is simple, if not always so easy in practice: We should let the Holy Spirit (or Jesus) guide our behavior. Our primary task is to work on healing our minds through Course practice, since the quality of our behavior depends on the quality of our thoughts. As our practice deepens, we will come to hear the Holy Spirit's voice with greater clarity, and so more and more we will allow our specific behaviors to be guided by Him. If we let Him, He will guide us in literally everything, down to the smallest detail (see, for instance, W-pII.275.2:3).

Given the obvious value of nonviolence, will the Holy Spirit always guide us to behave in a *totally* nonviolent way? My answer is: Not necessarily. I have no doubt that the Holy Spirit's guidance for our behavior will tend toward nonviolence, since His sole purpose for behavior is to communicate love. But I also believe that He will not make us bite off more than we can chew. The Course tells us that "the Holy Spirit cannot ask more than you are willing to do" (T-2.VI.6:2). It also says that "no response given by Him will ever be one that would increase fear" (T-9.II.3:3). And let's face it, the prospect of responding to all seeming attacks with total nonviolence is terrifying to those of us whose minds are far from totally healed. Jesus offered us an example of extreme nonviolence, but most of us simply aren't ready to follow him all the way just yet. Indeed, he tells us that even his own disciples "were not wholly ready to follow [him] at the time" (T-6.I.16:1).

Therefore, I believe that the Holy Spirit will guide us to do the most loving, nonviolent thing we are realistically capable of doing, *given our level of development*. Just as the Holy Spirit will sometimes guide us to take physical medicine if we are too afraid to accept a deeper healing (see T-2.IV.4-5), so He will sometimes guide us to act in ways which fall short of total nonviolence (but which *are* expressions of love, within our current limitations) if we are too afraid to practice the more radical nonviolence of the advanced teacher of God.

Strictly speaking, total nonviolence on a form level is impossible anyway, since even the simple act of eating involves doing violence to the body of another living thing. Since Jesus clearly ate and drank during his earthly life, even he was not totally nonviolent on a form level. We need not burden ourselves, then, with the impossible goal of total nonviolence in the world. All we need do is practice the Course, try our best to listen to the Holy Spirit, and act as much as possible from His guidance.

Frankly, I think that many times, particularly in the terrifying situations that tend to bring out our most violent impulses, we will simply fail to hear Him. I think that most acts of physical violence are egoic responses rooted in fear. But whatever opening we give the Holy Spirit, He will use. And to the extent that we are able to hear Him, our acts will be less violent than they would have been if we hadn't heard Him at all.

Applying this to daily life, I believe that each situation is unique, and that the guidance of the Holy Spirit—assuming we hear it—will be adjusted to our level of development. For instance, if I have a gun and

I'm attacked by a mugger, my ego may goad me to kill him, but the Holy Spirit may guide me to wound him so that I can run away and call the police, as well as the paramedics who can treat the injury I inflicted upon him. Perhaps that's the most loving thing I'm ready to do at that time. Perhaps a more advanced person with a higher degree of healing would have been guided to accept the mugger's beating without resistance in order to teach the mugger a profound lesson in love, but I'm not ready to do that yet.

I personally believe that even some of the wars we've fought, such as the fight against Hitler in World War II, may have been influenced by the Holy Spirit to some extent. Now, please don't get me wrong: I am not claiming that the Holy Spirit *advocates* war. There is no doubt in my mind that war is rooted in the ego, that the Holy Spirit is always calling us to a better way, that we always have the potential within us to choose that better way, and that the Course calls us to ultimately relinquish war in all its forms. But even so, perhaps World War II was truly the most loving response to the menace of Hitler that collective humanity was realistically capable of at the time. (And perhaps the current war on terrorism is the most loving response we are realistically capable of now, though personally I think we have it in us to make better choices in this situation.) Perhaps if we had been further along in our development we could have responded to Hitler with nonviolent Gandhi-style resistance—as some people, particularly in Denmark and the Netherlands, actually did with some success—but we just weren't ready for that yet. It is worth noting that even Gandhi contended that armed resistance to oppression was a more advanced option than fearful submission, though he certainly felt that loving, nonviolent resistance was far superior to both.

I believe that the Holy Spirit can take *anything* and use it for His purposes if we will let Him. The Course says that the advanced teacher of God sees only the Holy Spirit's lesson in the events of the past, which must include even the most violent events:

> The past...held no mistakes; nothing that did not serve to benefit the world, as well as him to whom it seemed to happen. Perhaps it was not understood at the time.
>
> (M-4.VIII.1:6-7)

Conclusion

To summarize, I think the Holy Spirit guides each of us to do the most loving, nonviolent thing we are realistically capable of doing at a given time. He takes into account our level of development, in particular our level of fear, and gears His guidance specifically to our needs. In doing so, He ensures that the best possible outcome will come about, given the limitations of the people involved. To the degree that our actions are truly guided by the Holy Spirit they will teach love, even if they fall short of total nonviolence on a form level. As we listen to His Voice we will advance in our development, and our actions will become increasingly nonviolent until the day that we become advanced teachers of God, shining exemplars of radical nonviolence in thought, word, and deed.

25

What is the Course's stance on competition? Would it have us refrain from all forms of competition?

Short Answer

According to the Course, the *idea* (content) of competition is wholly of the ego. However, the *form* of competition, like all forms, is neutral in itself, and it is impossible to refrain from all forms of competition in this world. Therefore, what the Course would have us do is make sure that the content of our minds is noncompetitive, even when we are engaging in forms that are competitive.

☽☽☽

According to the Course, the *idea* (content) of competition is wholly of the ego.

Competition is an idea entirely foreign to God. As He created us, we are limitless beings, who "both *have* everything and *are* everything" (T-4.III.9:5). Our only function in our Heavenly home is to share everything with one another, extending our abundance in creation. There is no lack, and therefore the whole idea of competition is inconceivable: "Because God's equal Sons have everything, they cannot compete" (T-7.III.3:3). We all share in the inheritance of God, and in His Kingdom, "there is no loss" (W-pI.76.9:3; this exact phrase appears seven times in the Course).

However, once we listened to the ego and made the physical world, we "lost" the inheritance of God, at least in our minds. The ego "is competitive rather than loving" (T-7.I.4:1), and the ego's world is a reflection of this. This world is a world of separation, and in such a world, everyone is limited, unequal, and lacking. Living as limited bodies in a separate world requires us to compete for physical resources such as food, shelter, mates, and territory. As human beings, we also compete for what might be called *mental* resources—special love, self-esteem, status, etc.—all of which fall under the Course's category of "specialness."

In short, competition is woven into the very fabric of this world. It is not an idea limited to more obvious human forms like war, athletics, or the quest for wealth, but rather a basic component of everyday life on earth. It is, in fact, the idea at the heart of the ego's "'laws' of chaos" (T-23.II.1:1), the laws that govern this world. In a world of differences, everything is enemy to everything else, and existence is a chaotic battle for survival. To be sure, some things join together in cooperative alliances, but only in order to defeat a common enemy. The law of Heaven is that everyone has everything; but the law of earth is the law of the jungle: "You have what you have taken" (T-23.II.9:3).

In this world, then, there are winners and losers. One's gain is another's loss. And through this ongoing battle for survival between separate entities, the ego ensures its own survival. Each separate entity loses in the end through death; only the ego itself—the thought of separation—wins in the long run.

However, the *form* of competition, like all forms, is neutral in itself, and it is impossible to refrain from all forms of competition in this world.

Upon hearing how grim and ego-ridden the idea of competition is, our first impulse may be to try to give up all forms of competition entirely. However, I think this is the wrong approach to the problem for at least two reasons—the reasons presented in my heading above. First, even though the *idea* of competition is of the ego, the *forms* in which competition takes place are neutral in themselves. They are simply empty vessels, which can be interpreted through the eyes of the ego or the eyes of the Holy Spirit. Thus, giving up the form of competition is not the crucial thing; giving up the mental content of competition behind the form is.

Greg Mackie

Second, it is simply impossible to give up every single form of competition in this world. Now, certainly there are many forms we can give up, and I think it's highly likely that we will be guided to give up certain forms as we progress on the spiritual journey. But as I said in my previous point, competition is woven into the very fabric of this world. Whenever we eat something, we are gaining at the expense of the thing being eaten. Whenever we recover from an illness, we win and the microbes that caused the illness on the physical level lose. Whenever we get a job or find a mate, we have defeated the others who competed for that job or that mate. Conversely, when we get eaten, don't recover from the illness, or fail to obtain the job or mate, we are the losers.

We can certainly live in ways that reduce the amount of competition we engage in, but no matter how we choose to live, we cannot help but engage in at least some of these forms. Competition is simply part of living in this world, and so it is impossible to give up all competition on a form level. Fortunately, it *is* possible to look at all of these competitive forms in a different way, which leads me to my next point.

Therefore, what the Course would have us do is make sure that the content of our minds is noncompetitive, even when we are engaging in forms that are competitive.

We may not be able to give up all forms of competition, but giving up forms is not the crucial thing anyway. The crucial thing is giving up competitive content in the mind, the *idea* of competition sponsored by the ego.

I think it's critical to realize that just giving up forms does not lead to a true change of mind. The Course tells us unequivocally, "You cannot change your mind by changing your behavior" (T-4.IV.2:1). It is so easy for us to give up certain more overt forms of competition like basketball games or the corporate rat race, and then think we've really given up competition. But if all we've done is give up a few forms, we haven't really given up competition, for two reasons. First, we're still engaging in all sorts of other forms of competition that are not so obvious to us, like the ones mentioned above. Second, and more important, we really haven't given up the content of competition in our minds.

Our main task, then, is not so much to give up competitive forms, though we certainly should give up specific forms if we feel so guided. Instead, our main task is to give up our competitive mindset through ongoing Course practice. Indeed, the Course considers giving up the idea of competition to be absolutely essential to its program. In the Text, we are told, "Do not underestimate your need to be vigilant *against* this idea, because all your conflicts come from it" (T-7.III.3:5). In a later discussion of the idea of justice (the idea that everyone must get what he deserves), the Course says, "The principle that justice means no one can lose is crucial to this course" (T-25.IX.5:4). In the Workbook, Lesson 133 tells us that if our motivation for acquiring something is to take something away from someone else, then what we are seeking is utterly valueless, and we should let it go. Finally, the Course material tells us again and again that salvation lies in joining with others, "and in so doing, [losing] all sense of separate interests" (P-2.II.8:4). Giving up the idea of separate interests and giving up the idea of competition are one and the same. This is the only way the ego thought of separation, and the competitive battle for survival based on that thought, can be undone.

How do we keep the content of our minds noncompetitive even while engaging in the inevitable competitive forms? Besides maintaining a regular regimen of Course practice, I can think of two Course-based attitudes we can cultivate. First, we can remind ourselves that all of these competitive forms we are engaging in are totally unreal. There may well be "winners" and "losers" on the level of form, but none of this has any effect at all on anyone's reality. No matter what the appearance, the fact remains that, in truth, there is no loss.

Second, we can allow the Holy Spirit to change our motivation for engaging in these forms. As long as we listen to the ego, we will engage in them for the purpose of fulfilling our lacks through taking from others. But if we listen to the Holy Spirit, we will engage in them for the purpose of serving the Holy Spirit's plan of salvation through *giving* to others.

The transformative power of these attitudes becomes evident if we apply them to some of the examples of competitive forms I presented above. As long as we listen to the ego, we will view eating, maintaining bodily health, and acquiring a job or mate as means to fulfill our perceived lacks at the expense of others. Our mindset will be competitive, and winning these things for ourselves will be extremely important to us. But if we listen to the Holy Spirit, we will see all of these things as unreal, and of no ultimate consequence. Eating well, maintaining bodily health, and acquiring the right job or mate will be important only to the extent that they allow us to do our part in the Holy Spirit's plan of salvation and be of service to others. Whether we win something or lose something on a form level, we will trust that all is well, because the Holy Spirit gives everyone everything they need. Our mindset will be noncompetitive, and so winning and losing will not be important to us at all.

A personal story: My relationship with competitive athletics

The whole question of competition and how to relate to it is a deeply personal one for me, as I have had a lifelong love for competitive athletics. I'd like to share a bit of my own personal journey in coming to terms with competition in this area, in the hope that it might be instructive. I make absolutely no claim to have transcended the ego-based desire for competition, but I have learned a few things over the years, and so I hope that what I'm about to share will be helpful.

As I said, I have loved competitive athletics all my life. I enjoyed (and still enjoy) both watching various sports and participating in them. In particular, I was a very good competitive distance runner in my younger years. And to be totally honest, my motivation for competing, especially in my high school and college years, was almost pure ego. My distance running success, in my eyes, was my ticket to special love, self-esteem, and status—those precious mental resources I referred to earlier.

But as I grew older and became drawn to the spiritual path, I slowly began to re-evaluate my relationship with competitive athletics. I began to realize that athletic success wasn't the key to happiness that I thought it was. Losing was painful, and even winning was not really all that satisfying. As I began to study the Course, what it said about the idea of competition hit very close to home. I had to really think about what I wanted to do concerning my competitive running career.

As a result of reflecting on this, I asked the Holy Spirit a number of times for guidance about whether to quit competitive distance running.

While I don't know how pure my reception of guidance was, the answer I always seemed to get was "You don't need to quit, but you do need to learn to look at it in a new way." So, for a period of several years, I kept running races, but really tried to bring a noncompetitive mindset to them. And while my success at this was far from perfect, I feel like I did make some progress. I continued with the form of competitive distance running, but over time, I learned to not take it so seriously. I began to remind myself of the unreality of it all, and place less importance on winning and losing. I learned how to love my "opponents," seeing them as compatriots rather than enemies. I began to see my road races as opportunities to connect with people, instead of opportunities to gain status at their expense. In short, I tried to use my races as means for joining and giving, rather than as means for separating and taking away.

Eventually, I gave up competitive distance running. There were a number of reasons for this, but the bottom line was that other things, like my work with the Course, had simply become more important to me. And even though I gave up this particular form of competition, I don't regret the time I spent doing it. In hindsight, I see that I learned things from it that continue to benefit me in my current work. One major benefit is that I learned self-discipline and training principles that are perfectly applicable to Course study and practice. The Holy Spirit has put the skills I developed through competitive running to good use, even though my original purpose for doing it was pure ego. As I look back on my running career, I can't help but think of this line from the Manual: "The past as well held no mistakes; nothing that did not serve to benefit the world, as well as him to whom it seemed to happen" (M-4.VIII.1:6).

To this day, I still run noncompetitively, and I still enjoy competitive athletics, though not with the zeal I had earlier in my life. I still watch my favorite sports, and I admire the dedication, skill, grace, and discipline of great athletes. Perhaps as I evolve, the day will come eventually when I give up competitive athletics entirely. I don't know. But for now, I continue to learn how to look at this form of competition in a different way, often doing Course practice as I watch, learning how to maintain the content of noncompetitiveness in my mind even as I partake of competition on the level of form. I certainly haven't transcended the ego in this area, but I am making progress. And that is the important thing.

Conclusion

Can you imagine what the world would be like without the idea of competition? It would be a vastly different place. While I've stressed that giving up particular forms of competition is not the answer in and of itself, I have no doubt that many of the most painful and unnecessary forms *will* be given up as our minds are healed. And even the forms that remain temporarily necessary while we live on this earth will be seen in a whole new light. Our world will be transformed from a place of war to a place of peace; from a place of lack to a place of plenty; from a place of fear to a place of love. From such a world, it is a small step back to Heaven, in which peace, plenty, and love are our eternal inheritance, and we are forever freed of the need to compete for what is rightfully ours.

26

What is the Course's view of sex?

Short Answer

Like every other form in the world, sex was made by the ego for the purpose of maintaining the separation, but can also be used by the Holy Spirit for the purpose of communicating joining. What sex is to us depends on the purpose that we give it.

☾☾☾

The Course says very little about sex per se, but it does say a lot about the body and how we use it. Sex, of course, is a body-centered phenomenon. Therefore, in the following answer, I will take what the Course says more generally about the body, and apply it to the specific topic of sex. I'll start with the "bad" news about sex (this gets pretty grim, so hang in there), and then move on to the good news. Finally, I'll share some of my own thoughts about how to deal with our sexuality from a Course perspective.

But before I get into the "bad" news, I want to stress that the "bad" news is only half the story—the ego's half. The Course is not *against* sex, but rather against the ego's *use* of sex. Sex, like the body, is neither good nor bad; it is nothing, neutral in itself. In the hands of the ego, sex is an unholy deception aimed at keeping us separate; but in the hands of the Holy Spirit, sex is a holy expression of joining. Let's keep this in mind as we now descend into the darkness of the ego's use of sex.

Sex was made by the ego for the purpose of maintaining the separation.

This is a startling idea, since we tend to associate sex with joining, but the Course tells us that the body "is clearly a separation device" (T-6.V(A).2:3) made by the ego. If this is so, then everything associated with the body, including sex, is a separation device, at least as long as we continue to identify with the ego. The following are some ways in which the ego uses the body—and special relationships rooted in the body—to maintain the separation.

Physical desires, including sexual desire, arise from the ego's need to confirm its reality. Physical impulses are egoic distortions of miracle impulses.

The Course tells us that all bodily appetites, including sexual desire, come not from the body, but rather from the ego:

> Appetites are "getting" mechanisms, representing the ego's need to confirm itself. This is as true of body appetites as it is of the so-called "higher ego needs." Body appetites are not physical in origin. The ego regards the body as its home, and tries to satisfy itself through the body.
>
> (T-4.II.7:5-8)

What a mind-bending idea! It seems a given that bodily appetites like sexual desire are driven by deep bodily instincts (for instance, the urge to procreate) and come upon us against our will. But according to the Course, bodily appetites are the expression of a decision made by the *mind,* a decision to identify with the ego and reinforce the ego's reality. Certainly this decision is not one that we are usually consciously aware of, but it is a decision nonetheless. Our decision to experience sexual desire is the decision to believe that we are limited, lacking beings who must seek outside ourselves, through sexual fantasies or through sexual encounters with other people, to fulfill our lack. Therefore, this decision reinforces the belief that we are separate.

But physical impulses are more than simply nonphysical in origin. The Course also tells us that they are actually miracle impulses in disguise:

Your distorted perceptions produce a dense cover over miracle impulses, making it hard for them to reach your own awareness. The confusion of miracle impulses with physical impulses is a major perceptual distortion. Physical impulses are misdirected miracle impulses. All real pleasure comes from doing God's Will.

(T-1.VII.1:1-4)

In the original dictation to Helen Schucman, "physical impulses" actually read "sexual impulses" (see *Absence from Felicity*, pp. 252-253), and the passage addressed Helen's own sexual fantasies. The idea here is that we all have miracle impulses deep within our minds, impulses which come from the Holy Spirit (and Jesus). But as those impulses rise to our conscious awareness, they are distorted by the ego, which of course wants nothing to do with miracles, and they become physical impulses. The real pleasure of doing God's Will is turned into the pseudo-pleasure of bodily stimulation. Thus the ego takes miracle impulses, which would *end* the ego if they were expressed in their pure form, and twists them into a means of reinforcing itself and maintaining the separation.

A couple of paragraphs later (T-1.VII.3), Jesus discusses the subject of fantasy, and given the original context of the dictation, I believe that sexual fantasies were originally targeted here. We are told that "fantasy is a distorted form of vision" (T-1.VII.3:1), which is another way of saying that physical impulses (like those associated with sexual fantasy) are distorted miracle impulses (which stem from spiritual vision). "Fantasy is an attempt to control reality according to false needs" (T-1.VII.3:4)—in the case of sexual fantasy, our false need for physical gratification. "Fantasies are a means of making false associations and attempting to obtain pleasure from them" (T-1.VII.3:6). This is exactly what we do in sexual fantasy: We concoct elaborate scenarios in our minds (we make "false associations") for the purpose of physical pleasure. In so doing, we indulge in a solitary activity in which there is no real joining at all.

Thus we refuse the miracle, which would end the need for fantasy by showing us the "wholly satisfying nature of reality" (T-1.VII.3:11)—that is, the reality of our nonphysical, non-egoic Self, and of our true union with others in that Self. In this way, the ego takes miracle impulses—impulses to extend and join with others in true vision—and turns them into sexual fantasies as a way of reinforcing and maintaining separation.

Special relationships, including sexual relationships, are the ego's substitute for real joining, which is the joining of minds. Striving for physical joining through special relationships is the ego's means of preventing *true joining.*

"The special love relationship is the ego's most boasted gift" (T-16.V.3:1). And based on my observation of the world's art, music, literature, and media, I would say that the *romantic* form of the special love relationship is the most sought-after version of that gift, and further that the *sexual* aspect of the romantic relationship is the crown jewel of the ego's gifts. (Oddly enough, the day before I began writing this answer, I heard a radio commercial for a local jeweler which exhorted men to give their romantic partners diamonds "to celebrate the fire and sparkle of your special relationship.")

Most of us believe that hot romantic relationships with great sex will save us from the slings and arrows of the world. They are our "haven in the storm of guilt" (T-16.IV.3:1), "a union made in Heaven" (T-16.V.8:3). Above all, we see romantic relationships and the sexual union that comes with them as the deepest, most profound experience of joining with another human being that the world offers. Even the majority of our religious traditions consider sexual love to be a God-given, holy thing, or a beautiful, life-affirming expression of divine Nature—at least as long as we keep it within certain moral parameters.

But can we truly join with each other by joining our bodies in romantic, sexual union? According to the Course, we cannot. Special relationships were invented by the ego as a means of fooling us into *thinking* that we are joining when in fact we are cementing the separation into place still further. They are "a kind of union from which union is excluded" (T-16.V.6:4). And this certainly applies to sexual union, one way in which we attempt the "union of bodies":

> For they [those who are afraid to truly communicate] think their minds must be kept private or they will lose them, but if their bodies are together their minds remain their own. The union of bodies thus becomes the way in which they would keep minds apart.   (T-15.VII.11:5-6)

True joining occurs between minds, not bodies. But the ego fears true joining, because that would mean the end of the separation, which means the end of the ego. Since the ego needs our allegiance in order to survive, and since all of us have a genuine yearning to join, the ego must give us something that looks like joining, but really isn't. Therefore, it offers us "the union of bodies," which is of course what we attempt to do through sex. Ego-directed sex makes us believe that we have really joined with another person, but in truth it keeps us apart, because it doesn't really involve the joining of minds. Joining our bodies is thus the ego's way of ensuring that our minds remain safely apart. Joining our bodies maintains the separation of our minds.

Sex promises joining, but ends up separating.

I think it is obvious that most of us think of sex as one of the great means of joining, perhaps the greatest of all. We practically worship sex. Romantic, sexual love is celebrated and exalted in our songs, poems, stories, and even in our religious literature (such as the Song of Solomon in the Bible, and the *Kama Sutra)*. But in truth, sexual impulses, as made and directed by the ego, are a distortion of the impulse to join. They distort miracle impulses, which are the only means of true joining. They promise joining with another, but actually end up excluding the mind of the other, which is the other's only reality. In short, while sex promises joining, it really ends up separating. It confirms that we are separate and alone. And this was the ego's purpose for it all along: to maintain the separation.

These ideas may sound far out, but I think we can see the truth of them in our experience, if we will really look. In America today, we are more sexually active than ever, and yet we are also lonelier than ever. Perhaps these ideas are not so far out after all. Perhaps it is true that, though we all seek joining with God and with each other, "physical closeness cannot achieve it" (T-1.II.1:3). Perhaps sex, under the ego's direction, really does make us feel more separate.

Sex can be used by the Holy Spirit for the purpose of communicating true joining.

The grim picture of sex painted above may send us all scurrying for the monastery and the convent. But there *is* some good news about sex: Nothing is too dirty for the Holy Spirit. The same body the ego uses to keep us separate, the Holy Spirit uses as a device for communicating true joining:

> Remember that the Holy Spirit interprets the body only as a means of communication. Being the Communication Link between God and His separated Sons, the Holy Spirit interprets everything you have made in the light of what He is. The ego separates through the body. The Holy Spirit reaches through it to others.
>
> (T-8.VII.2:1-4)

Therefore sex and romance, in the hands of the Holy Spirit, *can* be used to communicate a genuine joining of minds. This is similar to the belief of many religions that sex is holy when used in a loving way that is in accord with God's Will, or the rhythms of Nature. But there is a twist: Traditional religion usually sees sex as a God-given (or natural) thing that can be corrupted through improper use, but the Course sees sex as an ego-given (or unnatural) thing that can be made holy through proper use.

Is there anything in the Course that specifically describes the Holy Spirit's use of sex? I cannot find anything, but I think that the Course's statements about the Holy Spirit's use of the body can, by and large, be applied to sex. Here are a couple of examples:

> The Love of God, for a little while, must still be expressed through one body to another, because vision is still so dim.
>
> (T-1.VII.2:3)

> In the service of uniting [the body] becomes a beautiful lesson in communion, which has value until communion *is.*
>
> (T-8.VII.3:4)

The idea that sex can be used to communicate joining may seem to contradict the idea presented above that sex cannot bring about joining. I think the resolution of this seeming contradiction lies in the fact that the Holy Spirit uses the body to *communicate* a joining that has truly taken place mind-to-mind, while the ego uses the body to *prevent* mind-to-mind joining from taking place at all. The ego tries to convince us that we can use sex to *achieve* union; the Holy Spirit uses sex to *celebrate* union. The ego regards bodies as a means of separating minds, but Jesus tells us that the Holy Spirit regards bodies "solely as a means of joining minds and uniting them with yours and mine" (T-8.VII.2:5). Thus sex can prevent joining or facilitate joining, depending on who (or Who) is using it.

How, then, should we deal with our sexual desires?

This is the question we all want answered, is it not? In a nutshell, my answer is that we shouldn't try to suppress sexual desires or feel guilty about them, but we should be as honest as we can about the purpose behind them. We should try (through Course practice) to turn away from the ego's uses for sexual impulses, and allow the Holy Spirit to use them instead. As the Course tells us, "The Holy Spirit would not deprive you of your special relationships, but would transform them" (T-17.IV.2:3). We can let Him redirect our sexual impulses and transform them back into miracle impulses.

The following are some of my personal observations concerning sex from a Course perspective, along with a personal practice that I sometimes use when I experience sexual feelings:

Given the Course's dim view of sexual impulses (at least when those impulses are directed by the ego), should we practice celibacy? The Course itself doesn't give us any behavioral injunctions concerning sex, so I think our sexual choices are really between us and the Holy Spirit. I'm sure that there are people (like monks and nuns) who are truly called to celibacy, and by all means they should honor their calling. But I suspect that many, perhaps most of us are not called to this. For most of us, the path will involve transforming our sexual expression into a more loving expression, rather than eliminating it altogether.

If we don't opt for celibacy, should we at least adopt behavioral standards concerning sex? Again, the Course itself contains no behavioral standards about sex. But I don't think that means we are forbidden to adopt such standards ourselves if they are helpful. I personally believe that adopting behavioral standards concerning sex and teaching them to our children is wise and probably necessary, given the volatile and impulsive nature of sexuality, and the tragic consequences—unwanted pregnancy, sexually transmitted diseases, etc.—that result from unrestrained sexual behavior. Learning to listen to the Holy Spirit takes practice, mental discipline, and a fair level of maturity; many of us, especially younger people, simply haven't yet developed the ability to hear Him clearly, and as long as that is the case, most of our sexual responses will come from the ego. Adopting behavioral standards concerning sex can help protect us from the negative consequences of ego-driven sexuality as we work on healing our minds. Adopting such standards would be in line with the Course as long as we don't use them as a substitute for healing the mind, which the Course tells us is the only way to salvation.

To be frank, I myself am fairly traditional in regard to sexual mores (though since I fully affirm homosexual relationships, I guess I'm not *too* traditional). I personally believe that teenagers are best off being abstinent, and adults are best off limiting their sexual activity to serious, committed relationships. I speak only for myself here and not for the Course, but I just think that practicing self-discipline concerning sex is by far the most loving thing to do. The more our sexual behavior is an expression of real love for another person rather than simply an exercise in bodily gratification, the more closely it will reflect the Holy Spirit's purpose for sex.

That being said, I think that we should also recognize that sexual desire is very deeply rooted, and will not be transformed by the Holy Spirit overnight. The vast majority of us will probably continue to be driven by egoic sexual desires for quite some time; because of this, I think that while we should practice self-discipline, we should also cut ourselves some slack. Most of us, even if we are not promiscuous, will continue to indulge in private sexual fantasies and seek to gratify ourselves through them to some degree. And if we do choose to indulge such desires sometimes, I think the worst thing we can do is make it into a huge issue and wrack ourselves with guilt over it.

On those occasions when I indulge an egoic sexual desire, I find it helpful simply to remind myself that salvation doesn't hang in the balance. I try to treat that sexual desire the same way the Course would have us treat physical medicine: I remind myself that salvation does not lie in it, but it is no sin to partake of it if I am not ready to transcend it. Occasional sexual release need not be any different than taking a pill, a useful temporary expedient as we work on healing our minds. Simply recognizing that sex is not salvation is a positive step *toward* healing our minds.

I think it's honest and healthy to acknowledge that we will most likely be dealing with ego-based sexual desires for a long time. Even as our minds do begin to heal, our sexual expression will still most likely be a mix of Holy Spirit and ego. We need to let that be okay, even as we work to change it. Most of all, we shouldn't let ourselves feel guilty about it, since guilt, of course, just reinforces the ego.

Transforming our sexual desires: a practice

Here is a specific practice I sometimes use when confronted with a sexual desire. First, I ask myself, "'What is it *for*?' (T-17.VI.2:1, et. al.). What is the purpose for this desire? Which voice is prompting this feeling in me?" If it feels like the Holy Spirit is prompting the desire—as may well be the case, especially in the context of my marriage—I will go ahead and express it in some form that is consistent with my commitment to my marriage vows. (For those who are not in committed relationships, this would translate into expressing it in some form that is consistent with their own sexual ethics, a form guided by the Holy Spirit.)

If it feels like the ego, I move to the second step. I ask, "What is the miracle impulse that this sexual impulse is hiding?" I remind myself that "all real pleasure comes from doing God's Will" (T-1.VII.1:4). I try to find the miracle impulse and express that instead of the sexual impulse. What does this mean in everyday life terms? It means that, for example, if an attractive woman catches my eye, I might silently send her a blessing or perform an act of kindness for her instead of indulging in sexual fantasies about her. I find this powerful and effective, because rather than trying to *suppress* my desire, which just doesn't work, I *redirect* it by looking for the pure, Holy Spirit-inspired desire underneath. While I'm not always successful in doing this, I've succeeded often enough to know that sexual desires really can be transformed into miracles, and when they are, I'm a lot happier than I would have been if I had simply indulged the sexual desire.

I highly recommend this practice. It has worked wonders for me, and others who have tried it have reported positive results as well. The next time you are grappling with sexual desires, why not give it a try?

Conclusion

Above all, I think we should always remember that our only real desire is for God. Our sexual desires are only a dim reflection of the burning desire we have for our Father. Our sexual desires, when directed by the ego, pull us away from our true Love. Let us, then, do what we can to turn away from the ego's shabby "gifts" and seek out our true Love, Who alone will satisfy our deepest yearnings:

> *What can I seek for, Father, but Your Love? Perhaps I think I seek for something else; a something I have called by many names. Yet is Your Love the only thing I seek, or ever sought. For there is nothing else that I could ever really want to find. Let me remember You. What else could I desire but the truth about myself?* (W-pII.231.1:1-6)

27

What about our addictions? How would the Course address addictions and ways that we can heal them?

Short Answer

The Course aims at restoring to us the awareness of God's Love, our only real desire. Addictions are simply distorted ways of searching for God's Love. They are the ego's substitutes for that Love, its attempt to keep us from finding God's Love through getting us to seek for it where it is not. We can heal addictions by applying the Course's program specifically to those addictions (alongside whatever other recovery program may be appropriate), thus undoing them and ultimately restoring our awareness of God's Love.

☙☙☙

The topic of how to use the Course to heal addictions is a huge one, and an important one, since addictions are a life-or-death matter for many people. This brief answer will only scratch the surface of a topic that I think really deserves a fuller treatment. It is my hope that this topic will be more fully explored in the future, as I believe the Course has great potential for healing addictions, if used wisely. The following is a broad overview of how I believe the Course sees addictions, and how it can be successfully applied to them.

The Course heals addictions by restoring to us the awareness of God's Love, our only real desire.

Broadly speaking, "addiction" can be defined as a continual craving for something which we believe will fill a perceived lack. We seem to have many lacks, and so addiction takes many forms. Yet the Course tells us that "a sense of separation from God is the only lack you really need correct" (T-1.VI.2:1). The only thing really lacking in our lives is awareness of God's everlasting Love for us. Thus I believe that the Course offers us an excellent program for dealing with addictions, because it aims to *restore* to us the awareness of God's Love. If this, our only real desire, is fulfilled, then all of our addictions, which are simply distorted forms of that desire, will be healed.

The various addictions we experience—everything from drugs, to sex, to food, to watching TV—are simply misguided attempts to attain the happiness that only God's Love can really give us. They reflect our striving for what the Course calls *idols*, worldly things that the ego offers us as substitutes for God's Love. The ego provides these substitutes precisely because it doesn't *want* us to find God's Love, since if we did, the ego would be no more. In the words of the old song, it has us "lookin' for love in all the wrong places." This is in keeping with the ego's central dictum: "Seek but do not find" (T-16.V.6:5). It wants us to be permanently distracted by intensely seeking for happiness, but never finding it.

The Course material presents us with a number of specific examples of idols that we seek as substitutes for God's Love. Here are just a few of them (thanks to Robert Perry for this list): human love, being liked, status, prestige, power, influence, knowing the right people, fame, money, material things, going shopping, clothes, physical pleasure, physical protection, physical beauty, pills, other people's bodies, intelligence, finding your special gift in the world, and desired places/situations/circumstances. That's quite a list. I think all of us can find something on it that we have sought at one time or another.

For me, the whole idea of seeking but never finding describes perfectly the entire process of addiction. We don't have to be heroin addicts to see this process at work in our lives; since virtually all of us are seeking a number of the things on the above list, we are all addicts of one sort or another. Think for a moment of all the various things you have sought after eagerly in your life. They promised you happiness, did they not? Some you probably didn't attain, and if you are like most of us, you were probably bitterly disappointed. But what of those you did attain? Perhaps you had the realization that the Course describes in the following passage:

> You must have noticed an outstanding characteristic of every end that the ego has accepted as its own. When you have achieved it, *it has not satisfied you.* (T-8.VIII.2:5-6)

I know this is practically the story of my life. Some particular thing—in my case, athletic prowess, finding the right romantic partner, or being a great writer, just to name a few—seemed to promise happiness. I sought it diligently, and all too often, I didn't get it. When that happened, I was devastated. But even when I did get it, I found that it didn't satisfy me. It didn't deliver the happiness that it seemed to promise; as a good friend of mine once said, "The pizza never delivers." And so I would seek for something else, hoping that would do the trick. It is really no different than a drug addict seeking hit after hit, hoping to find satisfaction in it, yet sinking further and further into despair. Drug addicts and alcoholics are simply more extreme examples of a dynamic that runs most human lives every day. We are all addicted to seeking happiness from a world which cannot give it. And it is this very dynamic of addiction—our adherence to the ego's program of "seek but do not find"—that the Course aims to undo.

We can heal addictions by applying the Course's program specifically to those addictions, thus undoing them and ultimately restoring our awareness of God's Love.

As I've said, the Course is aimed at restoring our awareness of God's Love. How does this restoration come about? As every Course student knows, the Course's means for accomplishing this is "removing the blocks to the awareness of love's presence" (T-In.1:7). Our addictions *are* those blocks, since our addictions are our egoic substitutes for love. The Course's prescription for healing, then, is for us to apply its program to those addictions, so that they can be undone and our awareness of God's Love restored. As the Introduction to the Workbook says, we are to apply its lessons with "great specificity" (W-In.6:1) to the circumstances of our individual lives. Thus whatever form our particular addiction takes, that is the form we are to practice with.

What specific Course practices can we use? There are literally hundreds to choose from, and if we work the program, each of us will undoubtedly develop a "problem-solving repertoire" (W-pI.194.6:2) of practices that are particularly effective for us. But one example that comes immediately to mind is a practice from Chapter 30 of the Text. As mentioned above, what we call "addictions" the Course calls "idols." This practice, which I have put into the first person, is one that Jesus gives us to use whenever we are tempted by idols (for instance, if I am an alcoholic and I am tempted to take that first drink):

> *There never was a time an idol brought me anything except the "gift" of guilt. Not one was bought except at cost of pain, nor was it ever paid by me alone.*
>
> (T-30.V.10:3-4)

This, I think, would be a great line to memorize and apply to situations when we are tempted by our addictions.

What about the various treatments available for more serious addictions, like drug addiction and alcoholism? What about things like medical intervention, inpatient or outpatient drug rehab, psychotherapy, or Twelve Step support groups? I believe that such things are probably absolutely necessary for the majority of people with substance abuse problems, as well as for many who have other serious addictions. I think that each person should be advised by someone trained in substance abuse diagnosis and treatment (I certainly don't qualify) as to what treatment options are best for him or her. Alcoholism and addiction to drugs like heroin or cocaine are very serious matters. They wreak havoc on the lives of those afflicted and their loved ones. A wrong move in their treatment can lead to devastating consequences, even death. Most of us, especially those who are on the downward spiral of substance abuse, aren't anywhere near ready to heal such a serious and intense illness with Workbook lessons alone. Addicts need help, and they are best off turning to those who are truly qualified to provide it.

Thus when I say that we should apply the Course to our specific addictions, I don't mean that we should use it in place of other treatments. What I am saying is that, as Course students, we would do well to use the Course *along with* whatever other treatments may be needed, and to view those other treatments from the perspective of the Course's thought system. So as we seek medical intervention, we can remind ourselves that material means of treatment are simply useful temporary expedients as we work on healing our minds. As we work through the Twelve Steps, we can view them through the lens of the Course and adapt them if necessary; personally, I believe that the Twelve Steps are extremely compatible with the Course, and I know a number of people who have combined the two programs successfully. As we enter into psychotherapy, we can bring with us with the intention of confronting the ego within us honestly and unflinchingly, so that we can allow it to be undone through forgiveness. (According to *Psychotherapy: Purpose, Process, and Practice*, a supplement to the Course dictated by Jesus to Helen Schucman, forgiveness is the true purpose of psychotherapy.) The key is that as we go through these other treatments, we would also be doing the Course's own program: studying its teaching, doing its practice, and extending love and forgiveness to others. The program of the Course would serve as the larger framework into which all of our other treatments would fit.

Crucial to the success of this, I think, is getting *support*. "Salvation is a collaborative venture" (T-4.VI.8:2). In saying this, the Course is very much in agreement with virtually everyone involved in the field of addiction recovery: No one can do it alone. As I reflect on this, it doesn't surprise me that this is the case. If our root problem is separation, what other cure for it could there be than joining? Thus in joining together to heal our various addictions, we strike right at the heart of the ego's program of idolatry, and uproot our addictions at their source.

Above all, I think that we cannot remind ourselves often enough that our addictions are simply egoic distortions of a truly healthy desire: our desire for God's Love. "For still deeper than the ego's foundation, and much stronger than it will ever be, is your intense and burning love of God, and His for you" (T-13.III.2:8). As we walk the path of addiction recovery, we can hasten our steps by continually reminding ourselves of that which we truly seek:

> *What can I seek for, Father, but Your Love? Perhaps I think I seek for something else; a something I have called by many names. Yet is Your Love the only thing I seek, or ever sought. For there is nothing else that I could ever really want to find. Let me remember You. What else could I desire but the truth about myself?*

> (W-pII.231.1:1-6)

28

I have an illness, and am concerned about taking physical medicine. I know the Course does not forbid this, but since physical medicine is magic, won't taking it reinforce my ego?

Short Answer

While attempting to heal the body in any way other than healing the mind is magic—the belief that a power other than God can save us—it does not follow that using magic will necessarily reinforce the ego. It will only do so if we believe that magic is *truly healing*, and thus use it as a substitute for healing the mind. We can use magic in a way that does not reinforce the ego by practicing "conscious magic": taking physical remedies with the conscious understanding that we are doing so only to temporarily alleviate physical symptoms while we work on healing the mind. And as we practice conscious magic, we should remind ourselves that our real goal is not physical healing but rather the peace of God, which will allow us to ultimately transcend bodily concerns entirely.

Attempting to heal the body in any way other than healing the mind is magic—the belief that a power other than God can save us.

What is magic? Magic is the ego's substitute for the healing device that God Himself gave us, the only healing device that really works: the miracle. Magic is the mind's insane attempt to "give" healing power to everything *but* God—to our separate selves, to other people with "special" healing powers, or to various things in the physical world. The miracle works because it heals the *mind*; specifically, it heals the mind's belief that we are separate from God and from each other, the real source of all sickness and suffering of any kind. But magic is rooted in "the belief that there is a creative ability in matter which the mind cannot control" (T-2.IV.2:8). It focuses on healing the physical through physical means, and therefore it doesn't really heal at all, because it leaves the true source of all sickness (the mind's belief in separation) unhealed.

All magic can give us, then, is an illusion of healing. Like a stage magician who uses illusions to make things seem to disappear, our magic is an attempt to conjure an illusion of healing, in which our sickness and suffering seem to disappear. This illusion deceives us into believing that our problems are gone, so we will no longer seek true healing. This is the ego's whole purpose for magic: By turning us away from true healing, magic cements the ego further into place.

As most Course students know, one major form of magic discussed in the Course is physical medicine: "Physical medications are forms of 'spells'" (T-2.V.2:2). Physical medications are attempts to heal the body without healing the mind, and thus they are attempts to avoid the true healing that God's miracles would bring.

Yet it is worth noting that the term "magic," as the Course defines it, applies to much more than just physical medications. More broadly, it applies to anything other than God that we believe will keep us from harm or bring us happiness. (See W-pI.50.1:2-3 for one list of things that qualify as magic.) Even if we narrow the focus to physical health—which I will do from now on, since that is the focus of this question—the term "magic" refers to much more than just the pills and shots of conventional medicine. We are told that "all material means that you accept as remedies for bodily ills are restatements of magic principles" (T-2.IV.4:1). The implication of this sentence is that all physical means of treating bodily illness—including herbs, homeopathy, acupuncture, macrobiotic diets, exercise, colonics, aromatherapy, and any of hundreds of other forms—are also forms of magic.

But our investment in magic goes even deeper than that. The Course implies that *anything* we do physically to maintain the health of the body is a form of magic. It tells us that physical appetites were invented by the mind to maintain the ego (see T-4.II.7:5-9). Lesson 76 in the Workbook, "I am under no laws but God's," tells us that in truth we are not bound by the laws of medicine, nutrition, immunization, and bodily protection, among others. The Course also tells us, in this startling sentence, that when the mind is fully healed, the body will not be bound by any of the laws we normally think it must obey:

> The body's health is fully guaranteed, because it is not
> limited by time, by weather or fatigue, by food and drink,
> or any laws you made it serve before.   (W-pI.136.18:3)

This sentence is truly astounding. It tells us that if the mind were truly healed, then the body wouldn't age, wouldn't need protection against the elements, wouldn't need sleep, wouldn't need to eat or drink—in short, it really wouldn't need much of anything. The belief that it does need all these things is, by implication, a form of magic: a belief that we are under laws other than the laws of God, a belief that a power other than God can save (or harm) us.

Why am I bringing all this up? Because it is my impression that a number of Course students, once they read that physical medications are magic, try to give up taking physical medications as much as possible, in the mistaken belief that this is what the Course asks of them. They acknowledge that the Course permits physical medicine as a "compromise approach" (T-2.IV.4:6), but still believe that the way to give up our investment in magic—and thus the way to avoid ego reinforcement—is to make as little compromise in this area as possible. In other words, the way to avoid ego reinforcement is to physically give up all the different forms of magic that we use.

However, I really do not believe that this is what the Course is asking of us. Not only does this approach completely miss the point—

the mind is healed through miracles, not through physically giving up particular forms—but, given what we've seen, it is truly impossible for us to completely give up magic in our current, unhealed state. To really do this, we would have to give up much more than pills and shots; we would have to give up eating, drinking, and sleeping! None of us will be ready to give up these activities anytime soon. We do believe in the magic of physical laws, and as long as we do, we have to live by those laws. Therefore, the issue is not really *whether* we will use magic, but *how* we will use it. Which brings me to my next point.

Using magic does not necessarily reinforce the ego. It will only do so if we believe that magic is *truly healing*, and thus use it as a substitute for healing the mind.

We have seen that the ego made magic to reinforce itself. It is an ego trick designed to keep us away from true healing, the ego's substitute for healing the mind. Yet even though all this is true, magic is not *inherently* ego reinforcing; if it were, we'd be sunk, because as we saw above, using magic to a certain extent is unavoidable as long as our minds remain unhealed.

How, then, can we use magic in a way that does not reinforce the ego? By actively refusing (as best we can) to accept the lesson that the ego is trying to teach through magic: that we are separate from God, and that the physical realm is the source of sickness and healing. As long as we acknowledge to ourselves that magic does not truly heal and thus cannot be used as a replacement for healing the mind, we can use magic much more safely, because we have robbed it (at least to a certain extent) of its ego-reinforcing power.

In fact, the whole reason that the Course recommends a compromise approach concerning physical medicine is that this approach can help *prevent* ego reinforcement. In the passages which discuss this approach, we are given two main reasons for it:

1. Many sick people are afraid of mental healing (the miracle). Giving them a miracle would increase their fear, and thus prevent healing. Therefore, it is better to give them physical remedies to temporarily alleviate their symptoms, so that their fear will be reduced. (See T-2.IV.4.)

2. Miracle workers—people who give healing to others—can also sometimes be afraid of mental healing. When they are afraid, they will have a tendency to ascribe any healing they bring about to their own special powers rather than the power of God working through them. To avoid this, they should recommend physical remedies for their patients, because it is obvious that such physical remedies do not come from their own special powers. Miracle workers should take this approach as long as their fear of mental healing persists. (See T-2.V.2.)

Notice that in both cases, using physical remedies is an antidote to *fear*. And since fear is the emotion of the ego, this is just another way of saying that using physical remedies is an antidote to ego reinforcement. In the first case, physical remedies prevent the ego reinforcement that would happen as a result of the sick person's increased fear; in the second case, physical remedies prevent the ego reinforcement that would happen as a result of the miracle worker's fear (specifically, the ego reinforcement stemming from his belief that healing comes from his own special powers rather than from God). Thus in both cases, the magic of physical medicine serves as a means to avoid strengthening the ego. Used as a temporary alleviator of fear, it can help both the sick person and the miracle worker address their problems, at least on a surface level, until they are ready to fearlessly accept the miracle, the only source of true healing.

We can use magic in a way that does not reinforce the ego by practicing "conscious magic": taking physical remedies only to temporarily alleviate physical symptoms while we work on healing the mind.

The key to the effectiveness of the compromise approach above is the recognition that the magic being used *is* magic. Using magic blindly in the belief that it is truly healing does reinforce the ego; only by using magic with full awareness of what we are doing can we use it in a way that does not reinforce the ego. Which brings us to the idea of *conscious magic*.

"Conscious magic" is Robert Perry's term for this whole approach to magic. Practicing conscious magic means that as we take our physical remedies, we actively tell ourselves, "I am taking this medicine only for temporary relief of symptoms while I work on healing my mind. I understand that physical medicine is magic. I understand that the only true healing is the healing of the mind through miracles, and I am not using this medicine as a substitute for that." Most importantly, while we take our medications, we also do Course practices that will help us heal our minds. By focusing on healing our minds through Course practice, we consciously refuse to accept the lessons that the ego is trying to teach through magic, and we consciously refuse to allow magic to become a substitute for true healing. Therefore, the magic we use will be much less likely to deceive us.

Based on this approach, here is my advice for how to deal with any physical ailment in a way that is in harmony with the Course:

1. Go ahead and follow any treatment regimen you feel guided to pursue. There is no doubt that physical treatments can often relieve physical symptoms, and that is a good thing in the short term, even if it falls short of true healing. Of course, consult your health care professional(s) for advice on the best treatment options for your condition, and also ask the Holy Spirit for guidance about how best to proceed. Whatever physical remedies you use will be magic, but this is totally in line with the Course, as long as you also do the things described in the next point.

2. Practice conscious magic, as described above. As you follow your treatment regimen, do your Course practice, and remind yourself constantly that true healing is of the mind. Choose to see your physical treatment as a temporary expedient to help you alleviate symptoms as you work on healing your mind. If you do that, then taking physical medicine is much less likely to reinforce your ego. On the contrary, your conscious awareness of the fact that what you're doing is magic, combined with your commitment to mental healing, will tend to weaken the ego.

I personally believe that learning how to use magic consciously is a very important skill for Course students to develop. As I said above, the fact of the matter is that all of us use magic to some degree. We can't really escape magic until we are *very* advanced spiritually, so it is important for us to learn how to use it properly in the meantime. For some of us, that "temporary expedient" will be a medication that we will need to take for the rest of our lives, and even then totally physical healing may never come. We need to be okay with that. We do live by physical laws as long as we believe in them, but trying to give them up cold turkey is not the way for us rank beginners to undo that belief. Rather, the way to undo that belief is to begin realizing, through Course study and practice, that those laws are illusions, and to constantly remind ourselves of their illusory nature *even as we temporarily live by them.* This is what the practice of conscious magic allows us to do.

As we practice conscious magic, we should remind ourselves that our real goal is not physical healing but rather the peace of God, which will allow us to ultimately transcend bodily concerns entirely.

One more thing we can do to prevent magic from reinforcing the ego is to make sure that physical healing does not become our focus. Yes, magic can temporarily alleviate physical symptoms, and this is a desirable thing in the short term. Yes, "the miracle can heal all forms of sickness" (T-30.VI.7:1), and as we progress on the path, we will increasingly use the miracle instead of magic to truly heal physical illness, both in ourselves and in others. Yet we should always keep in mind that, from the Course's standpoint, the body is not "the proper aim of healing" (T-8.IX.1:5). The healing of the mind is what really matters. This healing brings with it the greatest gift of all—the peace of God—and finding this peace should always be our aim:

> *The peace of God is my one goal; the aim of all my living here, the end I seek, my purpose and my function and my life, while I abide where I am not at home.*
>
> (W-pI.205.1:3)

With this as our goal, bodily health will cease to be such a pressing issue. Oddly enough, however, giving up our concern about the body ultimately *ensures* its health. Sickness comes from our identification with the ego and the body; by not focusing on the body, we slowly but surely come to realize that we are *more* than the ego and the body. This growing recognition of our true Identity sets us on the path to the realization that will one day free us forever from the ego, the body, sickness, and every form of magic:

> *I am not a body. I am free.*
> *For I am still as God created me.*

(W-pI.rVI.In.3:3-5)

29

What does the Course have to say about depression? What causes it, and how can it be healed?

Short Answer

Speaking in general terms, depression is caused by our identification with the ego, which brings with it a sense of *deprivation*: the belief that due to forces beyond our control, we lack and cannot acquire the things we need to be happy. Depression is healed by choosing to renounce the ego and listen to the Holy Spirit, Who reminds us that our sense of deprivation comes only from our own decision to deprive *ourselves*, and restores to our awareness the fact that we already have everything we need to be happy.

☾☾☾

Note: Before going any further, I want to make clear that this Q & A should not be used as a substitute for getting treatment for depression. While getting "the blues" now and then is pretty normal for most of us, clinical depression is a serious illness that can have devastating consequences. Anyone whose depression is severe or lasts more than a few days should seek professional help. My intent with this Q & A is simply to draw out what the Course says about depression, so that we might be better able to work with depression from a Course perspective.

Depression is caused by our identification with the ego, which brings with it a sense of *deprivation*: the belief that due to forces beyond our control, we lack and cannot acquire the things we need to be happy.

The ego is the belief that we are separate from God and from our brothers, and "depression is an inevitable consequence of separation" (W-pI.41.1:2). Why? Because separation brings with it a sense of *deprivation*, and the belief that we are deprived is the root idea behind all forms of depression. This is the basic gist of what is perhaps the Course's most succinct definition of depression: "Depression comes from a sense of being deprived of something you want and do not have" (T-4.IV.3:2). To be deprived means not just to be without something, but to have something *taken* or *withheld* from us by someone or something beyond our control. (Webster's Dictionary says that to "deprive" is "to remove or withhold something from the enjoyment or possession of.")

Depression, then, comes from the belief that we are lacking something essential to our happiness, *and* that we have no real hope of acquiring that thing because we don't have the power to do so. We become depressed when the perceived source of our happiness seems forever beyond our reach. Depression is the emotional expression of the thought "I want it, but I cannot have it."

It is not difficult to see how identification with the ego leads to a sense of deprivation and depression. If we believe that we are limited, separate beings, we will inevitably feel deprived. In Heaven, we had everything we needed to be happy, but now it seems as if we have lost it all. We have seemingly fallen from limitless beings basking in the boundless joy of Heaven to needy little creatures who must fight a hostile world for every scrap of happiness we can find. What's more, it seems that there is absolutely no escape from our deprived condition; no matter how hard we search for happiness in this world and how much we seem to find it, in the end we are all doomed to suffer the ultimate deprivation: death. In such a condition, what could we be but depressed?

The sense of deprivation at the heart of our separate existence takes many forms in this world, and so depression takes many forms as well. The following are some of the specific causes of depression that the

Course mentions. (We will take a look at the specific remedies the Course offers further below.)

We become depressed because we are lonely, cut off from our Father, our brothers, and our true home.

Loneliness is one of the most profound deprivations we can experience, and one of the classic causes of depression. It can, of course, take the form of feeling cut off from family and friends in this world. But this form, sad as it is in itself, is an expression of a much sadder and deeper loneliness, an existential loneliness of cosmic proportions: By choosing to be separate, we have cut ourselves off from our *Heavenly* family, our one true home.

The Course speaks poignantly of this in a number of places. Lesson 182 of the Workbook tells us of the deep, unacknowledged sadness we feel as a result of our seeming exile in this world; the Christ in us is homesick, and yearns "to breathe again the holy air that fills His Father's house" (W-pI.182.5:4). The Text section "The Forgotten Song" paints a metaphorical picture of that home: a loving home shared with beloved brothers, in which is heard a Heavenly song so beautiful that it "would make you weep if you remembered how dear it was to you" (T-21.I.7:2). As much as we try to cover up our sadness by distracting ourselves with the "pleasures" of the world, something in us weeps at the terrible aloneness of our separate condition, and yearns to rejoin our Father and our brothers. As hard as we try to make a home for ourselves in this world, something in us just knows that we don't really belong here. Deep inside, we feel homeless, and so it is no surprise that we feel depressed.

We become depressed because we think we have lost our innocence, and can never get it back.

Believing that we have been deprived of our innocence is deeply depressing, for what hope of happiness is there if our very nature is black to the core? Yet identification with the ego must lead to guilt, because the belief that we have separated from God and our brothers leads inevitably to the belief that we are sinners: violators of God's law who have forever corrupted our pristine original nature. On earth, this can take the form of feeling guilty for the various "sins" we believe we have committed, the various ways in which we have hurt other people and ourselves.

Who among us does not yearn for lost innocence? I think this yearning runs very deep in the human psyche, and expresses itself in a number of ways. It is expressed in our desire to recapture what we see as the innocence of childhood. It is expressed in the perennial human belief that there was once a Golden Age in human history, a Paradise Lost which can perhaps be restored if only we return to the old ways. While the Course would not have us search for innocence in childhood or in a mythical Golden Age, it very much acknowledges the longing for innocence that motivates this search. The Course states plainly that innocence is our heart's desire: "It is for this you yearn" (W-pI.182.12:2). The belief that we have lost our innocence is behind every tear we have ever shed, for "who could weep but for his innocence?" (P-2.IV.1:7).

We become depressed because we are trying to accomplish the impossible.

As much as we lament our seeming separation from God and our brothers, the fact is that we lack the ability to really do this. At first glance, this seems like good news, and ultimately it is. However, as long as we identify with the ego, this very lack is, ironically, yet another source of depression. The ego offers us a curriculum of separation, but since we cannot really *be* separate, the ego's curriculum cannot really be learned. We are thus trying to accomplish the impossible, and "being faced with an impossible learning situation is the most depressing thing in the world" (T-8.VII.8:3). We are indissolubly joined beings diligently trying to learn how to be separate, which is kind of like a man diligently trying to learn how to get pregnant. As long as we persist in this goal, we will feel deprived, because we are placing our hope of happiness in something we can never have. We will be frustrated and depressed, because we've set ourselves up for failure.

We become depressed because we are confused, divided between conflicting goals.

This point follows from the previous one. Precisely because we lack the ability to really separate from God and our brothers, a part of our minds is forever on the side of union with God and our brothers. Thus whenever we identify with the ego, we inevitably set up a conflict between the part of our minds that is for God, and the illusory

Greg Mackie

part that is against Him. In everyday life, we can see this conflict at work in the constant tension between our desire for intimacy (joining with others) and our desire for autonomy (being separate from others). Our minds are split between two mutually irreconcilable goals, and in such a state, peace of mind is impossible:

> No one can serve contradicting goals and serve them well.
> Nor can he function without deep distress and great depression. (W-pII.257.1:2-3)

We want separation and union at the same time, and we can't possibly have both. To have one is to be deprived of the other. We are caught between the proverbial rock and a hard place. How could we possibly find happiness in such a state?

We become depressed because we feel inadequate and powerless, unable to solve our problems and find happiness in this world.

Just as we lack the ability to truly separate from God, so we lack the ability to solve the myriad problems that seem to confront us in the world. This is a very serious lack in our eyes, for once we identify with the ego, we place ourselves in a position where we seemingly must wrest our happiness from the outside world. Happiness, we believe, lies in solving the various problems the world confronts us with, and acquiring the things we need to support our separate existence. Yet the longer we try to win at this game, the more it begins to dawn on us that we are doomed to failure:

> No one could solve all the problems the world appears to hold. They seem to be on so many levels, in such varying forms and with such varied content, that they confront you with an impossible situation. Dismay and depression are inevitable as you regard them.
> (W-pI.79.5:1-3)

Who among us hasn't felt this dismay in the face of the tangled web of problems we have to deal with in this crazy world? We hope to solve them so that we can find some measure of peace and happiness, but once again, we are trying to accomplish the impossible. This is such a depressing realization that we work very hard to convince ourselves otherwise. We try to "empower" ourselves through acquiring various tools and abilities that we think will make us better able to "win the game of life." We grasp for one external thing after another—things that the Course calls "idols"—hoping that even though the last ten thousand things we tried didn't work, this new thing just might do the trick. Yet again and again, our idols disappoint us; as the Course says, we "weep each time an idol falls" (T-29.VII.1:2). One more idol has not given the happiness it promised, and so we run off to seek another.

Eventually, we begin to realize that nothing in this world can really provide the happiness we seek. There really is no way to win this game. And while this realization can actually be a valuable turning point on our road to God (see T-31.IV.4-6), the Course also acknowledges that seeing the hopelessness of the world can throw us into a very dark pit of depression. It goes so far as to say that "men have died on seeing this" (T-31.IV.3:4)—a reference, I believe, to suicide. Convinced of the futility of finding happiness in the world, some have chosen the ultimate deprivation of death. This is a cruel irony, since the Course tells us that death itself "is the one idea which underlies all feelings that are not supremely happy" (W-pI.167.2:4).

We become depressed because we think we have no rewarding function to fulfill.

One of the major causes of depression is a lack of meaning in our lives. I believe that all of us have a deep yearning to make a difference, to be of service, to dedicate our lives to a goal that is larger and more meaningful than the mere satisfaction of personal needs. In short, we need a meaningful *function*. Without such a function, all we have is the depressing game of idol chasing that was discussed in the last point.

The Course is clear that we cannot be happy unless we have a meaningful function to fulfill. In Heaven, our function is creation, and when we chose to identify with the ego, we rejected that function, which led to depression: "You are sad because you are not fulfilling your function as co-creator with God" (T-7.VI.13:1). Now that we're (seemingly) on earth, it seems that we don't have any function at all besides looking out for number one, which just makes us feel more sad, more useless, and more alone: "The lonely ones are those who see no function in the world for them to fill; no place where they are needed, and no aim which only they can perfectly fulfill" (T-25.VI.3:6). In the end, self-serving is just plain unsatisfying; we need something more if we are to find real happiness on earth.

If self-serving is so unsatisfying, then what function *would* bring us happiness on earth? Most Course students can probably guess the answer, I am sure, but I will save that for my next point. It is time, at last, to end our gloomy tour through the causes of depression, and turn to the Course's means of healing the sense of deprivation at the heart of all our sadness.

Depression is healed by choosing to renounce the ego and listen to the Holy Spirit, Who reminds us that our sense of deprivation comes only from our own decision to deprive *ourselves*, and restores to our awareness the fact that we already have everything we need to be happy.

If choosing to identify with the ego makes us feel deprived and thus depressed, then the obvious remedy for depression is to stop identifying with the ego. But of course, we can't do this without help, and so we must turn to the Holy Spirit, Who speaks for our true Self. And one of the most crucial lessons the Holy Spirit teaches us is the true nature of our seeming deprivation. As I mentioned above, we believe that to be deprived means to have something taken or withheld from us by someone or something beyond our control. But the Holy Spirit teaches that this is pure illusion. The truth is that, however much it may appear otherwise, we've been in control all along:

> *Only you can deprive yourself of anything.* Do not oppose this realization, for it is truly the beginning of the dawn of light. Remember also that the denial of this simple fact takes many forms, and these you must learn to recognize and to oppose steadfastly, without exception.
> (T-11.IV.4:1-3)

This is a radical teaching, one that completely pulls the rug out from under our sense of deprivation. Obviously, this is not a realization that we are going to get overnight, but equally obviously, it is one that the Course really wants us to practice diligently. The author of the Course clearly wants us to learn that we ourselves have made our seeming deprivation, and so we ourselves have "made the god of depression" (T-10.V.4:2). As difficult as this may be to swallow at first, it is ultimately wonderful news, for if we made our deprivation and depression, then we have the power to *unmake* it—or, better, to allow the Holy Spirit to unmake it.

This is exactly what the Holy Spirit does, whenever we turn to Him for help. And just as our depression takes many specific forms, so the Holy Spirit has a specific remedy for each of those forms. Whatever form our depression takes, He heals it by giving us the thing we seem to be deprived of, thus proving that we are not really deprived of it. Let's see how He does this with each of the specific causes of depression discussed above:

He heals our loneliness for our Heavenly family by reminding us that we are not really living in exile: "You travel but in dreams, while safe at home" (T-13.VII.17:7). Through the holy instant, He offers us the opportunity to temporarily step away from our seeming exile, to "be still an instant and go home" (W-pI.182.Heading). Through teaching us forgiveness, He teaches us that we are forever one with our Father and all our brothers: "Forgiveness lets me know that minds are joined" (W-pII.336.Heading).

He heals our sense of lost innocence by offering us the gift of forgiveness, which proves that no sin has ever occurred (all of our seeming "sins" are merely mistakes), and thus demonstrates that "you have not lost your innocence" (W-pI.182.12:1-2).

He heals our frustration at trying to achieve an impossible goal by giving us an achievable goal. He does this by replacing the ego's curriculum of separation with His "curriculum of joy" (T-8.VII.8:5): a curriculum of forgiveness and miracles, with the goal of learning who we really are. Not only *can* we attain the goal of His curriculum— attaining it is an absolute certainty.

He heals the confusion caused by our conflicting goals by reminding us that "joy is unified purpose" (T-8.VII.15:1). He unifies our minds by overlooking the ego's goals and replacing them with His goal: forgiveness, healing, salvation, and the peace of God.

He heals our sense of powerlessness in dealing with the problems of the world by giving us the one thing that will solve all of them: the miracle, which releases us from our "false sense of isolation, deprivation, and lack" (T-1.I.42:1). He gives us His perfect guidance, which tells us exactly what to think, say, and do in every situation that confronts us. "Under His guidance [we] will travel light and journey lightly" (T-13.VII.13:4), free of the burden of having to solve by ourselves the problems that seem to oppress us. The fact that He solves the problems of the world so easily ultimately teaches us that these problems are meaningless illusions that have no effect on the joyous truth of who we really are. Therefore, they have no power to deprive us of our happiness.

Finally, He heals our belief that we have no rewarding function to fulfill by giving us the most meaningful and fulfilling function we can have on earth. This function is—you guessed it—forgiveness, our "function as the light of the world" (W-pI.62.Heading). He trains us to become miracle workers, extenders of forgiveness and salvation to our brothers in need. He gives us our special function, the particular form in which we extend forgiveness in the world, a form tailored to our particular strengths and special needs (see T-25.VII.7:1-3 and W-pI.154.2). Not only will fulfilling this function make us happy, but in truth our function *is* to be happy (see W-pI.64.4:2). This is the means by which we are ultimately restored to our Heavenly function of creation.

Thus the Holy Spirit heals our depression by healing the sense of deprivation at the root of our depression. He restores to us the things that we have deprived ourselves of. In the light of His teaching, the thought "I want it, but I cannot have it"—the root thought behind depression in all its forms—is transformed into "What I *really* want, I *can* have," and finally into "What I *really* want, I *already* have." For in the end, the Holy Spirit restores to our awareness the joyful truth that "*God has given [us] everything*" (T-4.III.9:2). How can we be deprived of anything if we have everything? And if we realize we cannot be deprived of anything, how can we be depressed? "What can be more joyous than to perceive we are deprived of nothing?" (T-15.XI.8:3).

Conclusion

Depression is a universal phenomenon in this world, however unacknowledged it may be. As we have seen, it is not confined to those whom the world diagnoses as "clinically depressed," but rather is the inevitable experience of anyone who identifies with the ego, which means virtually all of us. That's the bad news.

But the good news is that there is hope. We have the power to stop depriving ourselves, and we have the Help we need to do so. The Holy Spirit stands ready to restore the joy that we have denied ourselves, awaiting only our invitation. Let us extend that invitation to Him, and allow Him to shine away our depression with the joyous light of truth. This may not happen right away; our sadness runs deep, and letting it go will likely be a long process for most of us. But the Course's promise is that however long it takes, the day will come when the light of truth shines our darkness away. No matter how dark things seem to be, "A happy outcome to all things is sure" (W-pII.292.Heading).

Jesus and Religion

30

The *Psychotherapy* supplement (P-2.II.2) speaks out strongly against formal religion. What specifically is it referring to when it mentions formal religion, how is formal religion "an ego attempt to reconcile the irreconcilable" (P-2.II.2:3), and what is the alternative to formal religion?

Short Answer

Formal religion is any kind of religion that aims to reach God through adhering to "proper" forms, such as prescribed beliefs, rituals, or behavioral ethics. This is "an ego attempt to reconcile the irreconcilable" because true religion is concerned with *content* (experience), not form, and thus formal religion is diametrically opposed to the true goal of religion. True religion, the alternative to formal religion, consists of 1) teaching and learning forgiveness, and 2) joining with another person in a truly common goal, even if that goal is not overtly religious. Forgiveness and joining bring about the experience of God at which all true religion aims.

ʊʊʊ

Note: The brief discussion of formal religion in the *Psychotherapy* supplement occurs in the context of a section dealing with the relationship between religion and psychotherapy (P-2.II). It is an absolutely fascinating section that says some striking things about religion, psychotherapy, and the true nature of healing. I recommend reading it in its entirety.

Formal religion is any kind of religion that aims to reach God through adhering to "proper" forms, such as prescribed beliefs, rituals, or behavioral ethics.

What is formal religion? While the section of *Psychotherapy* we are examining never gives an exact definition of formal religion, I think what Jesus has in mind becomes fairly obvious if we think about the meaning of the word "formal." Webster's Dictionary defines "formal" as, among other things, "marked by form or ceremony" and "observant of conventional requirements of behavior, procedure, etc." Formal religion, then, is religion that is "marked by form"—more specifically, religion that focuses on being observant of the proper forms as the means to reach God. Formal religion says that if only we affirm the right creeds, perform the proper rituals, and/or conform our behavior to the correct moral standards, we will sanctify ourselves in the eyes of God (or will be in proper alignment with the Absolute, by whatever name). Indeed, these kinds of things usually come immediately to mind when we hear the word "religion." They are part of the very definition of religion, as conventionally understood.

We can see examples of the importance of adhering to proper forms in many of the world's religions. Many religions have some sort of formal creed, statement of principles, or sacred scripture that followers are urged (or required) to believe in. Most every religion has some sort of ritual observance associated with it, such as the sacraments of Christianity, the five daily prayers of Islam, the elaborate rituals of Tibetan Buddhism, and the Sun Dance of Native Americans. Finally, virtually every religion has a moral code, such as the Ten Commandments of Judaism and Christianity, the *Sharia* (religious law) of Islam, the precepts of Buddhism, and the *Yamas* and *Niyamas* (restraints and observances) of Raja Yoga.

The term "formal religion" thus encompasses a great deal of the teachings and practices of most of the world's religions. But before I go on, I want to make very clear that the *Psychotherapy* supplement's indictment of formal religion does not mean that the forms practiced by the world's religions are inherently egoic blocks to salvation. It is not my intention here to trash the world's religions, and that is certainly not the intention of the author of the Course, who says that teachers of God "come from all religions and from no religion" (M-1.2:2). I believe that most of the forms discussed above (and many more) *can* be used in the service of what the *Psychotherapy* supplement calls "true religion" (P-2.II.7:1), if they are used in the right spirit. I will expand on that point below.

This is "an ego attempt to reconcile the irreconcilable" because true religion is concerned with *content* (experience), not form, and thus formal religion is diametrically opposed to the true goal of religion.

Formal religion is simply a particular expression of one of the ego's basic laws: *Form is everything*. In the ego's eyes, content—the real meaning or intention of a thought, word, or deed, regardless of the form in which it is expressed—is irrelevant. If we can just get our ducks lined up in a row, says the ego, then all is well: "If the form is acceptable the content must be" (T-14.X.8:2).

But the Holy Spirit, as usual, completely reverses the ego's law. To the Holy Spirit, *content* is everything. Thus in His eyes, true religion aims at content—specifically, the *experience* of God or truth (P-2.II.2:4)—not adherence to proper forms. Just getting the forms right while disregarding the actual mental content behind them does not lead to the experience of God; rather, it leads to a hollow religion devoid of any meaningful content, which is just the kind of religion the ego wants. Religion becomes, to borrow a few more definitions of the word "formal" from Webster's Dictionary, "a matter of form only; perfunctory," a religion marked by "excessive emphasis on empty form."

Now we can see why the *Psychotherapy* supplement claims that the words "formal" and "religion" are fundamentally at odds with one another (P-2.II.2:2). The word "formal" refers to form that is devoid of meaningful content, while the word "religion," in its true sense, refers to the *experience* of meaningful content. Therefore, the words "formal" and "religion" are mutually irreconcilable. The very term "formal religion" is a meaningless oxymoron. Formal religion, then, is not really religion at all.

Yet all religions and paths of awakening, including the Course, use forms. This is unavoidable, since we live in a world of form. How, then, can we use the forms of our chosen path in a truly helpful way, a way that avoids the error of formal religion? In my mind, the crucial issue here is how we *perceive* those forms. If we see those forms as having meaningful content in and of themselves, we will tend to think that just doing the forms will somehow magically deliver the experience of God, regardless of the content of our minds. If we think this way, then we are falling into the trap of formal religion. This trap can take some very subtle forms, and I think it is very easy for even those with the best of intentions to fall into it. I know I have at times.

Fortunately, there is another way to perceive those forms. If we see them instead as neutral, inherently meaningless things that can at best be used as temporary means for communicating the content of the experience of God to our minds, then they can be used in the service of true religion. As long as we focus on experiencing true content, then whatever forms we use to do that can serve us well. We avoid the trap of formal religion by remembering that it is the content of our minds that matters most, not the forms used to express that content.

True religion, the alternative to formal religion, consists of 1) teaching and learning forgiveness, and 2) joining with another person in a truly common goal, even if that goal is not overtly religious.

I said above that true religion aims at the experience of God or truth. Now we see the particular vehicle that carries us to that experience, a vehicle that has two closely related aspects, as noted above: 1) forgiveness, and 2) joining in a common goal (what the Course calls a holy relationship). Let's look at each of these aspects in turn.

The importance of forgiveness—primarily, forgiving others—can hardly be overstated. The Course expresses in no uncertain terms the vital role forgiveness plays in the spiritual journey: "The way to God is through forgiveness here. There is no other way" (W-pII.256.1:1-2). In the section of *Psychotherapy* we are examining, the paragraph immediately following the discussion of formal religion (P-2.II.3) reiterates this idea that forgiveness is *the* way to awaken to our true Heavenly home, and adds this chilling thought: "The world has marshalled all its forces against this one awareness, for in it lies the ending of the world and all it stands for" (P-2.II.3:5).

This last line really packs a wallop. It presents the shocking idea that the world we live in is specifically designed to prevent us from seeing that unforgiveness is the only problem, and forgiveness the only solution. It suggests that all the things of the ego's world—including formal religion—serve the aim of keeping us from finding the key that will unlock the prison cell of the world and set us free. I think we have to admit that the world has been very successful at doing this. Outside of the Course or things influenced by the Course, have you ever heard the idea that *forgiveness alone* is what awakens us to God? I know I haven't. It seems that the world's forces are doing an excellent job of keeping this idea under wraps.

Forgiveness, of course, can occur in any relationship. But one kind of relationship in particular is especially fertile ground for forgiveness, and this relationship is the second aspect of true religion: the holy relationship, a relationship in which two people join in a truly common goal. Again and again, the *Psychotherapy* supplement—and indeed, all of the Course material—emphasizes the crucial role this kind of relationship plays in the process of salvation. Our section of *Psychotherapy*, in fact, declares that such a relationship is an absolute prerequisite for awakening (see P-2.II.8).

This may seem to contradict the idea presented above that forgiveness is the only requirement for awakening to God. But in truth, forgiveness and joining in a common goal are simply two aspects of a single process. This process is the process of accepting the Atonement: the process of learning that we are not separate from one another, but in fact share a common Identity. Both forgiveness and joining affirm a shared Identity, and it doesn't really matter which seems to come first. Any time forgiveness is given and received, a joining will take place; any time a joining takes place, forgiveness will be given and received. The two aspects—forgiveness and joining—occur together.

What forms can a relationship between two people joined in a common goal take? Certainly there are innumerable forms. The goal itself can be anything, as long as it can be *truly* shared, both by the two people involved in the relationship and with the entire Sonship. (Thus, goals such as robbing a bank or killing someone cannot be truly shared goals.)

But though the forms such a relationship can take are many, both the *Psychotherapy* supplement and the Course material in general place a special emphasis on one particular form: the relationship between *teacher and pupil* (or, in the context of psychotherapy, therapist and patient). At one point in our section of *Psychotherapy*, Jesus says bluntly that some forms that religion can take are essentially worthless if our goal is truly to reach God. But immediately after he says that, he tells us of the one thing that, regardless of the particular form it takes, will absolutely guarantee that we reach God: "If pupil and teacher join in sharing one goal, God will enter into their relationship because He has been invited to come in" (P-2.II.5:3).

This is a truly amazing statement. What it suggests to me is that the wellspring of true religion is not beliefs, rituals, ethics, physical edifices, holy places, institutions, clerical hierarchies, or any of the other external trappings we normally associate with religion. Rather, the wellspring of true religion is *the relationship between the teacher of a path of awakening and his or her pupil*. This relationship is the place in which both forgiveness and joining, the twin aspects of true religion, are born. This relationship is and has always been the true temple of God at the heart of every religion, whatever that religion's outward forms. This relationship is the true bringer of enlightenment, the beacon of salvation that has shone in and through all the great religions of the world.

But not just in and through great religions. For our section of *Psychotherapy* tells us that *any* relationship marked by forgiveness and joining will awaken us to God, even if the goal is not overtly religious at all. Overt reference to "God" or "spiritual" ideas is not essential to the process. All that a teacher of God needs to do is "teach forgiveness rather than condemnation" (P-2.II.1:2), and join with another person in a common goal (as we saw in P-2.II.5:3). In other words, he must teach and learn forgiveness and joining, the twin aspects of true religion that we've discussed. If he does this, both he and his pupil are assured of finding the way to God.

And as we've seen, a relationship in which forgiveness and joining occur can take many forms. It can be a relationship between a spiritual teacher and his pupil. But it can just as easily be, as our section of *Psychotherapy* emphasizes, a relationship between a psychotherapist and her patient. It can be any relationship in which one person's call for help is answered by another person's offer of help, as when Helen Schucman agreed to help Bill Thetford find "another way." Or it can simply be any relationship in which two people have come together in a shared purpose, even if that shared purpose is not explicitly acknowledged. Whatever form the relationship takes, what makes it a holy expression of true religion is that it has the mental content of forgiveness and joining. Expressed another way, this relationship exemplifies the reversal of the ego dictum quoted above (T-14.X.8:2), a reversal that can be expressed as follows: If the content is acceptable, the form must be.

Forgiveness and joining bring about the experience of God at which all true religion aims.

The bottom line is that if we take what Jesus is saying here seriously, we are faced with a radical redefinition of what constitutes religion. In his eyes, anything that facilitates the experience of God through forgiveness and joining is true religion, even if it is not overtly religious; conversely, anything that doesn't facilitate this is *not* true religion, even if it *is* overtly religious. Those who forgive and join, even in non-religious contexts, "can succeed where many who believe they have found God will fail" (P-2.II.7:6).

But of course, even those who fail will only do so temporarily. Eventually, all of us will leave the emptiness of formal religion behind and set out on the path of true religion, whatever form that takes for us. And "once this journey is begun the end is certain" (C-Ep.1:1). In the end, all of us will forgive, all of us will join in holy relationship with one another, and all of us will experience the memory of God that is the goal of all true religion.

31

Why does Jesus repeatedly ask us in the Course to forgive him? To me, he is the epitome of innocence and perfect love, so why do I need to forgive him?

Short Answer

Jesus asks us to forgive him because how we see him determines how we see the entire Sonship, including ourselves. We need to forgive him because, while we have traditionally seen him as a symbol of innocence and love, we have also seen him as a symbol of sin. Forgiving the sins we have projected onto Jesus frees us to fully accept his love.

ᛣᛣᛣ

Jesus asks us to forgive him because how we see him determines how we see the entire Sonship, including ourselves.

This is simply a specific application of a basic Course principle: How we see any of our brothers determines how we see them all. This must be so, since the Sonship is one. Thus when we forgive Jesus, we forgive the rest of our brothers as well. The reverse is also true: When we forgive any of our brothers, we forgive Jesus as well. This idea is the basis for an unusual means of forgiving our brothers given in Chapter 19 of the Text:

> Let me be to you the symbol of the end of guilt, and
> look upon your brother as you would look on me. Forgive
> me all the sins you think the Son of God committed.
> (T-19.IV(B).6:1-2)

Amazingly, we can forgive Jesus for all the rotten things we think other people have done to us. We can forgive Jesus for that snide remark our spouse made, for all the things our parents did to ruin our childhood, even for what Hitler did to the Jews.

How does this work? The underlying idea here, I think, is that most of us see Jesus as a symbol of innocence (though not without reservation, as we will see below). To those of us who grew up in a Judeo-Christian culture, he *is* the innocent, holy Son of God; we are steeped in a biblical heritage which tells us that "in him is no sin" (1 John 3:5). Because we already see him as innocent, it is easier to forgive him than it is to forgive our more "guilty" brothers. Thus he can serve as a kind of "stand in" for the people who have seemingly sinned against us. Forgiving him for the sins our brothers have seemingly committed allows his innocence and holiness to rub off on them. Because the Sonship is one, if we truly see Jesus' innocence, we will also see the innocence of those who have "sinned" against us.

And because the Sonship is one, forgiving Jesus can even help us forgive *ourselves*:

> I ask for your forgiveness, for if you are guilty, so must I
> be. But if I surmounted guilt and overcame the world, you
> were with me.　　　　　　　　　　　(T-19.IV(B).6:4-5)

If we see ourselves as sinners, we will see Jesus as a sinner too. Thus we need to forgive him. But he reminds us here that just as our perception of ourselves as sinners will project onto him, so will our perception of him as innocent extend to us, if we allow it. By choosing to forgive him and fully accept the fact that he released the world from the illusion of sin forever, we will find that we ourselves share in his innocence.

Both of the above passages draw upon our traditional image of Jesus as the innocent Son of God. Indeed, Jesus has become the single most powerful symbol in our culture (and perhaps the entire world) for the Son of God, and this, I believe, is the key to understanding why he asks us to forgive him. The very goal of the Course is to help us forgive the Son of God. Of course, we can do this by forgiving any of our brothers, since all of us are equal parts of the unified Sonship. Yet even though the Course expands the term "Son of God" to include all of us, Jesus is still the prime exemplar of the Son of God for many of us. As the Course says, "The whole relationship of the Son to the Father lies in him" (M-23.3:3). He is our primary image of God, as well as our primary image of the Son's relationship with God. Thus, how we see him will have a particularly powerful impact on how we see God and the entire Sonship, including ourselves. Forgiving Jesus, then, can be a particularly effective means of forgiving the Sonship as a whole.

We need to forgive Jesus because, while we have traditionally seen him as a symbol of innocence and love, we have also seen him as a symbol of sin.

In the previous point, we saw how we can draw upon our traditional image of Jesus as the innocent Son of God to help us forgive all of our brothers and ourselves. But while we do see Jesus as innocent, this is not a complete picture of all that Jesus symbolizes to us. As symbol of the Son of God, Jesus carries all of the baggage we have associated with the Son of God, both positive and negative. And so, given the fact that the ego has gotten its two cents in concerning Jesus, he has unfortunately become to us not only a symbol of innocence, but also a symbol of *sin*.

How has Jesus become a symbol of sin? For starters, our traditional image of Jesus depicts him as such, in several ways. First, he is seen as inherently superior to us and separate from us; innocence is an attribute that belongs to him alone, while we who stand below him are hopeless sinners in comparison. Second, he is seen as a punitive judge who justly sends us to hell for our sins if we are unrepentant. Finally, he is seen as the innocent Lamb of God who died on the cross for our sins.

Of course, this last image is seen by Christian tradition as a symbol of *release* from sin, but in the Course's view, this image simply cements the reality of sin more firmly into place. The very "fact" that Jesus had to be punished for our sins "proves" that our sins are dreadfully real: "What must be punished, must be true" (T-19.III.2:5). The whole idea of atonement through sacrificial death is pure ego, as the following passage makes clear:

I became the symbol of your sin, and so I had to die instead of you. To the ego sin means death, and so atonement is achieved through murder. Salvation is looked upon as a way by which the Son of God was killed instead of you.   (T-19.IV(A)17:2-4)

Thus, while we may see Jesus himself as innocent, our traditional image of him confirms from several angles the ego's gloomy verdict that *we* are sinners. Seen in this way, the innocent Jesus is an ever-present reminder of just how guilty and black with sin the rest of us really are—he is the symbol of our sin. It is not difficult to see that this must have a huge effect on our relationship with him. Even though many of us profess to love him, if all Jesus does is remind us of how vile and sinful we are, won't we feel subtly (or not so subtly) attacked by him? If we feel attacked by him can we really see him as innocent? And if we can't really see him as innocent, is it possible, deep down, to really love him?

Yet there is an even deeper sense in which Jesus is a symbol of sin. We have seen how Jesus' innocence, viewed through the ego's eyes, condemns us all as sinners in comparison with him. But on a deeper level of the ego's thought system, Jesus' innocence makes *him* the ultimate sinner; in the ego's upside-down view of things, his very innocence is seen as the greatest of sins.

Why does the ego see his innocence this way? Because "to the ego, *the guiltless are guilty*" (T-13.II.4:2). This idea sounds very bizarre, but it is quite consistent with the ego's insane attempt to usurp God's throne and totally reverse His laws. The ego has set itself up as the god of this world, and its reign depends entirely on maintaining sin and guilt. Real innocence is thus a huge threat to the ego's rule, a major violation of its upside-down laws. Therefore, from the ego's perspective, innocence is the ultimate crime. The inevitable result of this twisted point of view is that for anyone who identifies with the ego, Jesus—the innocent Son of God—is Public Enemy Number One. According to the Course, the real underlying motivation of those who crucified Jesus was to punish him for the "crime" of being innocent:

When [the ego] was confronted with the real guiltlessness of God's Son [in Jesus] it did attempt to kill him, and the reason it gave was that guiltlessness is blasphemous to

God. To the ego, the *ego* is God, and guiltlessness must be interpreted as the final guilt that fully justifies murder.

(T-13.II.6:2-3)

Thus the very proof of the unreality of sin—the innocence of God's Son, exemplified in Jesus—became the ultimate proof of sin's reality. In the ego's insane kingdom, Jesus' very innocence was and is the ultimate symbol of sin.

The bottom line in all this is that there are many ways in which we see Jesus as a symbol of sin, and as I said above, this cannot help but have an impact on our relationship with him. I think it's safe to say that, whatever surface feelings we may have about Jesus, deep down many of us may carry a lot of fear, anger, and resentment toward him. Even those of us who have consciously given up the traditional images of him may still bear the wounds of those traditional images within us. Unconsciously driven by these images, we try not to dwell on his virtues, so that we can avoid the bitter reminder of just how unworthy we are compared to him. We recoil from his judgment, fearful that he will condemn us. We push away any thought that he might be a savior to us, not wanting to be reminded of his bloody sacrifice, which hammers home just how horribly guilty we really are. And even deeper down, the ego in us hates him for his very innocence, seeing it as the ultimate threat that must be blotted out at all costs.

In short, we have a lot to forgive Jesus for. In truth, he has not committed any sin, just as none of our brothers has committed any sin. But we have projected our own seeming sins onto him, and so we see him as a fearful witness to the reality of those sins. And it is this fearful image of him, this false god we have made of him, that must be forgiven:

> Some bitter idols have been made of him [Jesus] who would be only brother to the world. Forgive him your illusions, and behold how dear a brother he would be to you.
>
> (C-5.5:7-8)

We must choose what Jesus will symbolize to us: sin or innocence. Jesus wants us to forgive him because forgiveness is the choice to see him as innocent, and how we see him determines how we see the entire Sonship, including ourselves. Thus he asks us, "Would you see in me the symbol of guilt or of the end of guilt, remembering that what I signify to you you see within yourself?" (T-19.IV(B).6:6).

How do we forgive Jesus?

One way to forgive Jesus, suggested above, is to forgive someone else. At one point, Jesus even tells us that our forgiveness of our brother is evidence that we have forgiven him (Jesus):

> Forgive me, then, today. And you will know you have forgiven me if you behold your brother in the light of holiness. He cannot be less holy than can I, and you can not be holier than he. (W-pII.288.2:1-3)

The last line of this passage is a beautiful statement of our absolute equality, a real contrast with the inequality inherent in the traditional view of Jesus discussed above. When we forgive, we recognize that all of us—Jesus, our brothers, ourselves—are equally holy, equally innocent Sons of God.

Of course, we can also forgive Jesus directly, and we forgive him the same way we forgive anyone else: By withdrawing the sins we have projected onto him and asking the Holy Spirit to reveal to us our savior, the Christ in him. Applying to himself the Course's instruction to "forgive the Son of God for what he did not do" (T-17.III.1:5), Jesus says, "Forgive me your illusions, and release me from punishment for what I have not done" (T-19.IV(B).8:1). Let's take a moment to do that right now, using the following forgiveness exercise:

1. Call to mind your current image of Jesus. Visualize his appearance, whatever that might be to you. Allow whatever attributes you associate with him to come to mind. Notice any emotions that arise as you think of him. Look especially for any painful memories, ideas, or emotions you associate with him, and any hidden resentments you might have against him. These may be hard to find if you normally see Jesus as innocent and loving, but look for them with as much open-mindedness as you can muster. See also if you can get in touch with that part of your mind that condemns him for his very innocence. In this process, be gentle. Don't strain to dig up things from deep within your mind, but simply allow whatever is there right now to surface.

Greg Mackie

2. Once you have your current image of Jesus in mind, ask the Holy Spirit for a new vision of Jesus as the Christ, your savior. To do this, you might use a line from the Course, such as "Let me behold my savior in this one" (W-pI.78.7:3). Forgive Jesus for all of the sins you have seen in him, and ask that the innocent Son of God be revealed to you in all his glory. Allow whatever dark images you have of Jesus to be shined away by the light of the Christ in him.

3. Finally, invite Jesus himself to shine salvation into your mind. Again, you might use a line from the Course to do this, such as "Give me your blessing, holy Son of God" (W-pI.161.11:7). See him offering you salvation, in whatever way appeals to you. Invite him to join with you. Give thanks that the bitter idols you have made of him have been replaced by the recognition of him as your beloved elder brother, who yearns only to share his love with you. Join with him, and accept that love now.

I hope this exercise has allowed you to get in touch with and chip away at some of the unforgiveness you may have toward Jesus. I hope that it allows you to catch a glimpse of the joy that comes as a result of joining with him. I recommend doing it often, especially if you have a lot of negative memories or emotions associated with Jesus or traditional churches. A final note: In addition to the forgiveness exercise we've just completed, I also recommend doing the practice discussed earlier: Forgiving Jesus for the sins that other people have committed. I've tried this out myself, and it really works.

Forgiving the sins we have projected onto Jesus frees us to fully accept his love.

This is one of the greatest benefits of forgiving Jesus, for as hard as this may be to believe, the root cause of our unforgiveness of Jesus is our *fear of his love*. Yes, on one level our fear of Jesus is based on our traditional images of him as superior being, punitive judge, and sacrificial lamb. But on a deeper level, as we saw above, we identify with the ego's fear of his very innocence, its terror in the face of the purity of his love. The dark images of Jesus that cause us to recoil from him are simply things that the ego gives us as a rationale for recoiling from him, thus keeping us away from his love. In his earthly lifetime, those who feared his love crucified him; in our time, we who fear his love "crucify" him simply by trying to forget about him, by pushing him out of our minds and out of our lives.

But when we withdraw the ego's dark projections from Jesus by forgiving him, we open our minds to receive his love without reservation. As a passage I quoted earlier said, we discover "how dear a brother he would be to [us]." We allow him to be the elder brother, helper, and savior that he so yearns to be for us. He asks us to forgive him only so that he can fully share his love with us, and give us the help we need to awaken to our Father once again:

> Brother, forgive me now. I come to you to take you home with me. And as we go, the world goes with us on our way to God. (W-pII.342.2:1-3)

Conclusion

For some of us, forgiving Jesus may seem easy, so easy that we can use our vision of his innocence to forgive the brothers who seem less innocent in our sight. For others, forgiving Jesus may require confronting our deepest wounds and our greatest fears. Yet the good news is that whatever our current feelings about Jesus, in truth our forgiveness of him is already accomplished; he assures us, "You *have* forgiven me" (T-20.II.6:2). In the deepest part of our minds the entire Sonship, including Jesus, has already been forgiven, and all we need do is recognize that fact. This recognition is all it takes to invite Jesus' boundless love into our hearts.

32

When Jesus was resurrected, were we resurrected with him? If so, then why do we still experience ourselves as living in a dream of separation?

Short Answer

When Jesus was resurrected, the entire Sonship was resurrected with him. We still experience ourselves as living in a dream of separation because we have refused to *accept* the fact that we have been resurrected along with Jesus, and that therefore the dream is over. We come to accept this fact by *joining* in Jesus' resurrection through forgiving our brothers.

ᚉᚉᚉ

When Jesus was resurrected, the entire Sonship was resurrected with him.

The Course is pretty clear that when Jesus was resurrected two thousand years ago, he didn't go alone. As mind-boggling as this idea may be, the Course's teaching is that when Jesus arose, the entire Sonship went with him: "You arose with him when he began to save the world" (C-6.5:5; see also T-19.IV(B).6:5 and M-23.6:8-10).

To understand the huge ramifications of Jesus' resurrection, a brief overview of the plan of Atonement presented by the Course may be helpful. Here is how I understand it. In truth, all of us were saved—one might say "resurrected"—the instant the separation seemed to happen. Our error was immediately corrected by the Atonement: "The instant the idea of separation entered the mind of God's Son, in that same instant was God's Answer given" (M-2.2:6). In the blink of an eye, our minds were restored to the oneness of Heaven.

However, as inconsequential as that brief instant of separation was, our minds had really latched onto it. We were so lost in the illusion of separation that accessing the Atonement (through accessing the Voice of the Holy Spirit, Who offers us the Atonement) was extremely difficult at best, and for all practical purposes impossible for most of us. The seeming chasm between us and God had become "too great for [us] to encompass" (T-1.II.4:4).

What we needed to bridge this chasm was a *teacher*, one teacher who could rise above the illusion and fully awaken to the truth. If one teacher could pierce the darkness and let in the light, then the entire world would be saved, because the Sonship is not separate: Whatever one experiences, all the others will share. This is why the Course says, in Section 12 of the Manual, that the awakening of only one teacher of God is enough to bring about complete salvation for all:

> One wholly perfect teacher, whose learning is complete, suffices. This one, sanctified and redeemed, becomes the Self Who is the Son of God.   (M-12.1:2-3)

Many Course students have wondered just who this one teacher is, but it seems clear to me that this one teacher is Jesus himself. In Section 23 of the Manual, we read the following, which refers specifically to Jesus. Notice how similar it is to the passage just cited from M-12:

> We have repeatedly said that one who has perfectly accepted the Atonement for himself can heal the world. Indeed, he [Jesus] has already done so....He has become the risen Son of God.   (M-23.2:1-2,4)

The first passage tells us that a single perfected teacher would save the world; the second passage tells us that there *is* such a teacher:

Jesus. The logical conclusion is that Jesus saved the world. He is the one teacher who bridged the chasm between us and God (see T-1.II.4:3-5). His awakening made the Atonement accessible to us. It did so by opening our minds to the Holy Spirit, making His Voice accessible to us in a way that It hadn't been before (see C-6.1:1-3). And it was his resurrection that brought all of this about. His resurrection was the event that made the Atonement, given to us the instant we separated but obscured by our attachment to the illusions of the world, a living reality on earth: "The crucifixion did not establish the Atonement; the resurrection did" (T-3.I.1:2).

Thus, as nontraditional as the Course generally is in its depiction of Jesus, it shares with traditional Christianity the conviction that an event of enormous import took place in Jerusalem two thousand years ago, an event which literally saved the world. For traditional Christians, that event is Jesus' crucifixion, but in the Course, it is Jesus' resurrection. Through his resurrection, Jesus demonstrated his complete awakening, and through his awakening, we all were awakened. When Jesus left the tomb empty on Easter morning, he took the whole world with him. In this sense, he truly is our savior.

Personally, I find this idea that the *historical event* of Jesus' resurrection literally saved the world to be surprising and thought provoking. I find that the Course often bucks the trends of modern alternative spirituality, and here is one more place where it does so. Most New Age and alternative spiritual teachings depict Jesus as simply a teacher or wayshower, rather than a literal savior. In this view, the historical event of Jesus' resurrection—if it happened at all—has no saving power in itself (except, of course, that it was his own salvation), but was simply a demonstration on his part of what all of us have the potential to do.

The Course wholeheartedly agrees that Jesus was a teacher and wayshower, and that his resurrection was a demonstration of what we ourselves can do. But there is more to it, in the Course's view. Not only was Jesus a teacher and wayshower, but he was also a literal savior; not only was the resurrection a demonstration, but it was also a literally saving event. Surprisingly, the Course, in its own unique way, echoes the popular slogan of evangelical Christians everywhere: "Jesus saves."

We still experience ourselves as living in a dream of separation because we have refused to *accept* the fact that we have been resurrected along with Jesus, and that therefore the dream is over.

Being told that we are already awakened leads to the obvious question: If I'm really awake, why am I still stuck in this painful world? We still experience the dream of separation because, just as our attachment to the illusions of the world had prevented us from accessing the Atonement before Jesus awakened, that same attachment now keeps us from *accepting* the fact that when Jesus awakened, we all awakened with him. Before, we couldn't *access* the Atonement; now, we refuse to *accept* the Atonement. Jesus tells us that his purpose in coming to earth was to restore to us the awareness of our Father's Will, and that "your problem in accepting it is the problem of this world" (T-8.IV.3:5). He fulfilled his mission perfectly, and the awareness of our Father's Will has been restored to us. But we are a stubborn lot (the Biblical phrase "stiff-necked people" comes to mind), and part of our minds simply refuses to accept that Atonement has come, and the dream is over.

Why do we refuse to accept that the dream is over? The shocking answer is this: Because we fear awakening. This is a major theme of the Course, and in fact an entire section of the Text is devoted to it (T-13.III). Why do we fear awakening? In a nutshell, we fear it because awakening is death to the ego, and we identify with the ego. Therefore, we believe that awakening would be *our* death. We recoil from God's Love because we "think it would crush [us] into nothingness" (T-13.III.4:1).

This fear is what causes our minds to cling to the separation—or better, a *memory* of the separation, since in fact the separation is over: "You keep an ancient memory before your eyes" (T-26.V.5:6). The world really did end when Jesus arose on Easter morning, but we don't want to believe it. And so, like a child watching *The Lion King* on video for the ten thousandth time, we replay the saga of separation over and over again, trying to delude ourselves into believing that it is still happening, when in fact it has long since vanished into the nothingness from whence it came.

We come to accept our resurrection by choosing to *join* Jesus' resurrection through forgiving our brothers.

Fortunately, we still have the power to change our minds and accept the fact that the separation is over. How can we let go of our fear of awakening and accept our resurrection? Essentially, by choosing to *join* Jesus' resurrection through forgiving our brothers. (This includes forgiving Jesus himself, as a number of Course passages tell us; see Q & A #31, entitled "Why does Jesus repeatedly ask us in the Course to forgive him? To me, he is the epitome of innocence and perfect love, so why do I need to forgive him?")

Of course, as we've seen, we were already joined with him at the moment of his resurrection, and so this new joining is simply a matter of giving our mind's assent to a joining that has already happened. Yet this assent is important, for until we give our whole mind to the resurrection, it is in some sense incomplete: "Nor can the resurrection be complete till your forgiveness rests on Christ, along with mine" (T-20.I.2:10). Through forgiveness, we complete the process of awakening that began when Jesus rose two thousand years ago.

The choice to join Jesus' resurrection is ultimately an absolute, unequivocal choice; one day, we will fully commit our minds to the resurrection, and at that moment we will leave the dream behind forever. But the path to that final choice is one of gradual progress, in which we are confronted with the choice to accept or reject the resurrection on a moment-to-moment basis. Each moment of our lives, in every encounter with our brothers, we are choosing whether to be our brother's executioner or his savior:

> Would you join in the resurrection or the crucifixion?
> Would you condemn your brothers or free them?
> (T-11.VI.2:1-2)

This may all sound very abstract and metaphysical, far removed from everyday life. What on earth does it mean to choose between crucifixion and resurrection? In truth, this choice is not so far removed from our lives; indeed, it is presented to us in the guise of our most mundane everyday situations. Do we curse the driver who cuts us off, or do we bless her? Do we attack the husband who leaves the toilet seat up, or do we let it go? Do we hate those who have different political views than us, or do we strive for joining in spite of the differences? In all of these seemingly ordinary situations is the choice to nail our brothers to a cross, or to free them to rise from the tomb of the limitations our egos see in them. The choices we make as we go through our day are of no little consequence; they are literally the choice between the agony of crucifixion, and the joy of resurrection. For whatever we choose to offer our brothers, that is what we ourselves will experience.

This choice can be a difficult one for us, since we are so committed to the ego and thus still gripped with the ego's fear of awakening. Fortunately, Jesus himself is here to help us, if we are willing to invite him into our minds. He himself will lead us to our own resurrection, and doing so is his joy, because it allows the light of his own resurrection to shine once again upon the world: "My resurrection comes again each time I lead a brother safely to the place at which the journey ends and is forgot" (W-pI.rV.In.7:1). Let us choose to make his resurrection complete by answering his invitation to join him in forgiving the holy Son of God.

Subject Index

*Headings in **bold print** indicate an entire Q & A devoted to the subject.*
After the initial listing, A Course in Miracles *is referred to as "ACIM."*

Gender
 differences, illusion/reality of, 83-84
 language and, 75-84
 separation and, 77, 83-84
Gentle firmness, 110-111
Giving and receiving
 "giving to get," 58
 God's peace, 113-122
 laws of, 55-62
 material needs and, 204-205
 miracles, 11, 13-19, 25-27, 118, 136
 see also Extension
Goal(s)
 common, 136, 141, 144-148, 259, 262-265
 conflicting, 250-51, 254
 ego's, 98, **141-148**
 of God, 232, 239, 245-246
 of universal salvation, 146-148
 separate, 141-148, 218
 true religion and, 262-265
God
 as goal, 232, 239, 245-246
 denial of, 6-7
 laws of, *see* Laws, God's
 peace of, 113, 116-122, 239, 245-246
 resistance to, 97-102
 separation and, 3-9, 69-70
God's Love, 59, 65, 69, 79-80, 93-94, 148,
  202, 228
 as goal, 232
 fear of, 278
 specialness and, 3-5
 substitutes for, 198, 233-237
Guidance, 123-129
 a practice, 169-170
Guilt
 depression and, 249-250
 ego's voice and, 100, 124-127
 responsibility and, 35-40
 sex and, 230-231
 sin and, 268-272
Guiltlessness, *see* Innocence

Happiness
 depression and, 248-251
 function and, 252-253, 255
 search for, 22, 32, 187, 198, 220, 234-235,
  240
Harm/harmlessness, *see* Nonviolence
Healing 47, 50-53
 extension of, 37-38, 47, 50-53, 62, 137,
  149-157, 180
 fear of, 242-243
 illusion of, 240

see also Perception; Relationships;
  Sickness
Help, *see* Love, call for
Holy instant, 24-25, 254
Holy Spirit, the
 as Voice for God, 123-129
 behavior and, 207-213
 ego and, 123-129
 forgiveness and, 165-172
 free choice and, 11-18
 function in world, 63-74
 guidance of, 23, 66-67, **123-129, 149-157,**
  207-213
 healing depression, 247, 253-256
 judgment of, 131-134, 162-163, **173-180**
 lesson of, 101-102
 perception and, 60-61, 64-65, 151
 relationships and, 149-157
 saving time and, 22-23
 script of, 11-18
 use of joining, 223, 227-232
 use of money, 197, 199-206
 use of sex, 223, 227-232
 working with the illusion, 64, 67-68, 70
 a practice, 101-102

"I Need Do Nothing," 24-25, 119
Identity
 true, 35, 39, 44, 55, 58-59, 98, 133-134,
  165, 168, 172, 174-175, 189-196, 218,
  225, 227, 237, 255-256
 see also Christ; Son of God
Idols
 addictions and, 234-237
 as substitutes for God's Love, 234-237
 money and, 198-199
 search for, 32, 187, 198-199, 252
Illness, *see* Sickness
Illusion, 35, 57, 89
 belief in separation and, 58, 185-188, 200
 conflict and, 114-119
 hierarchy of, 87, 90-92, 161
 laws of, 57, 91-92
 of differences, 87-95
 physical form as, 49
 preference for, 88-93
 "reality" of, 91-95, 193-196
 truth and, 83, 87-95, 116, 123, 193
 world of, 185-188
 a practice in overcoming, 94-95
 see also Money; Problems, as illusions;
  Time, illusion of
Inadequacy, *see* Powerlessness
Inclusiveness, 47-53, 75-84

Order of difficulty, 87-95
    a practice, 94-95
    see also Miracles, no order of difficulty in

Pain, 12-13, 30-31, 34, 98, 101
    death as escape from, 43
    denial of, 189-196
    guilt and, 100
    illusion/reality of, 189-192, 195
    see also Suffering
Pantheism, 49
Peace, 113-122
    as goal, 239, 245-246, 254
    death and, 42-43
    false/true, 127-128, 167-168
    giving and receiving, 116-122
    journey to, 121-122
    loss of, 126, 251
    world and, 221
    practices, 115, 117, 118, 119, 120-121
Perception
    behavior and, 208
    forgiveness and, 165-169, 171, 174, 177
    healing relationships and, 149-157
    law of, 60-62
    miracles and, 14-17, 195
    of events, 14, 29-31
    selective, 90-91
Physical appetites/desires, 223-232
Physical needs, 56-57, 200-204
Possessions, *see* Money
Powerlessness, 251-252, 254-255
Prayer, 113-122
Predetermination, 11-18
Prejudice, 91, 160-162
    see also Differences
Problem(s),
    as illusions, 94-95, 255
    core, 237, 263, 278
    denial of, 127, 190, 240, 243
Problem-solving, 88, 236, 251, 254-255
    repertoire, 108-109, 236
    a practice, 94-95
Projection, 60-61, 125
    of sinfulness, 159-164, 175, 268
Punishment, 32, 43, 58, 165-168, 174-175, 269
Purpose in life, *see* Function

Racism, *see* Prejudice
Rapists, forgiveness of, 173-181
Reality
    laws of, 57, 91-92
    see also under specific subjects

Reincarnation, 44, 187-188
Relationships
    healing, 149-157
    holy, 145-147, 262-265
    romantic, 142-144, 226
    sex and, 223-232
    special, 143-144, 147, 226-227
    see also Forgiveness; Joining; Salvation;
        Sex
Religion
    laws of, 57
    formal, 259-265
    true, 259, 261-265
Responsibility, 29-40
    guilt and, 35-40
Resurrection, *see* Jesus, crucifixion and
    resurrection
Romance, *see* Relationships, romantic

Sacrifice
    Jesus and, 271
    love and forgiveness, and, 165-166, 175
    self-sacrifice, 56-57, 126
Salvation
    giving and receiving, 61
    joining and, 218
    plan for, 65-66, 197, 199-205, 219
    secret of, 31
    universality of, 146-148, 275-276
    see also Atonement; Forgiveness
Separate interests, *see* Goals, separate
Separation, the
    addictions and, 234, 237
    **awakening from dream of, 19-27,
        275-280**
    belief in, 83-84, 185-188, 240, 276
    birth and, 185-188
    cause of, 3-9
    competition and, 216, 218-221
    denial of self and, 195-196
    depression and, 248-251
    dream of, 19-21, **275-280**
    false forgiveness and, 167
    false joining and, 141-148
    gender and, 77, 83-84
    God's knowing about, 69-71, 73-74
    God's response to, 65, 73-74
    Holy Spirit and, 70-71, 73-74
    money and, 187, 199-202
    reality of, 6
    sex and, 223-227
    sickness and, 240
    world of, 185-188
    see also Ego, the

The Circle's Mission Statement

To discern the author's vision of *A Course in Miracles* and manifest that in our lives, in the lives of students, and in the world.

1
To faithfully discern the author's vision of *A Course in Miracles*.

In interpreting the Course we strive for total fidelity to its words and the meanings they express. We thereby seek to discover the Course as the author saw it.

2
To be an instrument in Jesus' plan to manifest his vision of the Course in the lives of students and in the world.

We consider this to be Jesus' organization and therefore we attempt to follow his guidance in all we do. Our goal is to help students understand, as well as discern for themselves, the Course's thought system as he intended, and use it as he meant it to be used—as a literal program in spiritual awakening. Through doing so we hope to help ground in the world the intended way of doing the Course, here at the beginning of its history.

3
To help spark an enduring tradition based entirely on students joining together in doing the Course as the author envisioned.

We have a vision of local Course support systems composed of teachers, students, healers, and groups, all there to support one another in making full use of the Course. These support systems, as they continue and multiply, will together comprise an enduring spiritual tradition, dedicated solely to doing the Course as the author intended. Our goal is to help spark this tradition, and to assist others in doing the same.

4
To become an embodiment, a birthplace of this enduring spiritual tradition.

To help spark this tradition we must first become a model for it ourselves. This requires that we at the Circle follow the Course as our individual path; that we ourselves learn forgiveness through its program. It requires that we join with each other in a group holy relationship dedicated to the common goal of awakening through the Course. It also requires that we cultivate a local support system here in Sedona, and that we have a facility where others could join with us in learning this approach to the Course. Through all of this we hope to become a seed for an ongoing spiritual tradition based on *A Course in Miracles*.

Books & Booklets in This Series

Commentaries on *A Course in Miracles*
by Robert Perry, Allen Watson & Greg Mackie

1. **Seeing the Face of Christ in All Our Brothers** *by Perry*. How we can see the Presence of God in others. $5.00

3. **Shrouded Vaults of the Mind** *by Perry*. Draws a map of the mind based on the Course, and takes you on a tour through its many levels. $5.00

4. **Guidance: Living the Inspired Life** *by Perry*. Sketches an overall perspective on guidance and its place on the spiritual path. $7.00

8. **A Healed Mind Does Not Plan** *by Watson*. Examines our approach to planning and decision-making, showing how it is possible to leave the direction of our lives up to the Holy Spirit. $5.00

9. **Through Fear to Love** *by Watson*. Explores two sections from the Course that deal with our fear of redemption. Leads the reader to see how it is possible to look upon ourselves with love. $5.00

10. **The Journey Home** *by Watson*. Presents a description of our spiritual destination and what we must go through to get there. $8.50

11. **Everything You Always Wanted to Know about Judgment but Were Too Busy Doing It to Notice** *by Perry and Watson*. A survey of various teachings about judgment in the Course. $8.00

12. **The Certainty of Salvation** *by Perry and Watson*. How we can become certain that we will find our way to God. $5.00

13. **What Is Death?** *by Watson*. The Course's view of what death really is. $5.00

14. **The Workbook as a Spiritual Practice** *by Perry*. A guide for getting the most out of the Workbook. $5.00

15. **I Need Do Nothing: Finding the Quiet Center** *by Watson*. An in-depth discussion of one of the most misunderstood sections of the Course. $5.00

16. **A Course Glossary** *by Perry*. 150 definitions of terms and phrases from the Course, for students and study groups. $7.00

17. **Seeing the Bible Differently: How *A Course in Miracles* Views the Bible** *by Watson*. Shows the similarities, differences, and continuity between the Course and the Bible. $6.00

18. **Relationships as a Spiritual Journey: From Specialness to Holiness** *by Perry*. Describes the Course's unique view of how we can find God through the transformation of our relationships. $11.00

19. **A Workbook Companion Volume I** *by Watson and Perry*. Commentaries on Lessons 1 - 120. $16.00

20. **A Workbook Companion Volume II** *by Watson and Perry*. Commentaries on Lessons 121 - 243. $16.00

21. **A Workbook Companion Volume III** *by Watson and Perry*. Commentaries on Lessons 244 - 365. $18.00

22. **The Answer Is a Miracle** *by Perry and Watson*. Looks at what the Course means by miracles, and how we can experience them in our lives. $7.00

23. **Let Me Remember You** *by Perry and Watson*. Regaining a sense of God's relevance, both in the Course and in our lives. $10.00

24. **Bringing the Course to Life: How to Unlock the Meaning of** *A Course in Miracles* **for Yourself** *by Watson and Perry*. Designed to teach the student, through instruction, example and exercises, how to read the Course so that the experience becomes a personal encounter with the truth. $12.00

25. **Reality and Illusion: An Overview of Course Metaphysics** *by Perry*. Examines the Course's lofty vision of reality, its account of the events which gave birth to our current existence, and how the Course views the relationship between ultimate reality and the illusory world of separation. $11.00

26. **How Can We Forgive Murderers? And Other Answers to Questions about** *A Course in Miracles* *by Mackie*. Insightful answers to perplexing Course questions, and practical tips for how to apply those answers to your personal life. $15.00

For shipping rates, a complete catalog of our products and services, or for information about events, please contact us at:

The Circle of Atonement
Teaching and Healing Center
P.O. Box 4238
W. Sedona, AZ 86340
(928) 282-0790 Fax: (928) 282-0523
E-mail: info@circleofa.com
Website: www.circleofa.com